Breaking Light

Breaking Light

Toward a Poetics of Opacity in Early Greek Thinking

D. M. SPITZER

SUNY PRESS

Published by State University of New York Press, Albany

EU GPSR Authorised Representative:
Logos Europe, 9 rue Nicolas Poussin, 17000, La Rochelle, France
contact@logoseurope.eu

For information, contact State University of New York Press, Albany, NY
www.sunypress.edu

Library of Congress Cataloging-in-Publication Data

Name: Spitzer, D. M., 1975– author.
Title: Breaking light : toward a poetics of opacity in early Greek thinking / D. M. Spitzer.
Description: Albany : State University of New York Press, [2026]. | Series: SUNY series in ancient Greek philosophy | Includes bibliographical references and index.
Identifiers: LCCN 2025049243 | ISBN 9798855807370 (hardcover : alk. paper) | ISBN 9798855807400 (epub) | ISBN 9798855807394 (PDF)
Subjects: LCSH: Thales, approximately 634 B.C.–approximately 546 B.C. | Anaximander. | Anaximenes, of Miletus. | Complexity (Philosophy). | Philosophy, Ancient.
Classification: LCC B253 .S65 2026
LC record available at https://lccn.loc.gov/2025049243

Contents

Acknowledgments

Sara, Ani, and Luna, whose companionship during the most extreme phase of the COVID-19 pandemic in 2020–21 formed a generous and generative home atmosphere in which the preliminary research and writing for this book emerged: deepest gratitude and love. During that period Sara and I began our nightly walks along the banks of the Susquehanna River in Harrisburg, Pennsylvania—whose movements showed me daily and nightly many of the dimensions of opacity registered in Thalean ὕδωρ.

Many sparkling thanks to Olga Blomgren and the participants of the panel "Thinking On and With: Perspectives on Édouard Glissant" that convened online during the 2021 Northeast Modern Language Association annual meeting.

To the editors and reviewers at SUNY, I offer much gratitude and appreciation. The comments offered in those channels placed the emphasis on *peer* in the process of peer review, opening with support for the project and suggesting ways to improve.

An earlier version of chapter 1 appeared as "Divining: ΥΔΩΡ, Opacity, and Thalean Considerations" in *Research in Phenomenology*. Many thanks to the editors and peer reviewers at that journal; full bibliographic information is given in the bibliography.

I am profoundly grateful to Jeffner Allen, who introduced me to the radiant thinking of Édouard Glissant, and whose support and encouragement for my work has expanded through the years.

Tony Preus, whose openness to various and different ways of reading ancient thinking is a genuine inspiration, I offer numberless thanks and appreciation.

Notes, Editions, and Abbreviations

Unless otherwise indicated, all translations are my own.

References to ancient sources and to some frequently cited modern and contemporary sources appear in parenthetical abbreviated citations within the body of the text, while references to other sources, along with further discussions, appear in footnotes. For the Milesians the ancient sources are given (authors and texts), followed by a bracketed reference to the numbering assigned by Graham in his 2010 edition *The Texts of Early Greek Philosophy*. The texts of Pherekydes are primarily those presented in Kirk and Raven's 1957 *The Presocratic Philosophers* (abbreviated K-R), with occasional reference to the more recent 2016 edition by Laks and Most, *Beginnings and early Ionian Thinkers*, volume 2, part 1 of their edition *Early Greek Philosophy* (abbreviated L-M). For other early Greek thinkers, the abbreviated name and fragment number are followed by the editor's name. When I cite commentary from these editions, they are treated like other secondary sources in the footnotes. Full references for each of these sources appear in the bibliography.

Finally, a note on the spelling of names: in order to open a distance between the perhaps overly familiar early Greeks, a distance in which their sounding otherwise might resonate, I have elected to present proper names according to a different scheme for transliteration. For the more frequently used *Anaximander*, for instance, I use *Anaximandros*. If some of the names are thereby rendered even slightly unfamiliar, hopefully some measure of foreignness or strangeness might take place and serve as a reminder of that foreignness quickening the thinkings associated with these proper names. For a similar reason, in many cases I have preferred the adjectival forms *Thalean, Anaximandrean, Anaximenean*. Furthermore, adjectivally rendered, the highly and insurmountably mediated character of early Greek thinking takes a place in the foreground. Lastly, this way of naming centers the thinking as neither proprietary nor exclusive to individual historical persons but caught up in the *tourbillons* of a transhistorical imaginary. Giving voice to experience(s) releases voiced-experience(s) into the multiple imaginaries and opens multiple, unpredictable relays, translations, afterlives, shadows. Opacities.

Abbreviations

Abbreviations conform to those given in *The Oxford Classical Dictionary*, 3rd edition (*OCD3*). For those authors, texts, and sources without *OCD3* abbreviations, such as the early Greek thinkers, I have applied the abbreviation system in Graham's table of contents. Other abbreviations of less frequently cited texts, such as the ancient Egyptian *Leiden Hymns* and the Indian *Upanishads,* are given in the text when these sources are introduced.

Introduction

Breaking Light

Clarity and intelligibility, guiding research into the earliest Greek philosophers, enclose the polestars of Milesian thinking—ὕδωρ, ἄπειρον, ἀήρ—and, muting those resonant words of Milesian thinking, limit the interpretive possibilities for approaching Thales, Anaximandros, and Anaximenes. *Breaking Light* intends to open a different way toward these early Greek thinkers, a way oriented by *opacity*, what Édouard Glissant thought as "that which cannot be reduced, which is the most perennial guarantee of participation and confluence."[1] What new insights and interpretive directions might unfold from engaging the opacities of early Greek thinking? How might the radiant thinkings of Thales, Anaximandros, and Anaximenes reverberate otherwise than as the breaking light (or, the dawn) of clarity and intelligibility? Encountered otherwise, the basic terms of Milesian thinking spread in manifold directions in relation to other key terms and ideas for ancient Greek thinking, but they also share a characteristic aura and ambience of opacity. As a reorientation away from the presupposition of clarity and intelligibility, thinking *opacity*, rather than clarity, can help to reanimate Milesian philosophy.

---

1. Édouard Glissant, *Poetics of Relation*, trans. Betsy Wing (University of Michigan Press, 1997), 191; originally published as *Poétique de la Relation* (Gallimard, 1990). Throughout, Wing's translation will be abbreviated *PR*, while the French text will be abbreviated *PdR*. Unless noted otherwise, parentheses or square brackets indicate my interpolations on Wing's translation, and citations are to her translation first, then to the French text. When I have given my own translation of a passage from *PdR*, the citation is reversed: to the French edition first, then to the English translation.

Light: Beginnings

Like light breaking over the archaic Greek world, according to the conventional narrative, clarity and intelligibility inaugurate philosophy, differentiate philosophic inquiry from mythic-poetic traditions: "Thales *is said* (λέγεται) to have brought out the light (ἀποφήνασθαι) of the first cause" (Arist. *Metaph*. 984a.2–3). The theme of light, illumination, darkness, and (un-)clarity operate in this passage, first in the movement of ἀποφήνασθαι, a compound verb of showing and speaking in which the sense of bringing forth or out of (ἀπο-) joins with the connection of light and speech animating the word φαίνω (speak) and its register of *giving-light, shining, breaking light,* as the dawn casts light (φάνη ῥοδοδάκτυλος Ἠώς, Hom. *Od*. 2.1). That of which Thales is said to have brought out the light had, in Aristotle's discussion, already sounded in very early theologizers and in the Homeric rendering of Okeanos and Tethys as "fathers of coming-forth" (γενέσεως πατέρας) as well as the river Styx as oldest and most revered (Arist. *Metaph*. 983b.27–33). "Yet," Aristotle continues, "if an archaic and early belief (ἡ δόξα) such as this would happen to be a belief about nature (περὶ τῆς φύσεως), it would be most unclear (τάχ' ἂν ἄδηλον εἴη)" (983b.33–984a.2). The attempt to bring light and clarity to an archaic and early belief inaugurates philosophy in its earliest named figure, Thales.

Philosophy's original movement of illumination occurs *from* (ἀπο-) the early belief and its unclear voicing in poetries and early theologizing, out, that is, from the darkness of mythic-poetic speech. In one sense, the criteria of clarity and intelligibility are unstable and dynamic, turning within the atmosphere in which they are thought. On a cultural tapestry whose fabric is myth and poetry, what appears more intelligible and clear to those on the other side of the rift opened by philosophy—and later still, as Gadamer observes, by Christianity[2]—would appear instead less clear, less intelligible in its unfamiliarity, in its seeming ruptures upon that mythic fabric. While in the fragments that pull apart divine beings from their various representations a sense does arise in Xenophanes of the fabric *as* fabric, that is, of the situatedness of the prevailing tapestry of divinities through which the world is engaged (Xns. 14–16 Lesher), nevertheless Xenophanean thinking still works on and in that fabric, enriching and

---

2. Gadamer understands this distinction to result from the thinking of Christianity, "das mythische Weltbild als Gegenbegriff zum wissenschaftlichen Weltbild zu denken." Hans-Georg Gadamer, "Mythos und Vernunft," in *Kleine Schriften IV: Variationen* (J. C. B. Mohr, 1977), 51.

adding subtly to the tapestry. Similarly, early Milesian thinking weaves itself within this fabric while also twisting against it, knotting and straining it. The meaning-network, that is, in which Milesian thinking sounds comes forward as the poetries and mythic imaginary of the archaic period and the imaginaries of the broader Mediterranean basin, Egypt, and the Near East cultural matrix.

CLARITY

Traditional interpretation of the Milesians unfolds within the area marked off explicitly by Aristotle with clarity and intelligibility. With only a few exceptions, the prevailing approach to early Greek thinking assumes clarity as an organizational, compositional, and expressive principle.[3] Drew A. Hyland, for instance, views clarity in the form of intelligibility as a fundamental aspect of Thalean—and philosophic—thinking.[4] More recently, based on a sensitive reading of Aristotle's comments in *Metaphysics* A, Maria Michela Sassi argues that clarity of expression, as well as clarity of the "new content" for thinking, sets apart early Greek philosophies from whatever prehistory may be found in mythico-religious thought.[5] Yet, clarity appears to be a criterion for Aristotle's thinking transferred onto his critical encounters with earlier thinkers.[6] Or, perhaps more suitably, Aristotle's

---

3. In the case of Herakleitos, Parmenides, and Empedokles, Mansfeld has argued that a deliberate "unclarity" guides the proems of these thinkers. Jaap Mansfeld, "Insight by Hindsight: Intentional Unclarity in Presocratic Proems," *Bulletin of the Institute of Classical Studies* 40 (1995): 225–32, JSTOR. More recently, Bryan has published a study of the Parmenidean poem illustrating "the way that the assumption of clarity has informed analysis of the specifics of Parmenides' argument" and suggesting that intentional obscurities in the poem serve as a provocation to reason through these obscurities toward clarity. Jenny Bryan, "The Pursuit of Parmenidean Clarity," *Rhizomata* 8, no. 2 (2021): 230, EBSCOhost. This would nevertheless amount to an ultimate valuation of clarity and intelligibility.

4. Drew A. Hyland, *The Origins of Philosophy: Its Rise in Myth and the Pre-Socratics: A Collection of Early Writings* (Humanities Press, 1973), 99–102.

5. Maria Michela Sassi, *The Beginnings of Philosophy in Greece*, trans. Michele Asuni (Princeton University Press, 2018), 26, 41.

6. On clarity as an Aristotelian criterion for distinguishing between philosophy and poetry and between "accomplished" and "primitive" philosophies, see Jaap Mansfeld, "Aristotle, Plato, and the Preplatonic Doxography and Chronography," in *Storiografia e dossografia nella filosofia antica*, ed. Giuseppe Cambiano (Tirrenia, 1986), 19–22 (quotations from 21). Mansfeld identifies the criterion in Plato, too (30–31).

dialectical interaction with, as John Russon has put it, *"the history of the human engagement with the reality in question"* works at clarification,[7] and this clarification typically involves separating the thought from the way it is said. The way it is said, in turn, may have a meaning-rich, if not an inextricable, linkage with the thought. Aristotle's reduction in the name of clarity of those features of the texts by or traditions related to the Milesian *physiologoi* that resembled his own concept of ὕλη—namely ὕδωρ, ἀπεί-ρον,[8] ἀήρ—not only establishes contours for philosophy as a discourse,[9] it also eliminates the multiple ways those features operate, determining them instead as semantically stable variables within the category of ἀρχή.

Clarity and Unity

The reduction through clarity and intelligibility of the radiantly polyvalent Milesian thinking also takes place as a stabilization and simplification to a single, unified position that can be neatly epitomized. From the early fifth century BCE to the present a whole tradition of interpretation has settled over those thinkers now called pre-Socratic philosophers. The Sophists Gorgias (485–380), Hippias (fl. mid-fifth c.), and Protagoras (490–420) all produced compendia of earlier thinkings: Gorgias's presentation was oriented, according to Jaap Mansfeld, by a "systematical point of view," while Hippias arranged thinkers in relation to questions, and Protagoras's collection aimed specifically at a critical assessment of Eleatic monism.[10] Such handbooks of epitomes, whatever their specific organizational princi-ples, depend on the idea of positions or views as in some way constituting

---

7. John Russon, "To Account for the Appearances: Phenomenology and Existential Change in Aristotle and Plato," *Journal of the British Society for Phenomenology* 52, no. 2 (2021): 161, Taylor and Francis Journals. For a concise and good discussion of the dialectical character of Aristotle's engagement with early Greek thinking in *Metaphysics* A, see also Pavel Hobza, "Anaximenes' ἀήρ as Generating Mist and Generated Air," *Apeiron* 53, no. 2 (2020): 100–105, De Gruyter Journals.

8. Among ancient interpreters Anaximandrean ἄπειρον was associated with ὕλη, possibly by Aristotle as an elemental source thicker (πυκνότερον) than ἀήρ and thinner (λεπτότερον) than ὕδωρ (*Metaph.* 989a.13–15) and explicitly in the summary given by Stobaios (τὸ δ᾿ἄπειρον οὐδὲν ἄλλο ἢ ἡ ὕλη ἐσίν [*sic*], Stob. *Ecl.* 1.11.12).

9. Mansfeld has written, "Thales was a philosopher because there can be no doubt that his 'water' is material, i.e., is a body." Jaap Mansfeld, "Aristotle on Thales and Others, or the Beginnings of Natural Philosophy," *Mnemosyne* 38, no. 1–2 (1985): 122, JSTOR.

10. Mansfeld, "Aristotle, Plato," 6.

philosophy. John Sallis has problematized the assumption of "holding a view" that operates in Aristotelian and subsequent philosophic thinking, showing how it seems to implicate a Platonic orientation governed by εἶδος (typically translated as *form*), such that the idea of *holding a view* itself already superimposes onto archaic Greek thinking the conceptual apparatus of Platonic and Peripatetic philosophy.[11] The stirrings, perhaps, of the εἶδος-view orientation can be heard in the introduction to Hippias's compendium quoted by Klemens of Alexandria (ca. 150–215 CE): "Having collected (συνθείς) what is greatest and most alike from all these thinkers [sc. Orpheus, Musaios, Hesiod, Homer, other poets, et al.], I will produce this gathering (λόγον) new and with many views (πολυειδῆ)" (Clem. Al. *Strom* 6.2.228C). Compendia present stabilized and unitary accounts—*views*—of earlier thinkers. In so doing, a concomitant levelling and flattening occurs, a translational protocol that transforms vibrant, dynamic thinking into fixed statements of doctrine.[12]

The views Aristotle assigns to Thales, Anaximandros, and Anaximenes operate on Aristotelian interpretive grounds, chiefly, that of ἀρχή, which he takes to register chiefly source, cause, and principle.[13] Present too is the overlapping zone of *philosophia*; Aristotle identifies Thales by name as the ἀρχηγός of a certain type of philosophy, that which seeks the ἀρχή as underlying thing (Arist. *Metaph.* 983b.6, 25). This type of philosophy pursues an ἀρχή of vast sweep:

> Most of those early philosophers believed there to be sources
> or causes (ἀρχάς) of all beings and things only in the form
> of material (ὕλη). That out of which all beings are and out of
> which they arise in the first place and into which they perish
> in the end—this substance (οὐσία) both remaining beneath
> (ὑπομενούσης) and altering (μεταβαλλούσης) in conditions,

11. John Sallis, *The Figure of Nature: On Greek Origins* (Indiana University Press, 2016), 15–16.

12. On this protocol, see D. M. Spitzer, *Parmenides and Translation: Figures of Motion, Figures of Being* (Peter Lang Verlag, 2025), 38–39, 47–60.

13. See Schofield's study of the term's history and its particular register in Aristotle. Malcolm Schofield, "ΑΡΧΗ," *Hyperboreus* 3 (1997): 218–36. See also Morano, who argues that the sense of ἀρχή as applied to Thales should be restricted to, and is best understood as expressing, origin. Donald V. Morano, "Thales and the Dawn of Western Philosophy," *Journal of Thought* 10, no. 3 (1975): 201, JSTOR.

> they say this element is this ἀρχή of all beings, also because they
> do not think it arises or is destroyed, since this is a certain type
> of φύσις always remaining secure (ἀεὶ σωζομένης, 983b.6–13).

In its earliest moments, philosophy seeks to reduce a totality of beings to a single, unified source.

The traditional modern narrative reinforces the stabilized and unitary views held by the archaic Milesians. In Hegel's account, Thales inaugurates philosophy by way of a reduction to a single simple substance (*auf eine einfach Substanz zu reducieren*), articulating a unity, a universal unity (*Ein allgemeines*) that remains in and for itself (*Anundfürsichseiende*) as a simple view *without* imagination (*die einfache phantasielose Anschauung*). While the history of philosophy unfolds through Anaximandros, in his having posited an infinite principle that "negates the finite" (*das Endliche negierende*), and Anaximenes, whose contribution involves the opening of a transition from nature to consciousness, it remains the aim to identify a single principle that is a unity with itself (*Einheit mit sich in sich selbst*).[14]

Departing from conventional *diadokhic* (διαδοχή) narratives that give a tradition of Milesian master-student relations beginning with Thales as a mentor to Anaximandros, Anaximandros to Anaximenes (Simpl. *in Phys.* 1.2, 24.13–14, 26–27), Nietzsche's early study *Philosophy in the Tragic Age of the Greeks* instead turns from Thales to Anaximandros, then from Anaximandros to Herakleitos, eliminating Anaximenes from the tradition. On Sean D. Kirkland's insightful reading, Nietzsche overturns the conventional narrative along which philosophy progresses out from the earliest and least developed to its later and more fully realized instantiation in Plato and Aristotle. Nietzsche's concentration on the personalities of the early Greeks opens up, as Kirkland shows, personality not as an accumulation of memories, behaviors, idiosyncrasies, and the like, but instead as a specific moment or locus of experiencing the movements of φύσις as both a groundless abyss "unthinkable *per definitionem*" and an imaginative, ordering generativity.[15] The great achievements of the early

---

14. G. W. F. Hegel, *Vorlesungen über die Geschichte der Philosophie*, ed. G. J. P. J. Bolland (A. H. Adriani, 1908), 138–39 (on Thales), 143–44 (Anaximandros), 148 (Anaximenes), HathiTrust; *Lectures on the History of Philosophy*, vol. 1, *Greek Philosophy to Plato*, trans. E. S. Haldane (Lincoln and London, 1892), 178–79 (on Thales), 186–87 (Anaximandros), 191 (Anaximenes).

15. Sean D. Kirkland, "Nietzsche and Drawing Near to the Personalities of the Pre-Platonic Greeks," *Continental Philosophy Review* 44, no. 4 (2011): 422 (on reversal of

Greeks will not be handing down a system or doctrine that provides steps—inchoate, primitive—in the advance of philosophy, or that advances solutions to logical or metaphysical problems, but a willingness to remain open to an experience of the double motion of φύσις and the provocation to one's own resolute movement into imagination out of abyss.[16] Even so, much of Nietzsche's treatment places stress on *unity* as the distinguishing mark of both the philosophers, in their "*monolithic*" responses that "they *single-mindedly* attempt to express,"[17] and philosophic thinking (*der Satz "Alles ist Eins"*): the unity of that which is worthy of thought, the one "greatest knowledge of all" (*die größte Erkenntniß*) and "the unity of all that is" (*die Einheit des Seienden*).[18]

Alongside this emphasis on unity sounds an emphasis on a sort of clarity in the non-allegorical or mythic mode of expression Nietzsche attributes (partially) to Thales.[19] Yet, Nietzsche sounds a complexity on the figure of clarity, where the unity experienced, what Kirkland has articulated as "overwhelming, abyssal, and excessive, a terrifying withdrawal of order and meaning,"[20] only comes to speech reluctantly and with difficulty, like a "metaphoric and entirely unfaithful translation into a totally different sphere and speech."[21] In *Breaking Light*, these translations—specifically the radiant, polyvalent terms ὕδωρ, ἄπειρον, ἀήρ—come forward not as attempts to grasp (*greift*) and petrify (*petrificiren*)[22] "an original experience of what must be somehow unintelligible, contradictory, dynamic, or singular" of the opening-closing movements of φύσις,[23] but rather as poetic speech seeking to activate the sense of those very movements. Gaining

---

the traditional narrative), 433 (describing personality/-ies in Nietzsche's early work), Springer Nature Link.

16. Kirkland, "Nietzsche," 435–36.

17. Kirkland, "Nietzsche," 421–22; italics added for emphasis.

18. Friedrich Nietzsche, *Philosophy in the Tragic Age of the Greeks*, trans. Marianne Cowan (Regnery, 1962), 39, 43, 45, respectively; *Die Philosophie im tragischen Zeitalter der Griechen*, in *Die Geburt der Tragödie und weitere Schriften zur griechischen Literatur und Philosophie*, ed. Bernhard Greiner (Alfred Kröner Verlag, 2014), 164, 167, 168, respectively. In the following discussion, Cowan's translation will be abbreviated *PTAG*, while the Kröner edition will be *PZG*.

19. *PTAG*, 44–45; *PZG*, 166–67.

20. Kirkland, "Nietzsche," 430.

21. *PTAG*, 45; *PZG*, 168.

22. *PTAG*, 44; *PZG*, 168.

23. Kirkland, "Nietzsche," 431.

some clarity that distinguishes it from allegorical and mythic modes, in Nietzsche's early account philosophic thinking also resists clarity of expression, even if it can seemingly be glossed somewhat simply as an expression of unity.

Not only do the conventionally narrated views of the Milesians come forward as transparently clear, reduced to a simple core of unity, the conventional narrative also encapsulates the thinkers themselves, situating them perhaps in a *school*,[24] but one in which competition and overcoming of the earlier takes precedence. "To walk alone along a lonely street," writes Nietzsche in his discussion of Herakleitos, "is part of the philosopher's nature [*Wesen des Philosophen*]." As Nietzsche continues on the theme, he introduces another image of the self-enclosed, isolated thinker as requiring a "wall of self-sufficiency [*Selbstgenugsamkeit*]" built of diamond to protect again hostile others.[25] The images thrust unities, reduced—performatively, perhaps, as the thinkers themselves are understood as reductive with a strict interest in discovering *unity* and the *single principle*[26]—to self-identical and self-enclosed fixations on the *one* each thinker has declared, toward conflict with each other as enclosed unities. Approaching Milesian and other early Greek thinking as the sort of male-masculine site of contestations embedded in the conventional diadokhic and modern narratives and the mode of relation characterized by overthrow and competition they share, which isolate thinkers, not only reinscribes the palimpsest-like overwriting of *logos*, thinking, and conquest Luce Irigaray has unveiled,[27] it also forms a barrier to hearing something else outside of that ring of disputation insofar as the contest, however much it brings together different thinkers of the circle, more radically binds each one to a kind of closed circle of selfhood that contains and holds *views* in conflict with others.

Herodotos's ancient narrative involving Thales, on one reading, can be seen to perform the impulse to unity: one of the ἑπτὰ σοφοί (seven sages)—Bias or Thales—could have secured the Ionians from the Persian subjugation by means of unification, where Bias had urged the Ionians to a single city (πόλιν μίαν), while the sagacious utterance (γνώμη) of

---

24. Even in the school paradigm and its image of community persists an aura of competition among individuals espousing competing theories.

25. *PTAG*, 66; *PZG*, 184.

26. *PTAG*, 39; *PZG*, 164.

27. Luce Irigaray, *In the Beginning, She Was* (Bloomsbury, 2013), 44, 49.

Thales recommends ἓν βουλευτήριον (a single governing council) to be established in Teos because of its central position (Hdt. 1.170). In both cases (of Bias and of Thales), turned in one direction emphasis falls on a link between wisdom and the impulse to unity. On the other hand, the tale could also be heard as emphasizing Thales's interest in bringing into dialogue a multiplicity of voices and sustaining their diversity. In addition to Irigaray's reading of the mode of thinking with a keen interest in overcoming or outperforming others (by way of *logos*) as a substitute for armed combat, the mode of thinking on display in the conventional narrative has the bearing of what Glissant termed the *continental* way of being and thinking: continental thinking takes place as a *grasping* (*comprendre*),[28] as "the thought of the one,"[29] "imposing synthesis" like an aerial view. Continental thinking not only precedes every system,[30] it belongs to "atavistic cultures," potent, efficacious, "deadly, deadly for the life of the world's cultures" because of the tendency to reduce otherness into transparency,[31] to assimilate or annihilate as a decisive movement in the "whole principle of generalization and its entire process."[32] In an archaic Greek imaginary, this mode presents itself in the figure of Zeus, supreme overlord. The final chapter, "Breaking Light, Unclosing Opacity," develops the theme of Milesian thinking as interventions on the continental mode figured in Zeus by way of an *archipelago*.

Clarity and Translatability

Clarity as full intelligibility and availability for swift and unproblematic translation might be termed *transparency*. Settled as-in-around-among the

---

28. See Wing's discussions of this term and her translation, which analyze it to its Latin etymological components: *com-/con-* (together) and *prendo* (grasp or capture) (*PR*, 212n5; 220–21n1).

29. Glissant, "The Poetics of the World: Global Thinking and Unforeseeable Events," trans. Kate Cooper Leupin, Chancellor's Distinguished Lectureship Series, April 19, 2002, Louisiana State University, Baton Rouge, n.p., published online October 20, 2017, https://sites01.lsu.edu/wp/theglissanttranslationproject/2017/10/20/the-poetics-of-the-world-global-thinking-and-unforeseeable-events/. This is an unpaginated lecture available online. References therefore are to the lecture as a whole.

30. Glissant, *Philosophie de la relation: Poésie en étendue* (Gallimard, 2009), 45.

31. Glissant, "Poetics of the World."

32. *PR*, 49.

hermeneutic sediment covering early Greek thinking lies a petrified translational layer: ὕδωρ means *water*, the meaning of which can be expressed chemically, reduced to the materiality of the elements discovered since Thales and along a pathway opened by his proto-scientific inquiries. Its meaning is clear and so is its aspect: when in its pure state, water has a clear complexion, though it can become, as a dictionary phrases it, "bluish in thick layers."[33] Similarly, ἀήρ in Anaximenean thinking simply means *air*. English itself calls for such translations, the replacement of Greek terms with the phantoms of themselves that haunt even contemporary English. And if a cognate for the Anaximandrean word ἄπειρον does not arise in English, a drive for a single term or definition just as abruptly operates: ἄπειρον means *unlimited*, or *infinite, indeterminate*, or *boundless*, or some elaboration or combination of these. Churned through the interpretive apparatus of *Metaphysics* and *Physics* and the zone articulated in those texts within which the Milesians are to be read, the words scarcely matter in any event, effaced by the translative impulse—driven by a belief in transparency—"to communicate as quickly as possible the thing underlying the words, to reveal the unity of being under the differences of languages, to reduce multiplicity to the singular."[34] Within that rubric, the important dimension has to do with clarity and intelligibility of an account that reduces and explains without the mythic pageantry of the earlier theologians.

So long as pathways remain grounded in a Peripatetic view of material cause and underlying thing and a commitment to the possibility—rather, the promise, the project—of speaking the essence of a being enabled by the interpretive principles of clarity and intelligibility,[35] Milesian ὕδωρ and ἀήρ will remain mere matter, fully transparent, available to, and presented in, a simple translation: *water, air*; while ἄπειρον can be equally reduced and made available through a translation assuming a transparency and-or unity of meaning. However, prior to the conceptual and interpretative translation into matter (ὕλη), the early Greek considerations moved oth-

---

33. Merriam-Webster English Dictionary, s.v. *water*, https://www.merriam-webster.com/dictionary/water, accessed 14 March, 2023.

34. Barbara Cassin, "Philosophising in Languages," trans. Yves Gilonne, *Nottingham French Studies* 49, no. 2 (2010): 19, EUP Publishing.

35. For instance, in articulating various kinds of causes Aristotle calls the form (εἶδος) or shape (παράδειγμα) the λόγος of the *essence* (ὁ λόγος ὁ τοῦ τί ἦν εἶναι) of a thing (*Ph.* 194b.26–27).

erwise: ὕδωρ; ἀηρ, ἄπειρον. Translation of the central, radiant terms of Milesian thinking—ὕδωρ, ἄπειρον, ἀήρ—into the English words *water, indeterminate, air* tends to prevent further thinking on the meanings of the Greek terms.

In the case of Milesian thinking, the charged terms on which interpretation has been based appear so thoroughly transparent that rethinking the translations may seem a wasted effort. On the interpretive blockages formed from the sediment of tradition-translation, Sallis writes:

> To return from nature to φύσις is not merely to substitute for a modern word or concept its ancient equivalent. Rather, it is to reverse a history of translation that, beginning with the Latin rendering of φύσις as *natura*, has distanced what is said in the translation from what was once said in the word φύσις. In the modern designation there is borne a sedimented history of interpretation, which has both deposited senses alien to that of φύσις and rendered imperceptible much that originally sounded in the word, not least of all the echoes of mythic discourse.[36]

While Sallis looks to dislodge φύσις from the strictures imposed on it through translation, the more specific terms ὕδωρ, ἄπειρον, ἀήρ form the area of this inquiry. What else beyond *water* and *air* might translate ὕδωρ and ἀήρ? The responses to this begin through and after the work of this study; in a sense, then, *Breaking Light* attempts a preliminary effort in the direction of bringing into view some broader horizons of translational—and so interpretive—possibilities in which those terms can be thought.

Opacity: Another Beginning

> It is one of the truths of poetry that an *Art poétique* is always in the future, always marked with the sign of that which is to come.
>
> —Glissant, "What Was Us, What Is Us"[37]

---

36. Sallis, *Figure of Nature*, 1.

37. Glissant, "What Was Us, What Is Us," in *Treatise on the Whole-World*, trans. Celia Britton (Liverpool University Press, 2020), 89, ProQuest.

Breaking Light attempts to break away from the breaking light of clarity and intelligibility attributed to the dawn of philosophy. In this sense, *breaking* speaks not of the light that inaugurates day, but as a rupture of the critical emphasis on light (clarity and intelligibility) as the distinguishing feature of philosophy. Not light, but rather opacity, numerous and teeming—*opacities*—as a radiant aura of abundance and richness, animates the sayings of the Milesian circle. One way to attempt this other *breaking* involves highlighting the poetic atmosphere of early Greek thinking, an atmosphere, again, animated by opacity, or opacities. Unfolding this animating sense in early Greek thinking, specifically focused on Milesians, attempts another beginning that seeks to open a way for the poetic resonances of early thinking to spread manifold, unclosed, to inspire more and further (re-)beginnings that *de-light* in their spiraled, torqued unforeseeabilities, their numinous openings and relations yet-to-come.[38]

Opacity, elaborated by Martinican thinker Édouard Glissant (1928–2011), spreads in multiple directions, including political, epistemological, literary, and ontological zones of inquiry. While emphasis throughout *Breaking Light* falls primarily on literary and the jointure of epistemological-ontological opacities, firm or solid barriers do not neatly contain one valence or dimension from another. Indeed, one of the major reverberations of the poetic opacity of Milesian thinking involves an engaged reticence, an ethical sensibility in voicing the profound interconnectivities of totality in relation. A way of being with others seems to flow from opacity in its multiplicity, a way characterized by openness toward and engagement with differences beyond mere tolerance.[39]

As an active engagement or a "textual practice" indissolubly relational, literary opacity unfurls from what Glissant sees as an opaque relation between thought and language on account of which all language takes place as opacity. Literary texts activate two (or three) regions of opacity: an "irreducible opacity of the text" and an "always evolving opacity of the author or a reader."[40] In the case of the Milesians, whose texts—if any ever existed—only echo through numerous other literary opacities, the thinkers invoking, summarizing, (allegedly) quoting, and commenting on Milesian thinking and the texts where those echoes, as linguistic phenomena in a

---

38. Inspired by Glissant's discussion and phrasing on spiral in "What Was Us, What Is Us," 98.

39. *PR*, 17.

40. *PR*, 115.

highly mediated ancient language, sound and resound, opacities overlap and layer in a provocative literary richness. When an additional dimension of opacity emerges from exploring the literary relations, other literary texts from the eastern Aegean cultural matrix and beyond, through which the terms of Milesian thinking resonate, the approach to archaic Greek thinking comes forward as already saturated with opacities.

OPACITY

The robust energies of Glissantian opacity propel the following interpretations of early Greek thinking, giving voice to an important dimension of the central and most resonant terms in their thinking, a dimension lost to interpretation oriented by clarity and yet already there in the archaic network of meanings generated by those terms. Multiple ways the energies of opacity work in Milesian thinking emerge throughout the inquiry, but as a preliminary, let opacity name what is irreducible and indissoluble and, moreover, what moves continually in—and perhaps *as*—the openings of Relation: "that which cannot be reduced, which is the most perennial guarantee of participation and confluence."[41] Importantly, opacities do not constitute absolutes, fixed cores or substance-essences that remain ever-out-of-reach—as in the "wedge-shaped core of darkness" free of attachments imagined by Virginia Woolf's Mrs. Ramsay in *To the Lighthouse*,[42] or, perhaps more directly, what Nietzsche heard in Anaximandrean ἄπειρον that echoed "the Kantian thing-in-itself," an "ultimate unity" (*letzte Einheit*) radically unavailable and only indicated through a negative.[43] Instead, as Nicole Jenette Simek has phrased it, opacity works as "an impetus to open-ended interpretation,"[44] an energy in-of-for *relation* of multiplicities, not unities. Relation relays opacities in continual movements, overlapping with totality as "open" and "in movement on and

---

41. *PR*, 191.

42. Virginia Woolf, *To the Lighthouse* (Harcourt Brace, 1927), 95–96. Another study might bring out some ways Woolf's voicing of something like an *opacity* wavers between and among what this phrase suggests, an impenetrable essence, and a point and moment of entanglements and relations, a locus of and for rejoining relations otherwise.

43. *PTAG*, 47; *PZG*, 170.

44. Nicole Jenette Simek, "Stubborn Shadows," *Symplokē* 23, no. 1–2 (2015): 369, Project Muse.

towards itself" (*en mouvement sur elle-même*) without the "principle of unity."[45] Opacity teems and overflows, not as an unintelligible something or as irrationality, but as *other than* intelligible and rational, as generated by the interactions or "weaving and interweaving" of several strands: this weaving suitably describes both Glissant and the Milesians, sourced from "a poetic imaginary" and generating a textured way of thinking that defies simple generic categorization.[46] Not only crossing and blurring genres, opacity withdraws too from a full articulation, an instance of its own movements, characterized as "a process rather than a product," such that its actions and movements—its generative relations—emerge in the work of interpretation.[47]

Experiences of opacity-in-relation provoke a poetic language that leaves open a span in which multiplicities can shimmer in their passing. Poetic speech attempts to set in motion what Glissant described as errancy, a way of moving without grasping for control or dominion and that "challenges and discards the universal" as a feature of territorial striving, seeking instead a language that "plunges into the opacities" of an area accessible to the one writing and thinking.[48] Such openness of poetic speech that lets opacities shimmer forms a moment of relation joining Glissant's poetics and Heidegger's thinking of poetic speech as ever more poetic to the extent that it remains "more open and ready for the unforeseen" (*Unvermutete*),[49] a phrase gesturing to the Herakleitean saying that "unless one foresees (ἔλπηται) the unforeseeable (ἀνέλπιστον), one will not disclose (ἐξευρήσει) being (ἐόν)—what refuses disclosure (ἀνεξερεύνητον)

---

45. *PdR*, 206; *PR*, 192.

46. Alexandre Leupin, *Édouard Glissant, Philosopher: Heraclitus and Hegel in the Whole-World*, trans. Andrew Brown (State University of New York Press, 2021), 46.

47. Michael Wiedorn, *Think Like an Archipelago: Paradox in the Work of Édouard Glissant* (State University of New York Press, 2018), 110–11, EBSCOhost.

48. *PR*, 20.

49. Martin Heidegger, ". . . Poetically Man Dwells . . . ," trans. Albert Hofstadter in *Poetry, Language, Thought* (Harper and Row, 1971), 214. My interpolation from Heidegger, ". . . dichterisch wohnet der Mensch . . . ," in *Vorträge und Aufsätze* (Klett-Cotta, 1954), 194. The full statement in Hofstadter's translation says: "The more poetic a poet is—the freer (that is, the more open and ready for the unforeseen) his saying—the greater is the purity with which he submits (*um so reiner stellt er*) what he says to an ever more painstaking listening, and the further what he says is from the mere propositional statement that is dealt with solely in regard to its correctness or incorrectness."

and goes nowhere (ἄπορον)" (Hct. 18 Robinson).[50] Opening poetic speech as openness and preserving opacities, a distinction might surface where Heidegger thinks this way of speaking in terms of "purity," while Glissant, as Isabel Astrachan has noted, articulates, promotes, and enacts *créolisation* in his "advocacy for a 'cross-cultural poetics'" and its diverse formations.[51] Poetic language, ready for what Glissant calls an "unforeseeable whirl" (*les tourbillons imprévisibles*) of relation in its expanse, keeps active multiplicities of meanings and multiple, diverse interpretive possibilities—shelters and preserves opacities.[52] Seanna Sumalee Oakley has observed that the ontologically oriented disclosures of Heidegger require a certain privileging of transparency—the light of clearing, the "open that is lighted by it itself as it itself"[53]—while Glissant is willing to suspend a need for understanding and advances, instead, an orientation of living-with, allowing opacities to tremor in their motions unresolved or reduced by the settling action of understanding.[54] Yet here, too, relations with Heidegger's thinking on poetic speaking can be felt where poetic language infuses the "familiar appearances" (*den vertrauten Erscheinungen*) with the foreign (*das Fremde*) as a way to sustain the unseen in its shimmering, as unknown (*unbekannt*),[55] which is to say, to preserve the opacities in their radiant motions just as Glissantian—and Milesian—opacities hover in an appearing that does not simply disclose, a coming-to-light *as* opacities.

Throughout *Breaking Light* opacity is energized by and from both Glissant and Heidegger, and their thinkings on opacity and ἀλήθεια weave in relations with the early Greeks. When opacity sounds in early Greek

---

50. A version of this translation first appeared in Spitzer, "Envisioning In-Visibility," in *The Translator's Visibility: New Debates and Epistemologies*, ed. Larisa Cercel and Alice Leal (Routledge, 2025), 236.

51. Isabel Astrachan, "Language and Being(s): Édouard Glissant and Martin Heidegger," *CLR James Journal* 26, no. 1 (2020): 168, JSTOR.

52. *PR*, 62; *PdR*, 74–75.

53. Heidegger, *Parmenides*, trans. André Schuwer and Richard Rojcewicz (Indiana University Press, 1992), 162.

54. Seanna Sumalee Oakley, "Commonplaces: Rhetorical Figures of Difference in Heidegger and Glissant," *Philosophy and Rhetoric* 41, no. 1 (2008): 10–11, Project Muse. There may also emerge an important difference in the letting-appear and letting-sound of Heidegger's poetics in contrast to the more active producing at work in Glissant. Astrachan, "Language and Being(s)," 167–68; Oakley, "Commonplaces," 16.

55. Heidegger, ". . . Poetically Man Dwells . . . ," trans. Albert Hofstadter, 223; my interpolation from ". . . dichterisch wohnet der Mensch . . . ," 194.

thinking, so resounds the unthought or unsaid: ἀλήθεια. Opacities and ἀλήθεια share a dynamics, a way of moving, as David Farrell Krell has written about the thematic hauntings of ἀλήθεια in *Odyssey* 5, like intricately woven "cryptic, calyptic concealments, concealments that somehow *show themselves*, reveal (Heidegger would insist) the mysterious dimension of every showing."[56] Heidegger brings out the motions of this word, the twofold of concealing and unconcealing that animates the word and event of ἀλήθεια, a togetherness not in the apparent oppositional or cancelling sense in which one replaces the other, but in such a way that each belongs to and with the other.[57] The Milesians' ways of voicing the dynamics of ἀλήθεια emerge poetically, similar to how Glissant, according to Oakley, reimagines figures from Heidegger's writings "aslant" through his granting "the task of thinking to poetry;"[58] the Milesians do not speak the word (ἀλήθεια), but the radiant terms of their thinking pulse with its energies and overlap in their regions of meaning.

RELATION, TRANSVERSALITY

> . . . everything communicates with the rest of the universe
>
> —Glissant, "The Poetics of the World"

A circle opening and gaining dimension, spiralized, helical, *relation* links Édouard Glissant and the early Greek thinkers transversally, letting Glissant's thinking of opacity, relation, multiplicity open fresh perspectives on the early Greeks through a spread of meanings and meaning networks.[59] In *Poetics of Relation*, voicing a dialogue with early Greek thinking that is, as Alexandre Leupin writes, "made clear everywhere,"[60] Glissant

---

56. David Farrell Krell, "Kalypso: Homeric Concealments after Nietzsche, Heidegger, Derrida, and Lacan," in *The Presocratics after Heidegger*, ed. David C. Jacobs (State University of New York Press, 1999), 117.

57. Heidegger, "ALETHEIA: (Heraklit, Fragment 16)," in *Vorträge und Aufsätze*, 254, 268.

58. Oakley, "Commonplaces," 6.

59. In his reading of Michel Leiris's *Aurora*, Glissant articulates geographical relations ("collusions between places") and the generative tangle of meanings flowing from what he calls "supra-logical mysteries of semantics" as "tranversalities." Glissant, "What Was Us, What Is Us," 83.

60. Leupin, *Édouard Glissant, Philosopher*, 68.

suggests the early stirrings of an imaginary energized by opacity in "the Pre-Socratics," among several ancient sources, an imaginary that "had premonitions of its unforeseeable whirl" (*les tourbillons imprévisibles*).[61] The *tourbillons* of relation manifest in a poetic language and sensibility that draw into dialogue Glissant and the early Greeks, among others. Such language, when amplified, challenges the reduction to clear, transparent doctrines through a richness of image, incompleteness, and openness, "an endless finality, one that remains open to the unpredictable surprise of becoming."[62] Full of tensions, the poetic language spanning Glissant and the early Greek thinkers slows the pace, asks for multiple readings, tremulous prefigurations of totality: "We find, in the abrupt, fragmentary texts of the pre-Socratics—as though the fragment were a piece of vanished duration—this feeling that our period has renewed that pre-Socratic era, when the hybridities of islands, the archipelagic thinking and the dreams of the Great-Whole had connected human to the earthly, or the cosmic. We imagine that we are beginning again that encounter, at least as long as we are not afraid of its mystical excesses."[63] An excess, an abundance of connectivity resonates for Glissant from the echoes of early Greek thinking and its poetics. This provokes continual returns, just as Glissant's own work asks readers, in Michael Wiedorn's phrase, to "experience philosophy as a continuous unknowing, a repeated call to imagine anew."[64] Heard together, Milesians and Glissant amplify this call.

Poetry and philosophy permeate one another in Glissant, while in early Greek thinking they have not yet been fully differentiated. Instead, on the cusp of this distinction, on its fold, early Greek thinking might be understood as *folding* into these two folds not yet folded. More still turns in the turbines of both Glissant and the early Greeks: Glissant wrote poems, essays, philosophic texts (incorporating elements of poetry and prose, reportage and theory), dramas; Thales, if he wrote anything, may have composed in dactylic hexameters, the poetic measure of Homeric and Hesiodic poetries, though he was also said to have written nothing, engaged rather in an oral dialogue with Egyptians, with the Karians, Phoinikians, Persians, and Greeks in Miletos and abroad, developing a

---

61. *PR,* 62; *PdR,* 74–75.

62. Leupin, *Édouard Glissant, Philosopher,* 85.

63. Glissant, "What Was Us, What Is Us," 102.

64. Wiedorn, *Think Like an Archipelago,* 112.

ground-work or field-work (*geo-metry*) out of such dialogue; Anaximandros produced not only text but a gnomon and a map of the inhabited world, multimodal in his poetics; the language of Anaximenes that shows through the testimonies pulses with a concrete imagery, with the place-based work of felting and with the work of the forge. From his first book of poems to his last, from the first line—"to every tortured geography [. . .] persuading one to stop at the uncertain—that which trembles, wavers, and ceaselessly becomes—like a devastated land—scattered" (from the opening fragment of *Riveted Blood*, 1947–50)—to the last—"Like a sowing of *chadron*! . . . Like milk from a mad *bécune*! . . . All the way to raising the bucket of water, nacreous with a heaviness of words [. . .] *Knowledge in a genuine abyss*" (from the closing graph and notes of *The Great Chaoses*, 1993)[65]—lived and living place(s) propel Glissant, sound in the language-scape. Throughout *Breaking Light* Milesian thinking gathers itself and moves (at least implicitly) *in situ*, on the shore, the liminal region of earth and sea meeting, overlapping: the Aegean surge reflects and teems in Thalean considerations, spans and outspans in Anaximandrean thinking, pulses with its similarity-and-difference with the densities of mist in Anaximenean thinking. The Milesian circle orients itself, is set in motion with and beside, the Aegean at Miletos.

Transversally joining Glissant and the Milesians in a study toward a poetics of opacity hopefully opens an area for rethinking the early Greeks otherwise than as a Eurocentric assertion of "the universality of the rational,"[66] where the latter describes one mode of reasoning, thoughtful comportment developed in Europe, at the exclusion of other modes—accordingly, it might be regarded as the *continental* mode. Opacity voices a different mode and can be heard throughout Milesian thinking. Similarly, a broad cultural matrix and imaginary in which move ideas and images from a vast and diverse region dissolves the supposed or presumed boundaries of East and West, drawn more starkly in the aftermath of the Greek-Persian wars, that Herodotos articulated in the opening of (and

---

65. *The Collected Poems of Édouard Glissant*, ed. Jefferson Humphries, trans. Melissa Manolas (University of Minnesota Press, 2005), 5, 256–57, respectively. Glissant's notes explain that *bécune* and *chadron* "are species of Antillean fauna" (257). Dates of publication come from Humphries's introduction and, ultimately, were "provided by Glissant himself" (xxxiii), although some bibliographic information elsewhere differs from these dates.

66. Hwa Yol Jung, "Transversality and the Philosophical Politics of Multiculturalism in the Age of Globalization," *Research in Phenomenology* 39, no. 3 (2009): 418, JSTOR.

throughout) his *Inquiries*. Expansively transversal, the Milesian circle—the Milesian *archipelago*—gives voice to a thinking churned within an estuary of cultures in relation, a *tourbillon* of ideas and images, an imaginary of relation and diversity. Miletos, as a location of interactivity, relation, diversity, propels Thalean, Anaximandrean, and Anaximenean thinking. On such a site the Milesians and Glissant again meet: Milesian thinking resonates with Glissant's in "becoming entangled in a realm far from abstraction, individualization, and solitude, located amid the realities of the world, in the sharing of a community, even if this community is still to come."[67] The following section, "(Re-)Beginnings," sketches this *tourbillon* of an Aegean imaginary while the chapters whirl within its movements.

As Oakley has put it, "Relation is not uniform," does not insist on an equilibrium in its moments, taking place as "different and relative."[68] For the project of *Breaking Light*, the transversal relations do not occur as a reciprocal circuitry through which attention circulates equally to Glissant, the diverse sources of the broader Mediterranean basin, and the Milesians. Rather, activating these relations by associations, affiliations, resonances, thematic soundings turns ever back toward Milesian thinking, attending to how that thinking shows up differently through the turnings of these relations. Even where linkages just surface to momentary view in passing, the emphasis on in-relation deepens and adds to the sense of a poetics of μίξις (articulated below). Such associations add to the relational aura, the nimbus of multiple and diverse meaning-networks accompanying Milesian thinking in ever-varying degrees of intensity and radiant hues. If nothing else, these provisional and momentary contacts-in-relation might prompt further research with different trajectories and focal areas, listening for how early Greek thinking quickens, for instance, Persian or Indian thinking, or twentieth- and twenty-first-century Caribbean thinking.

Opacity and (Un-)Translatabilty

What pathways come into view when Milesian thinking—all of which spoken (or, perhaps, written) in a manner that sounded *poetic* to ancients—resonates as dynamically unstable and untranslatable?

Although on its face the term *untranslatable* would seem to suggest a foreclosure on the possibilities for translation, untranslatability describes

---

67. Leupin, *Édouard Glissant, Philosopher*, 3.

68. Oakley, "Commonplaces," 12–13.

"not," as Barbara Cassin has put it, "what one doesn't translate but what one doesn't stop (not) translating,"[69] those aspects of texts, phrases, or critical words whose energies quicken and provoke further and continual efforts along the double helix of translation-interpretation. The *energies of the untranslatables,* to borrow a luminous phrase from Cassin,[70] summon the task of rethinking and reimagining the widening zones of meaning that translation cannot exhaust. An important dimension of this task involves disrupting and undoing what H. L. Hix has termed "translation inertia," a form of "signostalgia" specific to translation according to which a cessation of the dynamics involved in translating and interpreting leads to stagnation, to repetition without rethinking, to a stasis of language and meaning that limits the range of further interpretive possibilities.[71] Rethinking through untranslatability forms a counter-movement to the presumed transparency available for translating the radiant terms of Milesian thinking.

While some apparent strain may arise in the effort, the inertia settled upon early Greek thinking cannot be countered without such strain, without the collisions of that thinking with the movements of imagination. Translation can return the living motions of thinking to the terms and phrases of early Greek thinking, can reawaken an oralcy not as a relic of ancient and outmoded activity, but as "an abiding and dynamic element of philosophy's practice" that creates and preserves multiple possibilities for meaning.[72] In so doing, the poetic dimensions and horizons of this thinking surge into renewals and afterlives. The locus of crossings where the poetic valences, gusts, and currents of the Milesian terms converge and spiral does not open as a clearing or bright expanse, however. Rather, it thickens, spreads, and rolls as a dense cloud heavy with fluidity on the edge of collapse, a storm of opacity. In response to this, part of this project's task is to release and articulate the overwhelming senses of *opacity*

---

69. Cassin, "Translation as Paradigm for Human Sciences," *Journal of Speculative Philosophy* 30, no. 3 (2016): 243, Project Muse. Cassin also importantly stresses that untranslatability is to be thought in the plural: *untranslatables.*

70. The phrase "energies of the untranslatables" draws on Barbara Cassin, "The Energy of the Untranslatables: Translation as a Paradigm for the Human Sciences," *Paragraph* 38, no. 2 (2015): 145–58, EBSCOhost.

71. H. L. Hix, "A 'Sneaky' Form of Non-Translation," On Non-Translation and Translation Panel, Annual Conference, American Literary Translators Association, Rochester, New York, 10 November, 2019.

72. Spitzer, "Trans-philosophy: Translating philosophy on and beyond the boundaries," *Journal of Speculative Philosophy* 37, no. 3 (2023): 579–80, Project Muse.

resonant in the Greek terms through a balance of non-translation and close interpretation of the meaning-networks through and out of which these pivotal words reverberated in Milesian thinking.[73] To serve as a reminder that *water, air, unlimited/boundless* do not exhaust translation and thinking of ὕδωρ, ἄπειρον, ἀήρ, the Greek terms are presented untranslated.

(Re-)Beginnings: Recoveries, (Re-)Sources, Relations

"Perhaps," as Walter Brogan has written on Herakleitos, "there is a problem with too much familiarity that blocks us from what is essential for thinking."[74] In order to move interpretation away from or around the obstacles of over-familiarity, the most basic words of the earliest philosophers undergo critical suspension throughout this work: the familiar and habitual manner of treating ὕδωρ, ἄπειρον, and ἀήρ as words that simply designate water, unlimited(-ness), and air now hovers in suspense. From that suspension, soundings can begin through and across archaic Greek literatures in such a way as to reanimate and reawaken the vast range of meanings resonating from these terms as well as the profound interrelatedness joining them. Alongside the words themselves the founding interpretive criteria of clarity and intelligibility, derived mostly from Aristotle and the sources on which his own familiarity with the archaic Greek thinkers drew, also rise into suspension and appear in that suspension as already orienting interpretation of these thinkers in particular directions.

Movement in the direction of another way to interpret early Greek thinking takes place as a gesture of imagination, a projection, a leap. A similar leap Nietzsche ascribes to the philosopher in his discussion of Thales, and while the ground does (or can) collapse beneath the imagination's (*die Phantasie*) rapid footfalls, and the philosopher's imagination crosses moving waters in Nietzsche's image, the image does not end in entering and being submerged in the flowing waters; solid, if unstable,

---

73. Unlike Bachelard's sense of *reverberation* as an originary experience of an image and prior to—or transcendent with respect to—that image's history, reverberation in this study builds from a sense that the meaning networks of images propel them, in the first place, bestowing their newness. Just as waves rising in the sea are not distinct from the sea, but rather, it may be said that the sea waves, so, too, the meaning-network *images*. Gaston Bachelard, *The Poetics of Space*, trans. Maria Jolas (Penguin, 1964), 2–9.

74. Walter A. Brogan, "Heraclitus, Philosopher of the Sign," in Jacobs, *The Presocratics after Heidegger*, 268.

ground forms the terrain of philosophy in Nietzsche's image. Nietzsche envisions such leaping, propelled by *ein genialisches Vorgefuhl* (Krell translates: "ingenious premonition"[75]), as constitutive of philosophy, while calculating reason (*rechnende Verstand*) falls behind as it seeks more secure footholds (*sucht bessere Stützen*).[76] Kirkland articulates Nietzsche's disclosure of the imaginative force animating a leap in early Greek thinking from the abyss opened after the traditional mythic structures collapse through an "attunement to Nature as a terrifying loss of order." This leap takes place as another movement of φύσις, the movement of (imaginative, creative) thinking *from* the abyssal opening *toward* and *into* the work of engendering a "beautifully ordered and powerful philosophical or poetic discourse."[77] As Krell has observed, this forms a tension in Nietzsche's early engagement with early Greek thinking: this premonition (*Vorgefuhl*), this imaginative force (*Phantasie*), "is not 'imaginative' in the usual sense," barring from Thalean considerations mythic and poetic dimensions.[78] Even while Nietzsche sees that the purported Thalean pronouncement that *all is water* does bear associations with the mythic and poetic imaginary of ancient Greece, he finds that, of the threefold directives of that thought, only the third and final renders it eligible for the title *philosophy*: the articulation of an underlying unity, which has already surfaced as one of the interpretive rays gleaming from the dual interpretive principles of clarity and intelligibility. *Breaking Light* leaps alongside or in the manner of Nietzsche's Thales in the sense that emphasis falls on an alien imaginative power moving early Greek thinking, though in another sense—on the point of clarity, intelligibility, and unity—this project leaps *away from* Nietzsche's interpretations (however secondary they may be in his project) and *toward* a recovery of a poetics in early Greek thinking oriented by opacity, relation, multiplicity.

RE: BEGINNINGS, RECOVERIES

The following chapters on Thalean, Anaximandrean, and Anaximenean thinking work to recover vital networks of meanings that surface in the

---

75. David Farrell Krell, *The Sea: A Philosophical Encounter* (Bloomsbury, 2019), 132.

76. *PTAG*, 39–41; *PZG*, 164–65.

77. Kirkland, "Nietzsche," 432.

78. Krell, *Sea*, 132.

tourbillon of cultural imaginaries beyond the limits of the conventional narratives, translations, and interpretations, so as to let the thinking register in expansive ways apart from the reduction to clarity, intelligibility, and unity. *Recovering* unfolds in a complex manner, its movement generating torque on itself. In one sense, by suspending the Aristotelian vocabulary and parameters for interpretation and thinking the Milesians within the mythic-poetic imaginary of the wider Mediterranean cultural matrix, a sense of recovery emerges as *retrieval* of pre-philosophic meanings—where *pre-philosophic* identifies a historical zone of pre-disciplinarity in which *philosophia*, in particular, has not yet formed into a discipline in contrast to other disciplines, like poetry. Pre-philosophic does not mean less than or on the way to philosophy, but *other than* and *in excess of* what philosophy in its later disciplinary determination will encompass, so that, in a sense, what Sallis has called "the echo of philosophy before philosophy"[79] already "exceeds the boundaries of what is recognized as philosophy."[80] These meanings may help animate rethinkings of how what comes to be called philosophy already extends beyond itself, contains within itself a multiplicity of practices and modes. Motivated by this point, the interpretations unfolded in *Breaking Light* do not seek to overcome or replace existing readings, but to complement them; indeed, an undercurrent throughout the study involves registering the multiplicities pulsing in archaic Greek thinking.

The second sense of *recovery* brings out the ways in which interpretations *cover again* (re-) their subjects; the intended *retrieval* (recovery) only occurs from a position and contemporary nexus of entanglements, commitments, expectations, perspectives. Mobilizing Glissant and other thinkers of the twentieth- and twenty-first-centuries in the direction of fresh readings of the early Greeks will result in *re-coverings* or what Hix calls "distortions,"[81] ways interpretation arises through the interactions of differently situated thinkers. All interpretation produces this: logical analysis, attempts to (re-)construct argumentation and/or consistent systems (by today's standards) from the sparse remains and the reports concerning these thinkers, philological investigation applying insights in linguistics

---

79. Sallis, *Figure of Nature*, 14.

80. Robert Bernasconi, "Almost Always More Than Philosophy Proper," *Research in Phenomenology* 30, no. 1 (2000): 5, JSTOR.

81. Hix, "Fire at Night: A Version of Herakleitos," *Yale Review* 103, no. 2 (2015): 6–7, Project Muse.

and languages developed many centuries after the Milesians and the other literatures of the archaic period. All such approaches *distort* and *cover* the areas of inquiry, not because they are inappropriate or misguided, but because the act of interpretation brings some elements into focus while minimizing or excising other elements and shapes what it interprets by its own contours. Such covering, too, does not take place as something additional, but rather in a way that cannot be separated from what is covered; said differently, the world is always-already interpreted, a manifold of re-coverings, an irreducible multiplicity of layers. *Breaking Light* stresses the poetic valences and reverberations of the Milesian sayings as they activate multiple traditions, the vast and diverse eastern Aegean and Near Eastern imaginary(-ies) churning in their home city of Miletos and the various locations on their different itineraries in an attempt to reawaken dimensions of early Greek thinking that too often remain dormant in interpretive engagements.

Drawn through language that provokes further interpretation and attempts to open possibilities for meanings, the interpretive limits might be set in motion such that they occur as a kind of hovering between act and acting, between said and saying. This might be termed *limiting* or *bordering*, an interpretive approach "transitory, like chalk-drawn contours,"[82] a pathway traced in fluid strokes that describe a moment in on-going relations, the movement of a sketch. In order to activate this way of engaging toward early Greek thinking, much of the discussions in the chapters develop, like the title itself, through gerunds and-or gerundives: *Divining, Spanning, Hovering*. From the dynamics of a participle, these mean to propel thinking through their own hovering between noun and verb, perhaps generating some friction upon those boundaries. Also, participles evocatively sustain a present tense and its ongoing, unfinished aspect, hopefully inspiring a live engagement, an ongoing thinking in the interaction of reading through which this book begins to become what it might be, to open possibilities. In a way, this language, hovering, attempts to set in motion the verbal sense Heidegger disclosed in his engagement with Herakleitean φύσις and its participial and verbal aspect of rising and emerging that works otherwise than according to the metaphysics

---

82. Spitzer, "Introduction: Bordering Approaches and Trans-bordering Themes in Dialogue with the Work of Rosemary Arrojo," in *Transfiction and Bordering Approaches to Theorizing Translation: Essays in Dialogue with the Work of Rosemary Arrojo*, ed. D. M. Spitzer and Paulo Oliveira (Routledge, 2023), 4.

of substance (embedded in substantives).[83] The stress on participles also summons what Glissant described as the errancy involved in a poetics of relation, a way of moving without grasping for control or dominion and that "challenges and discards the universal" as a feature of territorial striving, seeking instead a language that "plunges into the opacities" of an area accessible to the one writing and thinking.[84]

If the language at work throughout *Breaking Light* seems at times to draw on poetic or creative writing resources more than on more conventional conceptual-discursive modes of philosophy, this is also because one motivating notion of this study has to do with ways that the more technical and specialized vocabulary of philosophy as a discipline has produced narrow interpretive boundaries with respect to the early Greek thinkers. Straining, pivoting, resisting those boundaries, the poetic energies try to reawaken a sense of philosophy before philosophy, its voicing in the language and meaning-networks of multiple imaginaries and their poetries. Balancing these energies, hopefully, operates a sustained call to listen for the opacities—"the dark urn / of words"[85]—quickening both these poetries and Milesian thinking, which relates to and so differs from those poetries.

(Re-)Sources

Through the archaic Greek period (eighth to early fifth c. BCE) flow the literatures selected to develop a confluent hydroscape of meanings within which Milesian considerations roil and pulse. While most of the poets in this study are from eastern Aegean cities or islands, exceptions include Stesikhoros, Bakkhylides, and Hesiod (ca. 700 BCE), though the latter's father may have come from the eastern Aegean Greek settlement of Kyme and is clearly known in the Greek east at least by the time of Xenophanes (mid-sixth c. BCE). A working assumption throughout is that even the works of those poets from areas at considerable distance from Miletos would have made their ways on the wings of speech to widespread Greek-speaking populations over the centuries of the archaic period and its regular trade and migration; assuming that ideas do not

---

83. Heidegger, "The Inception of Occidental Thinking," in *Heraclitus: The Inception of Occidental Thinking and Logic: Heraclitus's Doctrine of the Logos,* trans. Julia Goesser Assaiante and S. Montgomery Ewegen (Bloomsbury, 2018), 56–72.

84. *PR,* 20.

85. From Glissant, "Acclamation," trans. Mary Ann Caws, *Callaloo* 36, no. 4 (2013), 854, Project Muse.

circulate through and across putative cultural and linguistic barriers seems less reasonable—and less promising—than assuming they do (see below for discussion of this topic). If the Milesians Thales, Anaximandros, and Anaximenes lived during the sixth century BCE, the poetries assembled here form a surrounding atmosphere of language and images, the "already-there" of early Greek thinking, the vastness of Mnemosyne.[86] In some cases sources from somewhat later thinkers, such as Xenophanes (mid-sixth c. BCE), Herakleitos (late sixth c. BCE), and Parmenides (late sixth to early fifth c. BCE), provide additional emphasis or slightly different aspects of meanings resonating from the terms ὕδωρ, ἄπειρον, ἀήρ and their associations with other terms central to ancient Greek philosophy: ἀλήθεια, φύσις, λόγος. Such cases also serve to contour the afterlives of Milesian thinkings as they spread out from the early thinkers.

Cycling through Homeric, Hesiodic, and lyric poetries from Greek sources, each chapter also moves in spirals that include some sources less frequently given critical and comparative attention beyond their standard treatments in collections such as Kirk and Raven's *The Presocratic Philosophers*: the Egyptian *Book of the Dead* (ca. third millennium BCE), the *Leiden Hymns* (ca. thirteenth c. BCE), and the Shabaka Stone (ca. eighth c. BCE); the Zarathustran *Greater Bundahishn*, a ninth-century CE composition built from a very ancient oral tradition (ca. mid-sixteenth c. BCE);[87] early *Upanishads* (ca. seventh–sixth c. BCE), also drawing from a much older *Vedic* tradition reaching into the second millennium BCE.[88] Though these traditions significantly predate the Milesians, the working understanding that guides *Breaking Light* is that such sources remained an active part of the Egyptian and wider Eastern Aegean-Anatolian-Near-Eastern matrix of imaginaries, active in the sense of continuing "to exercise the imaginations of thinkers" in direct and indirect contact with them.[89]

RELATIONS

Opening a broad zone for inquiry, something like an estuary and its shifting and variegated waters coursing together and gathering earth and

---

86. On the *already-there* of early Greek thinking, see Spitzer, *Parmenides and Translation*, 17–38.

87. Prods Oktor Skjaervo, *Spirit of Zoroastrianism* (Yale University Press, 2011), 2–3, 6.

88. Patrick Olivelle, *Upaniṣads* (Oxford University Press, 1996), xxxvi–xxxvii.

89. Spitzer, "Images in Archaic Thinking," *Epoché: A Journal for the History of Philosophy* 26, no. 1 (2021): 2.

sea and sky and light, lets some dimensions of early Greek thinking flow and glisten in the dappled light and shade of a wide area of literatures. Rather than thinking the Milesians according to the traditional break with the poetic and mythic imaginaries of the archaic Greek period—in Hegel's terms, "without image" and "not blemished (*behaftet*) with sensuous representations (*Vorstellungen der Sinnlichkeit*)"[90]—this study allows the multiple registers of early Greek thinking to sound and echo throughout a vast expanse of images from a diverse region. While the Milesian Greek philosophers Thales, Anaximandros, and Anaximenes configure the focal point(s) of *Breaking Light*, taken as a community or a circle, their thinking moves within a wider circle encompassing the Aegean and even wider Mediterranean, Levantine, Mesopotamian, Persian, and Indian communities in which considerations on totality reach into a period that among the Greeks is now called Mycenean. Yet, even as the primary focus within the widened (trans-)cultural area remains on the three Milesians, this does not intend to reduce relation to a single direction, but to acknowledge and make explicit that *Breaking Light* focuses on the ways these relations enhance understanding of archaic Greek thinking. Perhaps some other studies will follow these relations in other directions, investigating the ways early Greek thinking might activate transformations in, for instance, the traditions of Zarathustran thinking of later periods.

Théophile Obenga has laid out ways that Egyptian texts from the third millennium BCE formed "a set of teachings (*sebayit*) viewed as a coherent body of precedents influencing the present,"[91] and Phoinikians likely formed a conduit for the dissemination of Egyptian thinking into Greek and other communities of the eastern Aegean region.[92] The principal Phoinikian cities on the eastern Aegean—Byblos, Sidon, Tyre, Arados—formed "a westward-facing maritime region" operating as contact and launching zones through which the major regional powers (Egypt and Mesopotamia) passed.[93] In the early centuries of the first millennium BCE the vast trade

---

90. Hegel, *Vorlesungen über die Geschichte der Philosophie*, 148; *Lectures on the History of Philosophy*, 191–92.

91. Théophile Obenga, "Egypt: Ancient History of African Philosophy," in *A Companion to African Philosophy*, ed. Kwasi Wiredu (John Wiley and Sons, 2004), 35, ProQuest.

92. Marinatos has suggested this with respect to a theme of circular heroic journey to the edges of the kosmos. Nanno Marinatos, "The Cosmic Journey of Odysseus," *Numen* 48, no. 4 (2001): 382, JSTOR.

93. John C. Scott, "The Phoenicians and the Formation of the Western World," *Comparative Civilizations Review* 78 (2018): 24–26, EBSCOhost.

network configured by the Phoinikians—ranging from the Black Sea to the western islands of the Mediterranean, the Iberian peninsula, and possibly the Atlantic coasts of Africa and Europe[94]—may have enabled the eventual Greek commercial expansions of the archaic period, beginning around the early to mid-eighth century BCE. J. N. Coldstream imagines close association between early Western Greeks and Phoinikians to the extent that "in western waters the Phoenicians could have been mentors to the Greeks, guiding them eventually towards suitable sites for settlement."[95]

Miletos, where the record of early Greek thinking first emerges, embodies the cultural nexus and confluence through and into which manifold cultural imaginaries churn. The city's foundation story, as formulated by Herodotos, involves a violent overthrow of an existing population (Karians) by a group of Ionians migrating from Athens (Hdt. 1.146). Even if the archaeological record does not support in detail the foundation narration Herodotos offers, Alan Greaves takes it to be "highly likely that there was a mixed Greek and Karian population at Miletos from the earliest times."[96] As a metropolis of the archaic period, Miletos established trading centers and cities over the Mediterranean basin, including sites on the Black Sea and Egypt. From the seventh century BCE, Naukratis, in the Nile Delta of Egypt, thought both to be the first of its kind in Egypt and to be of particularly important standing (Hdt. 2.178–79),[97] formed as a site of relations among Greeks and Egyptians. The city of Miletos set up a sanctuary to Apollo there (Hdt. 2.178) and possibly founded, or assisted in the foundation of, the city.[98]

Through Miletos passed regularly inbound and outbound goods and the people transporting them, and with such peoples the ideas, images, and myths from many different regions. In the city's diverse atmosphere images and themes flowed together in areas of material import, distribution,

---

94. Scott, "Phoenicians," 29, 35.

95. J. N. Coldstream, "Prospectors and Pioneers: Pithekoussai, Kyme and Central Italy," in *The Archaeology of Greek Colonisation: Essays Dedicated to Sir John Boardman*, ed. Gocha R. Tsetskhladze and Franco De Angelis (Oxford Committee for Archaeology, 1994), 47.

96. Alan M. Greaves, *Miletos: Archaeology and History* (Taylor and Francis, 2002), 55–56, ProQuest.

97. Walter Eric Harold Cockle, "Naucratis," in *OCD3*.

98. See Gerard Naddaf, "Anthropogony and Politogony in Anaximander of Miletus," in *Anaximander in Context: New Studies in the Origins of Greek Philosophy* (State University of New York Press, 2003), 36–37 with notes.

and production, such as metalwork, jewelry, faience, and pottery. The streams of relation flow in multiple directions: other Greek cities of the islands, western, and mainland regions; Egypt; Syria and Asia Minor; Mesopotamia. Such streams, inundated too by those flowing to the nearby oracular sanctuary at Didyma, diversified the city's population.[99] Archaic Milesian culture suggests a readiness to formulate new relations through the dynamics of migrational patterns both into and out from the city. Such fluidity emerges too in the difficulties, or impossibility, related to the identification of certain objects (specifically amulets) produced within the Phoinikian-Egyptian confluence.[100] The doxographic tradition links Thales to Phoinikian culture by way of his genealogy (Diog. Laert. 1.1.22 [Ths. 1 Graham]) and, by way of voyaging, to Egypt, where he was said to have begun practicing philosophy (φιλοσοφήσας δ᾽ἐν Αἰγύπτῳ, Ps.-Plut. *Plac.* 1.3.1 [Ths. 11 Graham]; Diog. Laert. 1.1.27 [Ths. 1 Graham]).

Similarly, the tradition around Anaximandros narrates voyages to the Greek mainland, along with close associations with Babylon. At Sparta, Anaximandros reportedly "put in place among the Lakedaimonians [Spartans] a *gnomon*" (Diog. Laert. 2.1 [Axr. 1 Graham]), an association also linking him to Babylonians.[101] While direct contact between Sparta and Mesopotamia can be established archaeologically in the seventh century BCE,[102] that contact also appears to have occurred in the figure of the poet Alkman. During this period at Sparta, Alkman, who may have been born in Sardis, capital of Lydia,[103] composed choral songs with apparently theogonic elements pulsing with cross-cultural energies and intimating

---

99. Greaves, *Miletos*, 61–68 (material production); 88–92 (sanctuary).

100. Carolina López-Ruiz, "Near Eastern Precedents of the 'Orphic' Gold Tablets: The Phoenician Missing Link," *Journal of Ancient Near Eastern Religions* 15, no. 1 (2015): 64–65, with notes, EBSCOhost. López-Ruiz articulates an important interpretive principle related to this point, that by "depriving Phoenicians of agency in creatively adapting and appropriating Egyptian and other Near Eastern traditions in their own art" and so viewing such objects as mere "amalgams" made by Phoinikian imitators the area within which Phoinikian cultural production can be more meaningfully studied is severely diminished.

101. M. Laura Gemelli Marciano, "East and West," in *Ancient Philosophy: Textual Pathways and Historical Explorations*, ed. Lorenzo Perilli and Daniela P. Taormina (Routledge, 2018), 18–19.

102. M. L. West, *Early Greek Philosophy and the Orient* (Oxford University Press, 1971), 207.

103. David Campbell, *Greek Lyric Poetry: A Selection of Early Greek Lyric, Elegiac and Iambic Poetry* (Bristol Classical Press, 1982), 193.

some of the filaments along which those energies travel.[104] Similarly, a century after Alkman, the Lydian ruler Kroisos, in his campaigns of the middle sixth century BCE, intended to muster an armed force composed of Egyptians, Babylonians, and Lakedaimonians (Hdt. 1.77), calling attention to historical relations among those various populations specifically in Asia Minor. Moving from Miletos to Sparta, that is, from one site of cultural convergences to another, Anaximandros's voyage to Sparta would have activated new perspectives on the ways Greek and Mesopotamian imaginaries already flow in currents of relation.

Unlike those of the earlier Milesians, biographies of Anaximenes do not include narratives of migration. Situated like Thales and Anaximandros at Miletos, Anaximenes also dwells within the networks and diversities of relation. Even without testimonies concerning travel, transversal relations would have formed for Anaximenes within the city limits, since Miletos around the time of Anaximenes's *floruit* had been linked to a rising Persian empire, its treaty with Lydian Kroisos transferred to Kyros of Persia (Hdt. 1.22, 1.141). Via the invasions and expansions of Kyros a conduit opened from Ionia and the eastern Aegean to the Indus River; Herodotos tells of a satrap of Kyros's at Babylon who kept many (expensive) hunting dogs from India (Hdt. 1.192). With goods come people, and with people, ideas and images, which circulate and transform in widening and unpredictable relays.

Poetics of μίξις

Opacities can coexist and converge, weaving fabrics. To understand these truly one must focus on the texture of the weave and not on the nature of its components.

—Glissant, *Poetics of Relation*[105]

---

104. West, "Three Presocratic Cosmologies," *Classical Quarterly* 13, no. 2 (1963): 155–56, JSTOR; *Early Greek Philosophy and the Orient*, 207–8.
"Apparently" because Most has advanced a different interpretation of the Alkman cosmogonic fragment, arguing that the preserved text belongs to the practice of allegorical reading and imports cosmogonic significance into an otherwise thoroughly local, ritually performed choral song presenting a myth. Glenn W. Most, "Alcman's 'Cosmogonic' Fragment (fr. 5 Page, 81 Calame)," *Classical Quarterly* 37, no. 1 (1987): 9–11, JSTOR.

105. *PR*, 190.

Throughout this book a guiding interpretive principle is that Greek sources bring different perspectives on ways of thinking and areas of inquiry that flood the whole vast and differentiated, yet fluidly connected, field of ancient communities. An aspect of these sources' opacities lies in their cultural multiplicity, their poetics of μίξις (*mixis*: mix, composition). Here, *mixis* describes a poetics animating Milesian thinking of the archaic period. The poetics of *mixis*, which also converges with a poetics of opacity, finds an echo within the poetics Glissant unfolded through the term *créolisation*. Glissant unfurls *créolisation* as an expansion and elaboration of *métissage*, a critical multiplication and diffraction of "the meeting and synthesis of two differences" into, instead, the multiple directions granted by the open awareness of expansive dynamics of relation on every level of existence—indeed, inherent to the notion of *existence*. As Glissant writes, "*créolisation* comes into view as *métissage* without limits, in which the elements are multiplied, the results unpredictable";[106] as a dynamic of relation, *créolisation* in Glissant works "as process" that "surpasses the known to actualize what exceeds the unknown."[107] This transformation or expansion of the double of *métissage* or hybridity on and through the energies of multiplicity(-ies) animates the poetics of *mixis* so that a mere tracing of separate and discrete filaments of meaning and "influence" that can be discerned within Milesian thinking no longer suffices. "Relation is not an external form that imprints itself upon chaotic or formless being," as Clevis Headley writes of Glissant's thinking.[108] Instead, the ontological status of each filament manifests in its already conditioned being-in-relation, which is to say its dynamics of becoming-through-relation: a kind of quickening without a final result or termination into multiplicity(-ies) and without a starting point on the stable grounds of substance or essence. Relation of *créolisation* overflows the presumed temporal and cultural linearities embedded in *influence* in a motion both spiralized—a "circularity with

---

106. *PdR*, 46–47; *PR*, 34.

107. Clevis Headley, "Glissant's Existential Ontology of Difference," in *Theorizing Glissant: Sites and Citations*, ed. John E. Drabinski and Marisa Parham (Rowman and Littlefield, 2015), 76, ProQuest. Headley interrogates and distances Glissant from "simple-minded 'aesthetic' construals of creolization as mixture" (76–77), and in the discussion of creolization here the term μίξις/*mixis* intends to separate from a notion of mere combination of pure elements into a (sterile) mixture.

108. Headley, "Glissant's Existential Ontology of Difference," 72.

volume"[109]—and torqued, polytropic in its generative turnings and twistings "from poetry to poetry, where an immense expanse of time and space constantly produces a redefinition, a difference."[110]

Relating opacities in motion, a poetics of *créolisation*, translated toward an archaic Mediterranean sphere in the term *mixis*, in its movements agitates and discloses—through unsettling—the already frayed and strained filaments of fixed cultural identities. As it works toward varied articulations throughout *Breaking Light*, a poetics of *mixis* lets sound and appear some ways in which an experience of relation expands along and through the new contours and configurations energized by identities not yet fixed and bound into ontologically determining and determined cultural categories, but rather charged with the energies of "diffusion, not concentration" that Irad Malkin has identified as operative in the archaic Greek moment.[111] Rethinking beginnings by way of a poetics of *créolisation-mixis* attempts to see anew, located and glimpsed within the folds of what Claudia Baracchi has called "radical discontinuities and fissures of forgetfulness," that which has been suppressed in the constructions of a continuity, that which remains "more hidden than ever precisely in its alleged epigones, in the schools bearing the names of its key figures."[112] The beginning traditionally assigned to Thales of Miletos and his companions Anaximandros and Anaximenes undergoes elemental transfiguration through multiple diffractions—thinking horizontally and oceanically in the currents of meaning—with sources from the Mediterranean basin and beyond its shores yet already involved by and as the pulse of relations. Approached transversally, the early Greeks do not assert—or are not asserted—in a position of dominance or superiority, but rather in "their shared role in cultural diversity,"[113] caught up in the turbines of

---

109. *PR,* 32.

110. Leupin, *Édouard Glissant, Philosopher,* 85. Leupin in this passage reads Glissant through and with Hegel and early Greek thinking, tracing a tautology or tautologies that continually generates differentiation.

111. Irad Malkin, "Postcolonial Concepts and Ancient Greek Colonization," *MLQ: Modern Language Quarterly* 65, no. 3 (2004): 348, Project Muse.

112. Claudia Baracchi, "Contributions to the Coming-to-Be of Greek Beginnings: Heidegger's Inceptive Thinking," in *Heidegger and the Greeks: Interpretive Essays,* ed. Drew A. Hyland and John P. Manoussakis (Indiana University Press, 2006), 28.

113. Glissant, "Cross-Cultural Poetics," in *Caribbean Discourse: Selected Essays,* trans. J. Michael Dash (University Press of Virginia, 1989), 101–2.

relation and the opacities animating them. The beginning, that is, dissolves and recedes into a tidal movement of numerous beginnings illuminated partially on the gleaming crest of their surges and then breaking into the oceanic surge of continual (re-)beginnings.

1

Divining

Thalean ὕδωρ

Dowsing

Beginning at the confluences, crossings, Thalean considerations seek elemental jointures: of sky and earth, fire and waters (Ps. Plut. *Plac.* 1.3; Stob. *Ecl.* 1.11.12 [Ths. 16 Graham]), divine and human. On mountain heights the sources of rivers flow from the earth's depths, high places ringing with the music of Kybele, "Mother Goddess,"[1] who appears in relief images carved "on rock faces in the open countryside, almost always in the vicinity of springs and natural sources of water."[2] A ὕδωρ-sources-springs complex pulses with the energies of the Great Goddess, whose center near Mount Dindymon in Phrygia lies between Miletos and the Halys River where Thales reportedly diverted the river to enable a crossing for Kroisos's forces (Hdt. 1.75.3–5).[3] Tishtrya, a male-masculine divinity, bore in the Zarathustran cosmology a direct relation to the waters in several cosmic zones: a hymn to Tishtrya, identified with the star the Greeks

---

1. See the *Homeric Hymn to the Mother of Divinities*, where the din of musical instruments (βρόμος αὐλῶν) and wild animals flood the "mountains full of echoes and the wooded (mountain) river-beds (ἔναυλοι)" (*Hom. Hymn Ma. Th.* 14.5).

2. Mark Munn, "Earth and Water: The Foundations of Sovereignty in Ancient Thought," in *The Nature and Function of Water, Baths, Bathing, and Hygiene from Antiquity through the Renaissance*, ed. Anne Scott and Cynthia Kosso (Brill, 2009), 198, EBSCOhost.

3. Additional information on Kybele is from Stephen Mitchell, "Pessinus," in *OCD3*. Munn suggests other connections between Lydian views and Thalean considerations. Munn, "Earth and Water," 203, 206.

called Orion's Dog or Dog Star (κύν' Ὠρίωνος, Hom *Il.* 22.29), discloses the divinity's "water-nature" and his causal relationship to springs of water, sings of his power over the tides of the sea (Yasht 8.1, 5, 29, 31).[4] Among the Phoinikian-Canaanite pantheon Baal destroys and scatters the rival divinity Yamm, personification of the sea and via his other name Nahar of the rivers, prior to assuming something like an official station (III.AB.A).[5] Cuneiform tablets recovered from the site of Ras Shamrah and dated to the fourteenth century BCE unfold a "cult of the elements and of natural phenomena" governed by the great male-masculine deity El, "who made the rivers flow into the abyss of the Ocean."[6] One recurring phrase in the tablets refers to El as "the Sources [of the Floods, / In the midst of the headwaters of the Two Oceans" (e.g., VI.AB.3–4; II.AB.iv–v.21–22).[7]

Sky of darkness overflowing with stars, sources and springs where earth's fluidity rises through mountains—Thalean considerations divine a joining of diversities on the opacities of ὕδωρ. Joining sky, earth, and ὕδωρ, the upper and lower, divine and human undergo a transformation, transversal in their relations through the flow summoned by ὕδωρ. A kind of dowsing, opening awareness into the luminous air for the pull of earth-enclosed waters, guided by ὕδωρ the Thalean sayings reconfigure the constellation of elements and divinities.

Divining, water-witching, the instrument attunes to the elemental enfoldings of sky, earth, and water, extends one's senses and responds to living waters beneath the surface. A similar purpose guides this chapter. Concentrating attention in a downward direction toward the various manifestations of ὕδωρ coursing beneath the interpretive layer(s) that cover Thalean considerations, toward what Sallis has called "the echo of philosophy before philosophy" sounding faintly and at considerable distance and constituting one aspect of "a beginning before the beginning,"[8] the aim is to listen for the resonances of Thalean considerations beyond

---

4. Translation from Mary Boyce, *Textual Sources for the Study of Zoroastrianism* (University of Chicago Press, 1990), 32.

5. Based on the translations by H. L. Ginsberg in *The Ancient Near East*, ed. James B. Pritchard, vol. 1, *An Anthology of Texts and Pictures* (Princeton University Press, 1958), 97, and by John C. Gibson, *Canaanite Myths and Legends* (Bloomsbury, 1978), 44, EBSCOhost. In his introduction, Gibson glosses Nahar as *river* (3).

6. Felix Guirand, ed., *Larousse Encyclopedia of Mythology*, trans. Richard Aldington and Delano Ames (Prometheus Press, 1959), 75.

7. Translated by Ginsberg in Pritchard, *Ancient Near East*, 1:93, 101.

8. Sallis, *Figure of Nature*, 14.

ὕδωρ-as-water, water as unified source. As the inquiry opens attention to the possibility of another beginning it may at least locate some sites where, with further exploration, the subterranean ὕδωρ might be drawn up for reconsideration, for a sense of its radiant opacities.

To let the underground springs sound forth otherwise will involve attuning interpretation to the sites marking the early soundings of ὕδωρ: Homeric, Hesiodic, as well as other archaic Greek literatures, but also texts from the ancient Egyptian archive and the Near East. The rhythmic and manifold visions intoned by such poetries together form a hydroscape into which early Greek thinking flows. Two principal insights ascribed to Thales point the way to underground currents that might be identified by roaming the field—not the field tilled by Plato and Aristotle and their epitomizing predecessors, but an older field opening before and between Homeric poetries and Herakleitos:

1. that ὕδωρ names the originary dimension or force (ἀρχή) of all things (Stob. *Ecl.* 1. 11.12 [Ths. 16 Graham]);

2. that some other, divine force (θεῶν, δαιμόνων) fills (πλήρη, πλῆρες) and is mixed (μεμεῖχθαί) in all things (Stob. *Ecl.* 1.3.28; Diog. Laert. 1.1.27 [Ths. 37 Graham]; Arist. *de anim.* 411a.7–8 [Ths. 35 Graham]).[9]

Through listening for the multiple valences of ὕδωρ across early literatures, the presumed clarity and intelligibility of Thalean considerations—the alleged thought that all is One and that One is clear and distinct—recedes into a dusk of opacities that activate further relation.

Divining: The Look of ὕδωρ

Beginning reflections on the surface(s) of ὕδωρ opens a way toward thinking its manifold resonances otherwise muted by the principles of clarity and

---

9. Snell has raised into view the distance between this statement of Aristotle's—specifically that "some say" mixture constitutes the whole—and a reasoning of Thales, suggesting that what belongs to Thalean considerations is only the phrase πάντα πλήρη θεῶν, and not the notion of mixing. This remnant he dismisses as scarcely rational, reducing Thalean considerations that are "philosophisch bedeutsam" to the single thought concerning ὕδωρ. Bruno Snell, "Die Nachrichten über die Lehren des Thales und die Anfänge der griechischen Philosophie- und Literaturgeschichte," *Philologus* 96 (1944): 171–72.

intelligibility. Other ways of beginning present themselves: the ordinary ways of being with ὕδωρ, such as cleaning and ritual purification, gathering and carrying ὕδωρ, and various types of mixing. These beginnings spread the meanings of ὕδωρ into numerous and important pathways for thinking and call to attention the social, political, and gender differentiating and joining dynamics of ὕδωρ. Nevertheless, beginning on the surface of ὕδωρ concentrates on its ways of showing forth and appearing, ways that through reflection move toward more primordial meanings gathered around and in the task(s) of Thalean considerations. In this beginning, multiple ways of saying ὕδωρ, such as Πόντος (Pontos, sea) and Ὠκεάνος (Okeanos, ocean), bring out the range activated by Thalean considerations.

ὕδωρ AND SOURCE DARKNESS

Beginning on the surface of ὕδωρ, in the *Iliad* a simile connects ὕδωρ and darkness:

> up rose Agamemnon
> weeping like a dark-ὕδωρ spring (κρήνη μελάνυδρος) that pours
> ὕδωρ dark as night (δνοφερὸν . . . ὕδωρ) down a steep cliff
>   (Homer, *Il.* 9.13–15)[10]

Darkness associated with ὕδωρ in the adjective μελάνυδρος generates the atmosphere of the simile. ὕδωρ pouring down in the second line registers a darkness like night in the adjective δνοφερόν (dark).[11] The lyric poet Stesikhoros brings out this connection, too, in the image of Helios crossing Okeanos to arrive at the depths (βένθεα) and darkness of Nyx (8.2–3 Edmonds).

Further, ὕδωρ here surges from earth's depths, from recesses, hidden places, just as the tears flow in this instance of the Iliadic simile from Agamemnon's inner recesses and hidden places, from a source not visible,

---

10. The other appearance of this simile involves Patroklos weeping to Akhilleus over the Greek casualties (Hom. *Il.* 16.3–4).

11. Compare, for instance, Odysseus's speech to Athene when he has at last arrived on Ithaka but before the goddess has revealed herself: in the mendacious tale Odysseus tells of Idomeneos's son's murder the completeness of night's darkness (νὺξ δὲ μάλα δνοφερή) provides such a dense cover over the heavens that no one could perceive the men lying in ambush (Hom. *Od.* 13.269–70).

submerged in the opacity of bodied thickness. The compound adjective μελάνυδρος (with dark-ὕδωρ) not only emphasizes the darkness of ὕδωρ, it also points to the source of ὕδωρ, suggesting a close association between the source—a spring (κρήνη) originating beneath the surface of earth—and that which flows from it. This repeated simile of ὕδωρ flowing from a dark source brings out the association of the two and the sense that a notion of source—not spoken as ἀρχή (beginning, source, principle, etc.), but rather as the more chthonic κρήνη (spring, water enacting continuous movements of showing and withdrawing)—already forms part of what is meant by ὕδωρ.

Yet, the emphatic darkness of the source in the simile complicates the association: the source recedes from further articulation, suffusing the outflow and the source with an aura of the unknown, the hidden. While it may be that, as Rabun Taylor has suggested, ὕδωρ (thought as water) "connotes radical alterity—and so it mediates, on the one hand, poetic inspiration, and on the other, knowledge of dark and hidden things,"[12] such mediation does not result in full comprehensibility, but rather in an unassimilable dimension, a resistance to intelligibility: opacity, a "primordial resistance to illumination" Baracchi has discerned in the movements of φύσις.[13] Emblematic of the continually partial disclosure of "dark and hidden things," Menelaos's encounter with the sea-deity Proteus reveals some ways in which disclosure flows into and contours the limits of the questioner rather than taking place as a deluge of complete knowledge. Proteus's disclosure responds to—takes shape within the limits of—Menelaos's own interests and questions, first about which divinity is preventing his own return and then about the returns of his brother and other Greek warriors (Hom. *Od.* 4.415–24, 461–80, 485–569).

These specific registers of ὕδωρ extend Thalean considerations into relations with the ancient philosophic tradition of Egypt. The testimonia concur that Thales had some close contact with Egypt and likely visited there. For instance, one account records that Thales arrived at Miletos after having practiced philosophy in Egypt (Ps.-Plut. *Plac.* 1.3.1 [Ths. 11 Graham]), while Diogenes Laertios specifies that Thales had learned from Egyptian priests (τοῖς ἱερεῦσι συνδιέτριψεν, Diog. Laert. 1.1.27). Thales's

---

12. Rabun Taylor, "River Raptures: Containment and Control of Water in Greek and Roman Constructions of Identity," in Scott and Kosso, *Nature and Function of Water*, 22.

13. Baracchi, "Looking at the Sky: On Nature and Contemplation," *Research in Phenomenology* 39, no. 1 (2009): 14, JSTOR.

location at Miletos renders this plausible, as the city was involved in the establishment of the settlement at Naukratis in Egypt by the late seventh century BCE. Early Egyptian sources (ca. late third millennium BCE) circulate thinking around entities preceding the event of creation, called Nun, along with Nu and Nut. Even as the creative movement, according to James P. Allen, took place from one to many, that unity seems differentiated in its primordial condition into a fourfold: "wateriness (*nwj*), or inertia (*nnw*), the most basic qualities, enshrined in the names of the waters (Nu, Nun)," "infinity," "darkness," "uncertainty," or "hiddenness."[14] In the *Leiden Hymns* of the thirteenth century BCE, Nun is called "the swirling original waters" that contain the river Nile and constitute the body of the great divine being that is the hidden, ineffable source of all (*LH*.DC, 168).[15]

These valences of water—here translated from numerous sources not strictly identifiable as ὕδωρ—sound also in Near Eastern thinking on first beginnings. In the opening verse of the Hebrew cosmogony resounds the image of dark waters that form the place on, within, and above which the creative deity performs the first moments of world-making (Gen. 1.1–3). So too does the primordial condition of dark water appear in the composite epic *Enuma Elish*. In that text the primeval female-feminine divinity Tiamat, whose speaking name echoes of "salt, oceanic water,"[16] appears in the opening scene as one stream in an estuary of generative waters:

> When above the heaven had not (yet) been named,
> (And) below the earth had not (yet) been called by a name,
> (When) Apsû primeval, their begetter,
> Mummu, (and) Ti᾿âmat, she who gave birth to them all,
> (Still) mingled their waters together. (I.1–5)[17]

---

14. James P. Allen, "The Celestial Realm," in *Ancient Egypt*, ed. David P. Silverman (Oxford University Press, 1997), 120–21.

15. All translations of the *Leiden Hymns* are from John L. Foster, trans. *Ancient Egyptian Literature: An Anthology* (University of Texas Press, 2001). Throughout, *Leiden Hymns* will be cited in the text abbreviated *LH*, followed by the Roman numeral designations and then the page number in Foster's translation, as in the above citation.

16. Iris Furlong, "The Mythology of the Ancient Near East," in *The Feminist Companion to Mythology*, ed. Carolyne Larrington (Pandora, 1992), 5.

17. Alexander Heidel's translation, *The Babylonian Genesis: The Story of Creation*, 2nd ed. (University of Chicago Press, 1951), 18.

Though not explicit, the darkness of this condition is to be inferred from the undifferentiated—or differentiated as what Tessier has called "contact boundaries" that are "fluid and permeable"[18]—moment that forms the opening scene of *Enuma Elish*.

While these sources have long been noted as forming the overall atmosphere of Thalean considerations, just as they have since ancient times been identified as sites of philosophic thinking,[19] the specific dimensions attributed to the primordial waters tends to remain out of view. These waters, as with Thalean ὕδωρ, teem with a valence of opacity that takes shape as "a fertile and creative lack of certainty,"[20] a dimension of uncertainties that opens a distance within which thinking can flow unblocked by immobile commitments and the grasping mode holding them rigidly in place. Resonant in the vast cultural matrix involving Mediterranean, Levantine, and Mesopotamian cultural imaginaries, the association of waters with primeval darkness and cosmogenesis teems in the first stirrings of philosophy and forms a current flowing together with Homeric poetries as both streams run into Thalean considerations.

Returning to the scene of Menelaos and Proteus, the narrative highlights a connection not only of ὕδωρ with knowing, but also with ἀλήθεια. By way of attending, as Michael Naas has recommended, to "the relations between the characters," the association of "speech and action, and, finally, the narrative *mise en scène* of this concealment or unconcealment,"[21] this bond joining ὕδωρ and ἀλήθεια rises further to the surface.

---

18. Linda Tessier, "Boundary Crossing: The Chaos-Cosmos Dynamic in Cosmogonic Myth (Egypt; Japan; Babylonia)" (PhD. diss., Claremont Graduate School, 1987), 134, ProQuest.

19. For example, Diogenes Laertios includes traditions in the wider Aegean cultural matrix, including north Africa, the Levant, Mesopotamia, Persia, and India (Diog. Laert. prologue).

20. Wiedorn, *Think Like an Archipelago*, 102.

21. Michael Naas, "Keeping Homer's Word: Heidegger and the Epic of Truth," in Jacobs, *Presocratics after Heidegger*, 85. In developing Naas's interpretive insight further, a reading of this scene would bring out more ways the event of ἀλήθεια is enacted and staged: for instance, the site of the recollection of this narrative (Halls of Helen and Menelaos, Lakedaimon [Hom. *Od.* 4.1–2, etc.]), Telemakhos's questioning (imperative, not interrogative [4.316–31]) and, prior to that, Helen's unconcealment of his identity and her expression of the power to conceal (ψεύσομαι) or reveal this identity (ἔτυμον ἐρέω, 4.140 ff.), and then the narrative shift to the suitors' plot to conceal themselves in ambush in order to capture and slay Telemakhos (4.624–714).

Unless the divine being who has the power to disclose whatever Menelaos seeks to learn arises from the depths of his native ὕδωρ in a movement of unconcealment, the engagement with that being remains impossible, unavailable. Menelaos first, and as a condition of the happening of ἀλήθεια, must await the surfacing of this being, the coming to light out of the darkness and concealment of ὕδωρ (Hom. *Od.* 4.401). Furthermore, this awaiting involves a self-concealment (4.439–41); at least in the scene from the *Odyssey*, such self-concealment forms a condition of, or perhaps a moment of the happening of, ἀλήθεια. That is, both beings involved in the activity of ἀλήθεια as the *Odyssey* narrates it emerge from conditions of self-concealment, both undergo the transformation of coming-to-light and unconcealment. Proteus, the being whose disclosure is sought in the encounter, undergoes a further return to the condition of concealment following the activity of ἀλήθεια in his return to the depths of ὕδωρ (4.570).

That the activity takes place as an assault on another being to initiate that being's disclosure must not go unnoticed, for it keeps in view the male-masculine framework and its emphatic violence within which ἀλήθεια as unconcealment is manifest: the scene presents two patriarchs in violent struggle, one seeking the submission of the other as a condition of disclosure, ἀλήθεια. After springing out in a hostile manner from his place of concealment, Menelaos's first task, which forms another condition of Proteus's disclosure of what is sought, is to take hold of the other being and grasp him through all his rapid turnings across manifold ways of appearing, spoken in the *Odyssey* as a δόλιη τέχνη (cunning way of rendering appearance) that Proteus does *not* cover in concealment (οὐδ᾽ . . . ἐπελήθετο, Hom. *Od.* 4.455)—adding still another layer to the overall scene and unfolding meanings of ἀλήθεια in its association with ὕδωρ. The manifestations of Proteus prior to his submission and disclosure of that which is sought include lion, serpent, leopard, great boar, ὕδωρ, a tall tree (4.456–58). Prior to asking and listening for another's reply, the events of ἀλήθεια occur as male-masculine opposition strife, violence.[22] Insofar as Thalean considerations unfold within the framework shared and elaborated by Homeric poetries, they, too, will involve themselves in the male-masculine orientation toward the event of ἀλήθεια as a violent encounter.

---

22. Irigaray has disclosed the association of male-masculine (philosophic) discourse and violence, where interactions in speech work as a mime and substitute for armed combat. *In the Beginning, She Was,* 44, 49.

Circling now to the Iliadic simile voicing the associations of source-darkness-ὕδωρ, when the simile of the dark spring of ὕδωρ and the sheer cliff is repeated later in the *Iliad* it bears different associations as the weeping figure (this time Patroklos) undergoes interpretation by Akhilleus through a second simile:

> Why are you filled to overflowing with tears, Patroklos, just like
> a young girl who runs to her mother and urges her to pick
> her up, seizing her robes, and she stops her from rushing
> off, crying the girl fixes her gaze on her mother so that
> she could be picked up. (Hom. *Il.* 16.7–10)

Focalized through the taunting, bravado masculinity of Akhilleus, Patroklos's weeping—which resembles the dark ὕδωρ pouring from a dark spring—appears also as a feminine yearning for comfort, for closeness, for the intimacy of being with another or with others. Akhilleus himself, after Briseis has been taken, weeps on the shore and calls for his mother (1.348–60), just as he weeps and calls again for Thetis after the death of Patroklos (18.22–72); his taunt also speaks his own experience of the need for the intimacy of being with another or others, even as Akhilleus derogates it as feminine. In a way, the *Iliad* narrates the double edge of this logic in a hardening self-enclosure of identity, motivated by the conflict of self against self, and the intricate and inextricable confluences of selves, beings, places that surface in the *Iliad*—confluences that lead, in the extreme case of Akhilleus, to further self-enclosure devoid of empathic regard.

In the simile the inner recesses of the dark source pour out dark ὕδωρ in a continual departure without return, and in another dimension of that simile brought to speech by Akhilleus such a departure engenders grief and resistance and a longing for being with another or with others, all of which the "poem of force" (as Simone Weil called it) images as feminine.[23] For the *Iliad*, or at least the Iliadic Akhilleus, human ὕδωρ in the form of tears speaks something of what Irigaray has thought as

---

23. As, for instance, when the women grieve for Patroklos together, not only in community but also in such a way that their griefs for Patroklos entwine and overlap with their own personal griefs (Hom. *Il.* 19.301–02). Akhilleus, on the other hand, withdraws from community in his grief, though he does once more summon his divine mother (19.2).

the exile of man from the dual beings of his origination,[24] figured in this simile as coursing dark ὕδωρ ever *away from* its dark source and then in Akhilleus's remarks that cast this flow as feminine. Moreover, the longing for being with another or with others activates the bodied responsion Mielle Chandler and Astrida Neimanis have associated with aqueous gestational capabilities of the female body, the pull and outflow from within toward others "to fill their needs, and provide material conditions for their flourishing." Such gestationality, however, extends beyond female reproduction, encompassing, for Chandler and Neimanis, all life in its aqueous being and various forms of nourishment and generation.[25] This broadening sense associated with ὕδωρ might resonate in the Thalean vision of totality and ὕδωρ, locating the expansive aqueous possibilities everywhere.

ὕδωρ AND SUBTERRANEAN DARKNESS

Still inquiring on the surfaces of ὕδωρ, another expression from Homeric and Hesiodic poetries illustrates how ὕδωρ comes to light as a specific body: ἠεροειδέα πόντον (sea with the look of ἀήρ; e.g., Hom. *Il.* 23.744).[26] In speaking of the look or appearance (εἶδος)[27] of ἀήρ that comes to light also in ὕδωρ, this expression illuminates a certain closeness and resemblance binding together the great and ancient body of ὕδωρ, πόντος (sea), with ἀήρ, the thick and concealing registers of the sky as it remains near the surface of πόντος. The expression draws into view also the close connections joining Thales and Anaximenes, thinker of ἀήρ: might it be that Anaximenean thinking approaches what is there to be thought from a different perspective, drawing into sharper focus the upward orientation of beings and things as they rise, while Thalean considerations look to surfaces that tend downward, remaining below and showing the pathways into depths?

---

24. See Irigaray's extended discussion, "The Wandering of Man," in *In the Beginning, She Was*, 83–112.

25. Mielle Chandler and Astrida Neimanis, "Water and Gestationality: What Flows beneath Ethics," in *Thinking with Water*, ed. Cecilia Chen, Janine MacLeod, Astrida Neimanis, and Elab Gis'e Trudel (McGill-Queen's University Press, 2013), 67–76, ProQuest.

26. This is a frequently voiced expression in the *Odyssey* (e.g., Hom. *Od.* 2.263; 13.150) and occurs twice in *Theogony* (729, 853).

27. The word speaks of the manifest look of a being or thing, as when Odysseus compares the appearance of Nausikaä to Artemis (Hom. *Od.* 6.152).

How does this resemblance and closeness arise that joins ὕδωρ and ἀήρ? ἠεροειδὴς πόντος: ὕδωρ as πόντος has the look of ἀήρ. Homeric and Hesiodic poetries voice the look of ἀήρ as that which conceals: at distant moments of the *Iliad* Aphrodite and Apollo spirit away from Greek warlords Priam's finest two sons, concealing them (ἐκάλυψε) in ἠέρι πολλῇ, an abundance of opacity (Hom. *Il.* 3.380–81 [Paris by Aphrodite]; 20.443–44 [Hektor by Apollo]). In these scenes ἀήρ enables divine beings to safeguard mortals who are dear to them by offering its concealment. Such concealment turns not only upward toward the ἀήρ hovering above and thickening the surface of ὕδωρ, but also importantly downward into the deep places of earth, as the Hesiodic and Homeric associations of ἀήρ with the depths bring to light. Linking ἀήρ to subterranean darkness, *Theogony* tells of the goddess Night concealing herself in the world below with a cloud that has gathered unto itself the look of ἀήρ (Νὺξ ὀλοή, νεφέλη κεκαλυμμένη ἠεροειδεῖ, Hes. *Theog.* 757). The murk and thick dimness of ἀήρ fills the Homeric lower world.[28] The look of ἀήρ conceals. ἠεροειδὴς πόντος thus says that both ὕδωρ as πόντος and ἀήρ occlude in dense opacity. The look of ἀήρ gathered in πόντος also tends downward into the lower regions.

As ἠεροειδὴς πόντος speaks of concealment and subterranean regions, it also says that such dense opacity reverberates between the ancient phrase and Thalean and Anaximenean thinkings, disclosing πόντος-ὕδωρ and ἀήρ in and as their being-belonging-together.[29] Great

---

28. Opening Book 8, Zeus threatens the other Olympians, claiming he will punish anyone caught interfering with his plans by hurling them into the murk-filled gloom of the Underworld (ἐς Τάρταρον ἠερόεντα, Hom. *Il.* 8.13). Hektor, in *Iliad* 12, responding to Polydamas's vision of peril for the Trojan forces, describes the varying flight of birds of omen as to the right in the direction of dawn and the sun or to the left in the direction of the ἀήρ-filled dusk (ζόφον ἠερόεντα, Hom. *Il.* 12.240).

29. The *reverberation* here summons the performative and communal dimension(s) of early Greek thinking: if they are presenting thinking in the form of written texts, those texts are designed to be performed, to be heard in the voices of others. Such performance opens the texts to temporality, temporalizes them, in such a way as to infuse all that is said with another layer of meaning. It also touches the phenomenological aspect of reverberation in-from reading (or hearing) specific images unfurled by Bachelard, where each hearer becomes both "possessed" by the image and the source of its life. Bachelard, *Poetics of Space*, 7–8. For specific discussion of how performative dimensions unfolds in Herakleitean thinking, see Victorino Tejera, "Listening to Herakleitos," *Monist* 74, no. 4 (1991): 491–516, JSTOR; and in the Parmenidean poem, see Spitzer, "Figures of Motion, Figures of Being: On the Textualization of the

πόντος collects in its reflectivity the dense, concealing opacity of ἀήρ. The darkening concealment of ἀήρ forms a conduit between the three apportioned regions of the Homeric world: the above of the bright upper region of sky (αἰθήρ), the subterranean darknesses (ζόφον ἠερόεντα), and the in-between opaque surface of ὕδωρ as the grey sea (πολιὴν ἅλα, Hom. *Il.* 15.187–93).[30] While ἀήρ suffuses the in-between areas of this tripartite schema, it also condenses and coalesces in the lower region of subterranean darknesses (ζόφον ἠερόεντα). By the poetic expression ἠεροειδὴς πόντος that calls forth the subterranean region in naming a specific manifestation of ὕδωρ, ὕδωρ joins and works between its own surfaces and the depths of Gaia, Earth, joining in such a way that the sources in the very deepest subterranean places come to speech as both earthen and ὕδωρ-related, as ῥίζαι and as πηγαί (roots and springs, Hes. *Theog.* 728, 738).[31] Thalean considerations, through invoking ὕδωρ, place emphasis on the between-region, those variegated bodies of ὕδωρ (such as πόντος) where reflectivity opens passages in upward and downward directions. That is to say, the experience of living voiced in Thalean ὕδωρ has the character of a fluid being-between where upper and lower, inner and outer gather and join, shimmering.[32]

The resonance with Anaximenean thinking gains additional richness and complexity as the upper, lower, and between regions collect in the concealing opacity of ἀήρ: both Milesians would appear to voice an experience of a concealing opacity (ἀήρ and ὕδωρ) as it gathers totality, both would appear to speak of the way beings and things are joined in or as

Parmenidean Poem," *Ancient Philosophy* 40, no. 1 (2020): 1–18, and, more thoroughly and expansively, "Philosophy through Translation: A Weave of Voice and Text," chapter 2 in *Parmenides and Translation.*

30. Poseidon voices the tripartite schema of the Homeric cosmography in his affronted response to Zeus's command, delivered by Iris, that he withdraw from the war. The zones of Gaia and Olympos, as Poseidon tells it, are held in common by the three male-masculine divinities.

31. Compare Stesikhoros's phrase that gathers earthen and ὕδωρ in their sources: near the continuously withdrawing (ἀπείρονας) silver-touched roots (ἀργυρορίζους), sources (παγάς) of the River Tartassos (5.2–3 Edmonds). Compare also the term ὑδατόριζον (with roots of ὕδωρ) associated with earth in the Parmenidean poem (Prm. 15a Gallop), which activates a similar gathering.

32. This vision of shimmering draws on Kenneth Maly, "Echoes at the Edge: Shimmering Images in *Delimitations,*" in *The Path of Archaic Thinking: Unfolding the Work of John Sallis,* ed. Kenneth Maly (State University of New York Press, 1995), 124–25, EBSCOhost.

the opacities that pervade totality in its appearings and movements[33]—for both move with a similar dynamic, one brought out by the joining and likenesses of the phrase ἠεροειδὴς πόντος. A difference between the two thinkers opens as one of orientation and beginnings. One begins with the reflective surfaces of ὕδωρ that gather totality in the concealing-revealing surface-depth-reflection dynamic. The other begins with the similarly concealing action of ἀήρ that locates each being and thing in multiple sites and, as Sallis has disclosed, as already doubled and other than itself, as "the obscuring that doubles all manifestation, that shadows it."[34] While both involve some measure of concealment, in focalizing thinking through the reflective bodies of ὕδωρ Thalean considerations seem to begin in reflectivity, in and as reflection on reflecting, attending to the entrancing ways waters shimmer between showing reflections and withdrawing into depths, provocatively manifesting a "dimension of experience according to which visible and the invisible embrace one another, en- and un-fold one another."[35] Put differently: Thales appears to begin with thinking, Anaximenes with what is thought. But these two beginnings take place as moments on a circle of reverberations from the ancient phrase, circular in their beginnings just as later archaic Greek thinkers voice (e.g., Hct. 103 Robinson; Prm. 5 Gallop), providing different accesses and starting points for thinking. Both open zones of experience where beings and things gather in opacity and where thinking and thought belong inextricably together.

The phrase *Thalean considerations* now gains itself as showing a way in which thinking ὕδωρ summons both the upper and the lower:[36] Thales stargazer, Thales who joins (*con-*) with the stars (*sidera*), to whom was attributed a *Gathering of the Stars for Sailing* (Ναυτικὴ ἀστρολογία) and other astrological works (Diog. Laert. 1.1.23; Plut. *De Pyth. or.* 403a [L-M R6–7]), Thales speaks of ὕδωρ as a way to collect the upper region,

---

33. Compare Sallis's interpretation of Anaximenean thinking ἀήρ as "a way of pondering things in their manifestness, in their way of becoming manifest." *Figure of Nature*, 20.

34. Sallis, "Doubles of Anaximenes," in Jacobs, *Presocratics after Heidegger*, 151.

35. Spitzer, "Envisioning In-Visibility," 229.

36. The adjectival construction (Thalean considerations) is intended to be a reminder of the adjectival presence of "Thales," already by the time of Aristotle enshrouded, more descriptor than historical person, as well as a gesture toward the community of thinkers, including Anaximenes, surrounding and preceding his floruit. For this, see Simplikios's remark, which he attributes to Theophrastos, on the "many others who came before" Thales (Simpl. *in Phys.* 1.2.23.30 [Ths. 13 Graham]).

uppermost, that beyond ἀήρ, in the reflective surface of the lower region, a way experience arises full of resonances, pulsing with an already-active totality of meanings. What shines upon the surface of πόντος both undergoes transformations in that surface (as reflections) and recedes into its umber depths. A gathering of this sort is intimated, as Thomas Heyd has observed, in the story of the well, which involves a down-going and may suggest the reflectivity of ὕδωρ.[37] Thales at the well is also a tale of looking inward, as in the utterance Γνῶθι σαυτόν, know yourself, attributed to Thales (Diog. Laert. 1.1.40), in such a way that this inward look takes up the reflectivity of ὕδωρ into thinking as already in and with the world: the inward and the outward belong together within the same horizon, as the reflectivity spoken in ἠεροειδὴς πόντος brings to the surface.

"Looking at the sky," as Baracchi has written, "one beholds not only the inhuman, but the inhuman in oneself."[38] The reflectivity of ὕδωρ, that is, gathers not only a region in the kosmos, but also, and perhaps more profoundly, the ways this region discloses the movements and actions of thinking as indissolubly full of what is thought and as able to gain a perspective on that fullness: just as looking at reflections in water can clarify the layered appearings of water, on the surface and in the depths, *as* layered appearings (but not appearances overlaid upon a metaphysical substance), so taking a reflective orientation in thinking lets the appearings arise *as* appearings manifold, folded, ceaselessly folding. ὕδωρ, moreover, calls forth the belonging together of thinking and thought that comes to view through reflection, just as the earth and sky come to view in the reflectivity of ὕδωρ *along with*, and not irreconcilably divided from, its own depths and darknesses.

ὕδωρ and Unilluminated Darkness

The thinking of Herakleitos seems to take up this belonging together—where *taking up* involves the transformation of thinking, its differential torque. A turn to Herakleitean thinking recommends itself from such taking-up and torquing, the involvement in thinking Heidegger understood in

---

37. Thomas Heyd, "And Yet She Moves!—The Earth Rests on Water: Thales on the Role of Water in Earth's Mobility and in Nature's Transformations," *Apeiron* 47, no. 4 (2014): 501–2, De Gruyter. Another possibility Heyd recommends is that Thales used the well as a way to view "a restricted portion of the starscape by looking *out of*" it.

38. Baracchi, "Looking at the Sky," 25.

ὁμολογεῖν, an attentive hearkening to what already lies in gatheredness in|as λόγος, thinking and hearkening to the Same in which matters themselves arise for thinking differently.[39] The sayings of Herakleitos, as well as their reception, make evident enough that ὕδωρ rises as a matter for thinking.[40] It is not only a matter of historical or philological interest that ὕδωρ, the polestar of Thalean considerations, rises also in Herakleitean thinking.[41] The view from Herakleitean thinking and its way of (re-)configuring the reflectivity of Thalean ὕδωρ may grant access and perspective onto Thalean considerations even as it departs from the name and figure of ὕδωρ. Listening for what ὕδωρ says beyond "water," Sallis brings out its sense of "flowing" and makes visible "an otherwise invisible affinity" relating Thales and Herakleitos.[42] Something for thinking summons the gathering reflectivity of ὕδωρ to both Thales and Herakleitos; the task is to let that summons arise here, too.

In the initial moment of this task, the matter circles around how reflectivity, spoken in Thalean considerations as ὕδωρ, forms a site for the belonging together of the upper and the lower, of thinking and thought. While the stress in Thalean considerations appears to fall on the belonging together and gathering that comes forth in the reflectivity of ὕδωρ, in Herakleitean thinking emphasis instead falls on the differentiation within the thought that lets appearings arise as appearings under the name and figure of ὕδωρ. The reflectivity of ὕδωρ itself undergoes continual differentiation in Herakleitean thinking: even in the same rivers, repeatedly different and plural ὕδωρ (ἕτερα καὶ ἕτερα ὕδατα) flows over those who enter (Hct. 12 Robinson). As Baracchi has put it, Herakleitean thinking

---

39. Heidegger, "Logos (Heraklit, fragment 50)," in *Vorträge und Aufsätze*, 209–10. In that attentive joining as it is taken up by different thinkers the movement(s) of differing will unfold.

40. For ὕδωρ and related imagery in Herakleitean thinking, see fragments 12, 36, 61, and 91 (Robinson). The epitomizing phrase in Plato, "all things undergo displacement (χωρεῖ) and nothing remains, beings resembling the flow (ῥοῇ) of a river" (Pl. *Cra.* 402a.8–10), likely drawn from an earlier Sophist assemblage, and its famous derivative πάντα ῥεῖ, everything flows (as expressed by Simplikios [*in Phys.* 308v.11–12]), signal that ὕδωρ held a paradigmatic role in Herakleitean thinking.

41. Though on this Thales does appear in the historical constellation of Herakleitos's thinking, and does so within the upper region of stars, that is, as expressly associated by Herakleitos with a gathering of what is uppermost (ἀστρολογῆσαι, Diog. Laert. 1.23 [Ths. 12 Graham]).

42. Sallis, *Figure of Nature*, 17.

images the "origin and structure of all that is" in terms of "not so much the principle of difference but principle *as* difference."[43] If ὕδωρ addresses the way appearing occurs in the manner of reflectivity, Herakleitean thinking focuses on the movement and diversity of appearings constituting any sameness, the swift flow out from any singular appearing: "out of many one and out of one many" (Hct. 10 Robinson). The appearing *as* appearing in the reflectivity of ὕδωρ comes forward in Herakleitean thinking as in motion and differing.

Herakleitean thinking looks to the *movement* of the gathering that comes to speech in Thalean considerations as ὕδωρ and lets it appear as differing. In its very movement this gathering both joins and differentiates. The Herakleitean λόγος lets the gathering as differing come to speech as reflexive. In Thalean ὕδωρ occurs a way of appearing *as* appearing in manifold layers yet collected in the reflectivity and opacity of ὕδωρ. Herakleitean thinking *listens* for such a way of appearing in the rising and falling movements—like a tidal surge and retreat—as it gathers by its very movement(s) of differing.[44] Such movement sustains its own irreducibility through its differing (διαφερόμενον) that joins in its own gathering (ὁμολογέει), a re-turning or re-flexion (παλίντροπος) that constitutes self-joining (ἁρμονίη). On account of its irreducibility, λόγος takes place in the manners of bow *and* lyre (Hct. 51 Robinson)—the former, taut so as to release its tension in the direction of another,[45] the other kept taut in unreleased tension so as to release its harmony and music, its voice, in the direction of another. In this way Herakleitean thinking renders λόγος as something that breeches whatever limits contain anything apparently singular without erasing those limits:[46] "hearkening *not to me* but to the

---

43. Baracchi, "The ΠΟΛΕΜΟΣ That Gathers All: Heraclitus on War," *Research in Phenomenology* 45, no. 2 (2015): 269, JSTOR.

44. Perhaps most directly the motion of gathering comes to speech as "gatherings (συλλάψιες) whole not whole converging diverging (διαφερόμενον, differing) harmony disharmony and out of many one and out of one many" (Hct. 10 Robinson).

45. The image of the bow seems to imply that when tension is released violence occurs.

46. Again, Baracchi's linkage of πόλεμος and λόγος lets arise a similar important dimension of λόγος, namely, its "indeterminately exceeding human utterance" that renders it beyond a mere "human property." "The ΠΟΛΕΜΟΣ That Gathers All," 277. Brogan, too, brings out this character of λόγος, which he terms a "dis-owning" that unfolds as "non-appropriative and that gives resonance to what does not come from itself." "Heraclitus, Philosopher of the Sign," 270.

λόγος is to join in the gathering (ὁμολογεῖν) with discernment (σοφόν),[47] to see one all" (Hct. 50 Robinson). As a gathering of thinking and thought in reflectivity like Thalean ὕδωρ, Herakleitean λόγος moves as a speaking that gathers by way of the constitutive differing of its own activity, its own performance: the opening and closing of speech (as bodied vocalization) and the hearkening to that motion and what is spoken.[48] That is to say, λόγος gathers as thinking in its action, λέγειν, *and* as thought in its disclosure of *one-all*, ἕν πάντα. The unity of λόγος opens as its multiplicity, its gathering action as this very opening.[49]

The opening of λόγος is its reflexive differing that gathers all. In gathering all by reflexive differing, Herakleitean λόγος lets appearing surface *as* appearing; in this way it joins in the similar action of Thalean ὕδωρ. They join, too, in the letting appear of opacities. Since λόγος takes place in a way that discloses each being or thing according to its φύσις (Hct. 1 Robinson), and φύσις holds closest and dearest (φιλεῖ) its own self-concealment (κρύπτεσθαι, Hct. 123 Robinson), the gathering action of λόγος collects both the upsurge of φύσις—its coming to light and self-showing—along with its self-concealing, withholding.[50] Such is the

---

47. The translation of σοφόν as "with discernment" resonates with Nietzsche's insights on σοφόν-*sapio* in his writing on Thales; see below on the adverbial rendering. *Die Philosophie im tragischen Zeitalter der Griechen*, 167.

48. Baracchi, too, notes the performative dimension of λόγος in the speaking and listening. "The ΠΟΛΕΜΟΣ That Gathers All," 278–79. Here interpretation of λόγος diverges from Heidegger, who dismisses the hearing of λόγος in its vocalization or voicing as not a genuine (*eigentlich*) manner of hearing, as enmeshed in "Klang und Fluß einer menschlichen Stimme." Heidegger makes a choice between "*was der Λόγος aussagt*" (which he dismisses) and its manner of presencing. Heidegger, "Logos (Heraklit, fragment 50)," 208, 211–12, respectively. Yet, the rising and falling movement of sound—its very *Klang* and *Fluß*—forms one important dimension of λόγος and constitutes one moment of its self-presencing *as* presencing and, as such, forms another dimension of its disclosive force. Attention to this movement would quicken attention to what is said as and of presencing.

49. On this, Brogan has written, that "the movement from the multiple to the singular paradoxically opens up again the question of the manifold." "Heraclitus, Philosopher of the Sign," 267.

50. Here is a moment of convergence with Heidegger's work on Herakleitean λόγος: Heidegger thinks this double action as "*zumal* ein Entbergen und Verbergen." "Logos (Heraklit, fragment 50)," 213.

depth of λόγος,[51] deepening into an opacity that appears but does so *as* concealed, unavailable.

Because the disclosure achieved by λόγος entails a dimension of opacity, of non-disclosure, λόγος exceeds the limits of understanding as *comprendre*, the grasping mode of continental thinking articulated by Glissant. However, the withholding or non-disclosure of Herakleitean λόγος does not unfold as deficiency, nor as scarcity, nor diminishment. Rather, the withdrawing that withholds preserves the surplus and abundance of each thing and being, what breeches the limitations of λόγος. The address of λόγος, that is, always exceeds what is available to understanding: λόγος works as the lightning bolt (Hct. 64 Robinson), not only illuminating but contouring a darkness—obliquely related in the image to the opacity of ὕδωρ[52]—that remains dark as it is pushed to more remote edges by the radiant flash of λόγος. λόγος becomes both a gathering that discloses in illumination and an unavailable, unfathomable depth continually withdrawing,[53] drawing into taut suspension and harmony these two constitutive dimensions of Herakleitean φύσις.[54]

Letting this way of appearing show up *as* appearing takes place as the fitting together (ἁρμονίη) that can only appear in an unilluminated way (ἀφανής, Hct. 54 Robinson). This way of being characterizes divine beings,[55] and Thalean considerations locate such beings in everything,

---

51. The Herakleitean statement on plumbing the limits of a soul (ψυχῆς πείρατα), for instance, takes place as a descent into the depth (βαθύν) of λόγος (Hct. 45 Robinson). The phrase itself transposes the depths and opacities of ὕδωρ (βαθύν) into the zones of λόγος and soul.

52. This interpretation develops Tejera's insights on this fragment. "Listening to Herakleitos," 509–10. The Herakleitean saying is: totality-as-multiplicity (πάντα) lightning-flash steers (οἰακίζει, Hct. 64 Robinson). The oblique relation has to do with the image of the lightning flash steering (οἰακίζει) totality-as-multiplicity, as if totality-as-multiplicity were a ship. If totality-as-multiplicity is steered as by a ship's rudder (οἴαξ), it is steered in and through a body of ὕδωρ that remains other than the ship and un-steered by the light.

53. This withdrawal is made explicit in Herakleitean thinking: λόγος of the soul is increasing (αὔξων) itself (Hct. 115 Robinson).

54. The opening of Herakleitean thinking announces the relation of λόγος and φύσις, declaring that λόγος differentiates (διαιρέων) each thing according to its φύσις (Hct. 1 Robinson).

55. For example: Solon 17 Gerber; Hom. *Od.* 10.573–74; *Hom. Hymn Dem.* 2.94–95; Hct. 67, 78 Robinson.

coursing through totality: all things full of divine beings, θεῶν (Arist. *de anim.* 411a.7–8; Stob. *Ecl.* 1.3.28 [Ths. 37 Graham]); totality ensouled (ἔμψυχον) and altogether full of divine beings, δαιμόνων (Diog. Laert. 1.1.27 [Ths. 1 Graham]). What remains unilluminated as roots and springs, as harmony, as opacity—that ὕδωρ which courses and fills full all beings and things under the names of divinity (θεῶν and-or δαιμόνων)—comes at least partially into the light of thinking, speech, and song: "one—the select (σοφόν)—does not want and wants to let itself be gathered only as the name of Zeus" (Hct. 32 Robinson). Initially and in a more primary way this withheld dimension, the unilluminated opacity, does not willingly come to speech. Herakleitos specifies the type of speech for which the unwillingness is primary: the singular name (ὄνομα Ζηνός), spoken *only* as a unity—taking the μοῦνον adverbially in the phrase μοῦνον λέγεσθαι οὐκ ἐθέλει καὶ ἐθέλει—the one select thing allows itself and does not allow itself to be gathered into speech only as a simple unity.[56] Bringing out the way the one select thing surges out of the bonds of its own unity, Herakleitos says: "to understand awareness (γνώμην), the singular thing selected (ἕν τὸ σοφόν) that steers all things through all things" (41 Robinson). Here again Herakleitean thinking implicates ὕδωρ in the image of steering (ἐκυβέρνησε) totality-as-multiplicity, but this image allows no outside—not even the select one thing (τὸ σοφόν)—since what comes into view through discernment (σοφόν) is the vision of one-all (50 Robinson). The ship and ὕδωρ converge as totality-as-multiplicity in the motion of relation through totality-as-multiplicity (πάντα διὰ πάντων), a tumultuous confluence of living-beings in their tidal movements. The λόγος animates and presences in the saying as its subtle or unapparent jointure and reflexive gathering.

Because the diverse and plural ὕδωρ of rivers does and does not stay the same, because the movement or flow into and out of identity takes place in this manner,[57] the look toward movement, intimated by Thalean

---

56. For an excellent discussion of identity in Herakleitean thinking, see Jessica Elbert Decker, "The Roots of Life and Death in the Homeric Hymns and Presocratic Philosophy," in *Otherwise than the Binary: New Feminist Readings in Ancient Philosophy and Culture*, ed. Jessica Elbert Decker et al. (State University of New York Press, 2022), 91. For more on this, see the discussion below on identity in Herakleitean thinking and its resonances with Anaximenean thinking.

57. In Diogenes Laertios's paraphrase, the whole flows like a river (ῥεῖν τὸ ὄλα ποταμοῦ, Diog. Laert. 9.1.8).

ὕδωρ, remains in Herakleitean thinking "irreducible to one name."[58] As such, Herakleitean thinking calls for multiple names, working polycentrically around and within multiple central terms—λόγος, πῦρ, πόλεμος, σοφόν—and in the figures of bow and lyre (Hct. 51 Robinson), death (e.g., 36 Robinson), ὕδωρ (e.g., 12, 49a Robinson), and more.[59] Each of these activates the movement of gathering as differing.

In their shiftings between a singular and plural ὕδωρ, the epitomes in Pseudo-Plutarkhos and John of Stobi (aka Stobaios, fifth c. CE) intimate the fluidity of Thalean ὕδωρ as an opacity that spills over the edges of a determination as a *unity*. Forming from the multiplicity that ὕδωρ describes, each differentiation itself takes place as a unique multiplicity: an opacity. Indeed, even the fires of heaven, sun and stars—the kosmos itself—gain their luminosity from the multiplicities of ὕδωρ (τῶν ὑδάτων)[60] in their opacities (ἀναθυμιάσεσι, Ps. Plut. *Plac.* 1.3; Stob. *Ecl.* 1.11.12 [Ths. 16 Graham]). Based on θύω, the word ἀναθυμιάσεσι (rising vapors) gathers and releases the opacities of both ὕδωρ and πῦρ, joining in itself the jointure of luminosity and opacity: θύω activates the valences of ὕδωρ, as in the swift motions (θύων) of the river Skamandros (Hom. *Il.* 21.234); the term also speaks of the dense opacity of a burnt offering, as when Akhilleus urges Patroklos to make a burnt offering (θῦσαι) to the gods (Hom. *Il.* 9.219). To the sky-fires of the heavens, and to the kosmos and all its sources of light, the multiplicities of ὕδωρ (τῶν ὑδάτων) bestow a luminous flashing of an opacity that churns and swirls like a surging river, like the smoke and flame of an offering.

Even the singular ὕδωρ of Thalean considerations would flow toward other ways of saying its diverse manifestations—the variegated bodies of ὕδωρ such as Ὠκεάνος (Ocean), Πόντος (Sea), πόταμοι (rivers)—as well as toward and into the saying that uncloses the apparent singularity of ὕδωρ: πάντα πλήρη θεῶν and-or δαιμόνων, where the stress on plurality (θεῶν, δαιμόνων) opens each singularity into and as a multiplicity of (divine, other) beings filling each being, divine beings other than ὕδωρ and in indissoluble relations with it. If all is in some way ὕδωρ *and* all is full of

---

58. Baracchi, "The ΠΩΛΕΜΟΣ That Gathers All," 269.

59. Heidegger, "ALETHEIA," 268.

60. Graham indicates a textual variant in his presentation of this text: θυμιαμάτων in place of τῶν ὑδάτων. Daniel W. Graham, *The Texts of Early Greek Philosophy: The Complete Fragments and Selected Testimonies of the Major Presocratics,* vol. 1 (Cambridge University Press, 2010), 28n10.

powers of otherness (divine powers), totality and the entities composing it withhold in the confluences of their depths some of their vital powers and recede from transparency into opacities. The continuously partial coming to light renders the divine the most difficult measured part (μέτρον), as Solon puts it, to come into the open of a certain open awareness (νοῆ-σαι) human beings can open (Solon 16 Gerber).[61] This open awareness (νόος), again in Solon's thinking, remains also *the unappearing* (ἀφανής) that belongs to the divine beings (Solon 17 Gerber).[62] Such is the way of divine being. Locating within all beings the way of being that withholds and remains in withdrawnness from coming-to-light, Thalean consider-ations seem to provoke the Herakleitean "hanging together in tension and interpenetration" thought as "unity of the different beyond the categories of interiority and exteriority or belonging and non-belonging."[63] That is, what seemingly belongs to divine beings fills also non-divine beings, whose interiority is thereby full of otherness, such that differing gathers all, overflowing—or rather, flowing in a way *beyond*—boundaries. On the other hand, this way of being that remains withdrawn from coming to light enables and preserves boundaries or limits: the fragment from Solon says "yet it holds the limits (πείρατα) of all beings and things" (Solon 16 Gerber). Differing, even as it gathers, can only gather what is limited; limits are the movements of differing.

ὕδωρ and Concealing Darkness

In the texts of Pherekydes the broadest and uppermost manifestation ὕδωρ as Ogenos (Ὠγηνός), understood as a variation of Okeanos (Ὠκεάνος, Ocean),[64] adorns the cloth produced by Zas and bestowed on Khthonie (Χθονίη) prior to their wedding (Pherec. 2 [K-R 54, L-M D9]). Ogenos

---

61. The translation of νοῆσαι as "open awareness" builds on Gadamer's insight that "die primäre Bedeutung des Wortes [νοεῖν] nicht das Sich-in-sich-Versenken, nicht Reflexion ist, sondern im Gegenteil die reine Offenheit für alles." Hans-Georg Gadamer, *Der Anfang der Philosophie*, trans. Joachim Schulte (Reclam, 1996), 143. See also Spitzer, "Trans-philosophy," 571–73.

62. This fragment reads: πάντη δ' ἀθανάτων ἀφανὴς νόος ἀνθρώποισιν.

63. Baracchi, "The ΠΟΛΕΜΟΣ That Gathers All," 280.

64. G. S. Kirk and J. E. Raven, *The Presocratic Philosophers: A Critical History with a Selection of Texts* (Cambridge University Press, 1957), 62n2. For a more nuanced discussion of Ὠγηνός, see also West, *Early Greek Philosophy and the Orient*, 18–19, 50.

forms part of the covering fabric of the world that conceals Khthonie, the lower recesses and regions of earth. On this cosmic level Ogenos, as a body of ὕδωρ, works both to conceal a more primary being and to prepare a surface for other beings yet to come. At some other moment in the Pherekydean cosmogony Χρόνος (Khronos, measured time) generates ὕδωρ, which itself thereafter works as a generative force along with πῦρ and πνεῦμα (Dam. *de principiis* 124 [K-R 51]). Although this summary has been deemed inauthentic and infused with Peripatetic and Stoic interpolations,[65] it may still point to a Pherekydean insight concerning the temporal aspects of these three, two of which had or were to have technical associations with ancient timekeeping.[66] Similarly a passage from the *Iliad* suggests containment on the level of the whole world. Crafting arms for Akhilleus, Hephaistos encircles the rim of the shield with the "great might of Okeanos' river" (Hom. *Il.* 18.607). In both the Pherekydean and Homeric images, moreover, the vast, most voluminous body of ὕδωρ (Ogenos|Okeanos) appears as a divinely-wrought artifact.[67]

In these passages the primacy of ὕδωρ gives way to a still more primary being who renders a figure or image of ὕδωρ so as to contain and limit other entities (images or distinctly living beings). The Pherekydean scene depicts Zas as more primary the temporally expansive beings along a living span (ἀεί, Diog. Laert. 1.11.119, Pherec. 1 [L-M D5][68]), who fashions the garment on which ὕδωρ as Ogenos appears, and

---

65. Kirk and Raven, *Presocratic Philosophers*, 57–58.

66. The solar movements of πῦρ as the sun were marked by the gnomon and the flow of ὕδωρ in the early classical *klepsydra* limited the speeches given in the lawcourts. The non-technical temporal aspects of πνεῦμα become manifest as the living breath, the vitality and pulse of a specific living body. For human beings πνεῦμα also marks out an entire span of each specific living body, raising into view the limits of that span. On the *klepsydra*, see Danielle Allen, "The Flux of Time in ancient Greece," *Daedalus* 132, no. 2 (2003): 70–73, Gale Literature Resource Center.

67. For a discussion of these images of Okeanos, see Spitzer, "Archaic Images of Totality," in *Studies in Ancient Greek Philosophy in Honor of Professor Anthony Preus*, ed. D. M. Spitzer (Routledge, 2023), 44–45.

68. The translation here and throughout of ἀεί builds on the term's archaic sense of a measured span, a span of life. In an earlier sounding in the *Iliad*, for instance, the pyres burning the Akhaian dead do not burn *eternally*, not "ever, always" as in lexica entries (e.g., LSJ, s.v. ἀεί), but for the span of the affliction. In this it parallels αἰών, a spanning of a self-togetherness, as Sallis has disclosed of the term in Plato's *Timaios*, rather than of a sheer perduring presence. *Chorology: On Beginning in Plato's* Timaeus (Indiana University Press, 1999), 79.

Khthonie, who is clothed by the image of ὕδωρ as Ogenos and who is renamed upon or at some time after being so concealed: "Then, after Zas had given her γῆν as a gift, the name Γῆ arose (ἐγένετο) for Khthonie" (Pherec. 1 [L-M D5]). The more primary other images in the Homeric scene are not only other vast bodies, such as the light-spangled dome of heaven and earth, but a complex array of animal, human, and divine life around which, as a border or boundary, Hephaistos sets Okeanos. ὕδωρ appears to come last as a boundary, working to contain and limit other beings and the world they inhabit. Yet, containing in this way enables the whole work to be a whole and, thus, to arise as something determined and there, something that stands and shows itself and can be engaged in its own self-showing. In this sense the two images disclose not only a certain belonging together that takes place as a setting and putting together—a making or fitting together, a harmony—of a whole world, but also the determinations, brought forth in the manner of an artifact, and the *determining* within which a thinking toward wholeness seems to move. As a surface that covers and as a limit that contains, ὕδωρ lets rise not only other beings, but also a way of surfacing, a way of showing in the human engagements with other beings that takes place in the manner of concealing and producing, making. In these manifestations of ὕδωρ resonate the tensions involved in a way of thinking a totality as like an artifact: closed and (apparently) static, but also as a *poetic* event—made, provisional, imaged, polyvalent, dynamic.

From another perspective, this imaging of a totality-as-artifact addresses also a manner of thinking beings as manipulable, there to be shaped, to be transformed into implements that can be handled.[69] At least on the surface the Pherekydean image presents the concealment of an original body by and for the sake of the chief agent of patriarchy—Zas and Zeus.[70] Khthonie of the Pherekydean scene receives and dons the

---

69. This touches the depths of myths involving waters and their linkages to colonization explored by Rabun Taylor. In addition to "the myths of struggle and revelation" that form the focal point of Taylor's studies come forward now the scenes of ὕδωρ as (part of) an artifact; they converge on "the issue of constraint" and co-operate to "set forth a paradigm of control and management." "River Raptures," 34.

70. Though they have been identified by some (for example, Kirk and Raven, *Presocratic Philosophers*, 55–56), West gives sustained attention to the distances separating Pherekydean Ζάς from the Hellenic Ζεύς, favoring a closer tie to "the Luvian Šanta, who lived on in classical Cilicia as Sandes or Sandon" and whose name and language may have been familiar to Pherekydes through his paternal ancestry; Pherekydes in

garment Zas himself has fashioned for her on the occasion of their wedding, inscribing into the discourse on origins the rituals involved in the institution of marriage as determined by patriarchy and, moreover, the concealment of an original female-feminine body by a male-masculine being as closely implicated in this institution.[71]

Pherekydean and Hesiodic thinking render the earth, understood as a female-feminine body, a site for male-masculine world-building and its contestations, grounded in a (putative) control over the concealment and disclosure of a naked reality beneath the concealment. In one sense these narratives relate the founding of the regime of such control.[72] The Pherekydean cosmogony narrates Zas's assertion of dominion over Khthonie by way of the gift-giving gesture, concealing her and rendering her superficial, clothed body (the garment) in such a way as to sustain and promote generation in the service of patriarchy. Having established the female-feminine as a locus of world-building, the Pherekydean narrative reduces Γῆ-Ge-Gaia to a mere site, unfolding upon her male-masculine contestations involving a struggle between Khronos and Ophioneos and possibly another struggle between Khronos and Zas (Pherec. 4–5 [K-R 58–60]).[73] By way of the early and rapid transformation from εὐρύστερνος (broad-breasted) to "a steady and lasting foundation for all the immortals who hold the clouded peak of Olympos" (Hes. *Theog.* 117–18), *Theogony* similarly renders Gaia both the contested ground and the contest-ground, that is, the site of the male-masculine violence for power-over-others. Meanwhile, the narrative trajectory of the Hesiodic theogony covers such contestation in the succession myth that involves the violent overthrow of earlier patriarchs unto the reign of Zeus.

The Pherekydean scene quivers, however, with a certain tension and ambivalence, one shared in the Hesiodic theogony's early transformation and concealment of Gaia (Hes. *Theog.* 117–18, 126–28). Both scenes seem to provide support for the patriarchal arrangement of the world, while

---

that way may have taken a synchretic approach to naming the deity. *Early Greek Philosophy and the Orient*, 50–52.

71. Kirk and Raven discuss the aetiological layer of the Pherekydean scene as related both to the *anakalypteria* and "to the consummation of the marriage." *The Presocratic Philosophers* 61–62 with notes 1–4.

72. Here again surfaces the lineage articulated by Baracchi according to which the concealed mystery is extinguished "as if the body naked were mystery revealed." "Looking at the Sky," 21.

73. On the latter conflict, see Kirk and Raven, *Presocratic Philosophers,* 66–67.

they also open a possibility, however narrow, for a subversive dimension of the female-feminine beings whose original bodies are concealed and withdrawn from the domain of patriarchy. In Pherekydean thinking the earth as Khthonie withdraws beneath the superficial concealment granted by the garment and its image of ὕδωρ as Okeanos|Ogenos. The concealment of ὕδωρ, while covering earth and articulating a site for patriarchy to thrust itself into being, also works to let the primary body of Khthonie remain segregated from that site. Not belonging to the region of male-masculine dominion, this partition formulates and locates itself, in a manner like that which Jeffner Allen has articulated of lesbian bodies, "as a living depth that is outside a world of surface appearance."[74] This "outside," however, refuses neither *surface* nor *appearance*, but rather the ontological polarity of surface-depth and appearance-reality.

Similarly, the body active within the narrative of *Theogony* is Gaia's other body, the other called for by the violent grasping of patriarchy. Gaia's primary body, that withdrawn and withheld from the overlordship of male-masculine divinities, flashes almost unnoticed in the expression sung at the very moment of the event of her happening: εὐρύστερνος, broad-breasted (Hes. *Theog.* 117). Gaia's other body—that contained within and constituted as a stabilized foundation for the succession of the patriarchal regime—articulates herself through an act of self-differentiation that lets Pontos arise (131–32). A reproduction of Gaia's power for self-concealment and withholding, Pontos manifests ὕδωρ as ἠεροειδὴς πόντος (sea with the look of opaque ἀήρ) within or around passages where female-feminine beings churn and create disturbances to the patriarchal order.[75] As Pontos, ὕδωρ develops within *Theogony*'s patriarchal cosmological scheme in the direction of Nereus and a close association to ἀλήθεια,[76] while, in the moment of origination, Gaia remains concealed and harbored in

---

74. Jeffner Allen, *Lesbian Philosophy: Explorations* (Institute of Lesbian Studies, 1986), 105.

75. One instance of the phrase ἠεροειδὴς πόντος is related to Κυμοδόκη, one of the daughters of Doris and Nereus (Hes. *Theog.* 252), occurring between two important scenes that disturb the regime of Zeus: (1) the emergence of Aphrodite from the severed genitals of Ouranos (188–200); (2) the tale of Medousa, whose very emergence and destiny—as unfolded by the Mousai—not only disturbs but erases and exposes as arbitrary the ontological boundary separating mortals and immortals (275–86). The other instance (873) is spoken within the narrative of Zeus's destruction of Gaia's final self-produced entity, Typhoeus (869–76).

76. The Hesiodic *Theogony* makes explicit the bond of ὕδωρ and ἀλήθεια in naming Nereus, son of Pontos, ἀληθέα (Hes. *Theog.* 233).

the opening-closing movement that constitutes τὸ Χάος.[77] The action of opening-closing constituting τὸ Χάος encompasses the event of differentiation brought forward by Hyland as a "very difficult ontological principle that *difference somehow precedes identity or sameness.*"[78] To this valence of τὸ Χάος as difference would be added a stress on what Heidegger has thought, with respect to the Anaximandros fragment, as the edges of arrival and departure (*Hervorkommen und Hinweggehen*) within whose jointure (*Fuge*) occurs a while (*Weile*) as presencing (*Anwesen*).[79] This zone and the very movement of its edges harbor Gaia's primary body as broad-breasted (εὐρύστερνος) and not yet contained by the formalizing, stabilizing requirement of patriarchy narrated in her transformation into "an everlasting stable foundation (ἕδος ἀσφαλὲς αἰεί) of all / undying beings, those who keep in their grasp the summit of snow-touched Olympos" (Hes. *Theog.* 117–18). Such movement, the opening-closing of τὸ Χάος, suggests—perhaps translates—the motions of both ὕδωρ and ἀλήθεια in the double action of opening-closing—revealing-concealing.[80]

ὕδωρ, in its most expansive manifestation as Ogenos|Okeanos, works as part of a concealing surface, instrumentalized in the case of the Pherekydean image to enable the violence of patriarchy in its drive to have and hold a totality in stabilized containment. Herodotos associates Thales with both the instrumentalization of ὕδωρ and its relation to patriarchal violence in narrating Thales's redirection of the Halys River to enable a crossing for Kroisos's forces in their campaign against Kyros (Hdt. 1.75.3–5).

---

77. The connection to the verb χάσκω by way of XA/XAN, yields the valence of τὸ χάος as opening-closing. LSJ s.v. χάσκω. Sassi also recognizes the opening of this movement but does not attend to the constitutive closing of χάος. *Beginnings of Philosophy in Greece*, 35. On the connection of Thalean ὕδωρ and Hesiodic χάος, made by ancients and attributed to Zeno the Stoic, see also Mansfeld, "Aristotle and Others on Thales, or the Beginnings of Natural Philosophy," *Mnemosyne* 38, 1–2 (1985): 124–25 with notes, JSTOR.

78. Hyland, "First of all Came Chaos," in Hyland and Manoussakis, *Heidegger and the Greeks*, 14.

79. Heidegger, "Der Spruch des Anaximander," in *Holzwege* (Klostermann, 1950), 354–55.

80. τὸ Χάος in Pherekydean thinking names the movements of ὕδωρ: one report on Pherekydes declares that he called ὕδωρ χάος, drawing on an etymological resonance from the verb χεῖσθαι, to pour (Ach. Tat. *Introd. Arat.* 3 [L-M R22]). Kirk and Raven observe that this may be Stoic interpolation; they also note the etymological tendency in Pherekydean thinking. *Presocratic Philosophers*, 59n1; 56.

Yet, in speaking the primacy of ὕδωρ Thalean considerations would also invoke—or intimate—a female-feminine withdrawing and its defiance of such violence and the institutions enabling it.

Water-Witching: Locating ὕδωρ

In depths, upon and within currents, in reflections, ὕδωρ issues a figure more of opacity and abundance than clarity and intelligibility. Opacity in its resistance withdraws from the reach of the rapacious mode of knowing Glissant highlights in his charged use of the term *comprendre*. Yet, the withdrawal intimated in Thalean ὕδωρ occurs as surplus, overflowing the bounds within which comprehension would contain it. Thalean considerations may indeed involve the thought that, as Richard Rojcewicz has phrased it, "all things are gifts bestowed on us from a mysterious source."[81] Yet that mystery does not rest in the containing shelter of "mystery" as something toward which no further thinking moves. Rather more in the manner of an "untranslatable" in Cassin's sense as "not what one doesn't translate but what one doesn't stop (not) translating,"[82] the mystery spoken as ὕδωρ provokes continual attempts at articulation. Responsive openness to the abundances that summon more and further articulations may also, as part of this response, call for a reticent comportment unfolded from the sense of the richness of opacities; something like this may echo in the report that Thales only wrote sparingly because, apart from observations on the solstice and equinox, everything remained in a sense ungraspable (ἀκατάληπτα, Diog. Laert. 1.1.23 [Ths. 12 Graham]). Such articulations occur not—at least, not exclusively—according to the hostile attitude of patriarchy disclosed in the Menelaos-Proteus scene of ἀλήθεια, but in a comportment that unfurls in open recognition of its status as limited:[83] a hand opening, not closing.[84] The thought of ὕδωρ and its mysteries gestures toward an area outside the grip of patriarchy even as its own gestures unfold within that grip.

---

81. Richard Rojcewicz, "Everything Is Water," *Research in Phenomenology* 44, no. 2 (2014): 199, JSTOR.

82. Cassin, "Translation as Paradigm for Human Sciences," 243.

83. Irigaray stresses the importance of limitations. *In the Beginning, She Was*, 59, 62.

84. The image points to Glissant's considerations that mark a difference between *comprendre* as "a gesture of enclosure if not appropriation" and the relations of *donner-avec* that take place as openings. *PR*, 191–92; 212n5; 220–21n1.

In this condition of overflow, Thalean ὕδωρ promotes sensitivity and alertness to intricate and continually reconfiguring, yet increasingly fragile and threatened ecologies of beings and places—human and beyond-human—joined by the diverse and differentiating opacities alive within each member of what Astrida Neimanis has termed "hydrocommons."[85] Activating a hydrocommons-awareness, Thalean ὕδωρ, however remote its address may seem, can inspire "new creative resources" toward an ethics whose reach, in answer to the opacity named in ὕδωρ, exceeds any one group, species, or territory and relates indissolubly to "the myriad bodies of water with whom we share this planet."[86] One crucial dimension of this ethical expansion lies in the recognition and continual rearticulation of the limits to understanding drawn from the power of ὕδωρ "to safeguard infinity, and serve as a limit to mastery." This practice of recognition and rearticulation will limit, too, the provisional, "schematised" understandings from spilling over into the grasp of *comprendre,* and can provoke both "an attitude of humility" and an "ability to respond, not to master."[87]

It may be important also to observe that ὕδωρ appears frequently embedded in Homeric similes, so that much of the term's resonance in the Homeric poems sounds within the overall atmosphere of those similes. Perhaps because of its ubiquity combined with its variegated forms and bodies, ὕδωρ offers a multifarious and flexible point of comparison. As Glenn W. Most has observed, one task of the simile is to generate unforeseen linkages between seemingly disparate entities.[88] Simile formation also

---

85. The fragile and threatened condition of "hydrocommons" Neimanis outlines in her 2013 article with reference to a United Nations internet resource. That condition has intensified in 2025: see https://www.unwater.org/water-facts/, last accessed 6 July, 2025. Astrida Neimanis, "feminist subjectivity, watered," *Feminist Review,* no. 103 (2013): 28–29, JSTOR. Nemanis also investigates the differentiating force of her sixfold "hydro-logics" scheme. "feminist subjectivity, watered," 31–32.

86. Neimanis, "feminist subjectivity, watered," 28. The "myriad bodies" Neimanis has in mind include all bodies, not just lakes, rivers, oceans, and the like.

87. Neimanis, "feminist subjectivity, watered," 32, 30, 37, respectively. Neimanis intends her "schematisation of water's complex hydro-logics" to move beyond the "abstract conceptual trope" of fluidity toward a "figuration" that would cycle from what can be drawn from water(s) into a figure for feminist subjectivity and then back again to the waters from which the figure has been drawn (32–33).

88. Glenn W. Most, "The Poetics of Early Greek Philosophy," in *The Cambridge Companion to Early Greek Philosophy,* ed. A. A. Long (Cambridge University Press, 1999), 351.

intimates a vision of the world as continually opening through inexhaustible (re-)configurations of relations, repetitions in the continual iterations of what purports to sameness.

In one sense, an attentive openness to the ways beings come to presence would not only draw from phenomena the necessary conditions attributable to ὕδωρ, as Simplikios suggests in his epitome of Thalean considerations: guided (προαχθέντες) out of the showing forth of beings (ἐκ τῶν φαινομένων) according to aesthetic attention (αἴσθησιν), Thales names ὕδωρ as the source (ἀρχήν, Simpl. *in Phys.* 1.2, 23.22–24 [Ths. 17 Graham]). The vast interrelations flowing as and through the numerous manifestations of ὕδωρ rise into the awareness of sense and guide thinking also toward reflective considerations on the manifold ways ὕδωρ opens itself to other entities, activities, experiences. ὕδωρ urges similaic thinking.[89]

Would an attentive openness to the ways beings show forth reflect—both from and beyond—the ways ὕδωρ seems to be related to and mixed with numerous dimensions of ordinary living, toward the ways attention itself resembles the multiplicity of ὕδωρ showing up in the world? The ways attention is inseparably mixed with the world? Might the initial Thalean consideration say: all beings join *in likeness* to ὕδωρ? All flow together and apart as ὕδωρ? Might Thalean considerations, gathering also from the range of ὕδωρ-related images available and current in the archaic moment, look toward beginnings as source—thought in the chthonic manner of springs and their dark recedings—and observe the confluence of the beginnings in ὕδωρ and the seemingly endless fluid configurations of beings, experiences, and things in resemblance to ὕδωρ? And then, in so reflecting, might a way of being mirrored in the ways ὕδωρ moves in beings arise in awareness too? Beings emerge as already related and mixed, not only with divinity, but with the world of other beings. So too does awareness itself always come forward as already mixed, convergent fluidly with the world of other beings. This μίξις-*créolisation* is gathered into the name ὕδωρ. Simplikios credits Thales with just such attentive openness according to αἴσθησιν.

Urged by the principal valences of ὕδωρ toward darkness and withdrawal into depths, a poetics of opacity emerges from the currents of meaning that flow beneath the solid ground of tradition. Rethinking beginnings by way of a poetics of opacity opens different, unforeseen

---

89. On similaic thinking in early Greek thinking, see Spitzer, *Parmenides and Translation*, 27, 37.

dimensions of Thalean considerations. The beginning traditionally assigned to Thales of Miletos undergoes elemental transfiguration through recognizing the opacity of ὕδωρ, opening a path along a "lineage of beauty" that remains alert to the mysteries of opacity "not behind/beyond veils," as Barrachi has written, "but everywhere, manifest in everything."[90] Articulating and sustaining the opacity of Thalean ὕδωρ does not mean that Thalean considerations remain unintelligible. Rather, it involves interpretive movements along the ever-shifting borders where the intelligible and that which surpasses intelligibility touch and overlap, like the edges of land and sea, rivers and seas, seas and oceans—and, profoundly, within human embodied selves and modes of awareness.[91]

These edges mark sites of transformation and the joining of differences, not reduced to a sameness but sustained in their differing. For Glissant, too, this is a place of beauty, characterized by "the tension of something that is a difference in itself and also opens itself to other differences to be known and encountered." Such opening opens as and toward unpredictable relations, an "open field of the possible" where the beauty of differences-in-relation withdraws just past the edge of knowing,[92] driven by the force of an "unforeseeable *tourbillon*" toward a provisional and dynamic image of totality.[93] In the case of the Milesians, the images themselves awaken the opacities in relation toward a totality as they also set totality in motion toward its own continual transformations. The images of ὕδωρ and ἀήρ, that is, name a moment in the span of opening-closing, or arriving-departing, as Herakleitos brings to speech in the sayings on elemental transformation: death of fire birth of air (ἀέρι) and death of air birth of ὕδωρ (Hct. 76b Robinson).

---

90. Baracchi, "Looking at the Sky," 21.

91. This points both to Baracchi's thought on the "inhuman in oneself" and to Neimanis's exploration of the many valences (and risks) of a "watered subjectivity," the specificities of hydro-logics that form confluences in|as human bodies. Neimanis, "feminist subjectivity, watered," 35–37.

92. Glissant, "In Praise of the Different and of Difference," trans. Celia Britton, *Calalloo* 36, no. 4 (2013), 858–59, JSTOR.

93. *PR*, 62; *PdR*, 74–75.

2

Spanning

Anaximandrean ἄπειρον

Crossings

Crossing through the doxographies and epitomes and haunting the fragment of Anaximandros, the term ἄπειρον points in multiple directions. Variously translated "the Indefinite," "the boundless," "the unlimited,"[1] or the replete "huge, inexhaustible mass, stretching away endlessly in every direction,"[2] ἄπειρον orients and punctuates the transmissions of Anaximandrean thinking. Aristotle developed a sense of Anaximandrean ἄπειρον in terms of the one-many and limited-unlimited interpretive lenses for engaging the earlier thinkers of φύσις, *physikoi* (Arist. *Ph.* 184b.15–25). Through these pairs early Greek thinking becomes early Greek *philosophy of nature* taking its first steps in the direction of philosophy—away from thinking *totality* and toward thinking just one field of totality: *physis* as *nature* distinguished ontologically from human activities.[3] This formulation settles the radiant term ἄπειρον into the definitional limits of *the infinite* and enables a critical interpretation within Aristotle's pairs as "linked to

---

1. Respectively: Kirk and Raven, *Presocratic Philosophers*, e.g., 127; Graham, *The Texts of Early Greek Philosophy*, e.g., 1:51; Laks and Most, *Early Greek Philosophy*, vol. 2, part 1, *Beginnings and early Ionian Thinkers* (Harvard University Press, 2016), e.g., 283.

2. Charles H. Kahn, *Anaximander and the Origins of Greek Cosmology* (Hackett, 1985), 233.

3. Heidegger, "Der Spruch des Anaximander," 324.

65

matter, to privation, to the absence of *telos* [τέλος], to *dunamis* [δύναμις]" with the result that ἄπειρον becomes decisively unknowable,[4] at least according to the knowledge of constituents and their number (187b7–13). From this aperture ἄπειρον retains something like an opacity in the sense of unknowability, but does so in a reductive manner Glissant associates with the transparency of filiation by which opacities are either annihilated or assimilated.[5] In this case, the conceptual bond of ἄπειρον and matter-deprived-of-form cancels the unknowability by way of formalization, the yearning and hungering (ἐφίεσθαι καὶ ὀρέγεσθαι) of matter toward form and the partial destruction of the former through formalization (192a16–19, 25–29).

Rather than bringing to rest the movements of ἄπειρον in a wholly unknowable condition, depleted and lacking, thinking Anaximandrean ἄπειρον through Glissant's articulation of opacity in *Poetics of Relation* lets the term resonate as fullness and abundance, as a name for multiple sources energizing totality in and as relation (*PR*, 56). Because they propel totality and generate the imagined—not reductive—transparency of relation, opacities are decidedly *not* insulated substances, monads, or atoms (*PR*, 55), do not isolate but instead found Relation (*PR*, 190); opacities form moments and locations of relational involvement "with the reflected densities of existence" (*PR*, 195) that sustain diversity (*PR*, 62) and enable "the knowledge in motion of beings" (*PR*, 187), activating an expansive "weave without borders [*frontières*]" (*PdR*, 204; *PR*, 190) that "invokes," as Headley has phrased it, "circuitry and connectivity."[6] Within such knowledge churn unpredictabilities, what Glissant called "unpredictable *tourbillons*," the premonition of which he specifically associates with "Pre-Socratics" among others (*PdR*, 74–75; *PR*, 62).

Though all that remains consists of epitomes, paraphrases, and quotations often contained within the vocabulary of a later epoch, the thinking of Anaximandros resists an easy assimilation or interpretation. Drawing on Theophrastos (ca. 370–287 BCE), Aristotle's successor at the Lyceum, Simplikios in the sixth century CE presents the statement known as the Anaximander fragment, adding that Anaximandrean thinking

---

4. Cassin, " 'Whole' and 'Ensemble': *Pan* Open / *Holon* Closed," in *Dictionary of Untranslatables: A Philosophical Lexicon*, eds. Barbara Cassin et al. (Princeton University Press, 2014), 1219–20, ProQuest.

5. *PR*, 49.

6. Headley, "Glissant's Existential Ontology of Difference," 54.

unfurled as especially poetic phrases (ποιητικωτέροις . . . ὀνόμασιν, Simp. *in Phys.* 1.2.24.20–21 [Axr. 9 Graham]). Other sources seem to offer some of the radiant Anaximandrean *poetic* terms embedded in summaries and descriptions that unfold within the Aristotelean interpretive matrix. Thinking toward Anaximandrean ἄπειρον necessitates a *crossing,* or *crossings,* away from the later reception and into and out of the currents of other early Greek thinkers. Both because of the sparse remains of Anaximandrean thinking and, more importantly, because of the release from the Aristotelean interpretive categories confining Anaximandrean ἄπειρον that becomes available through literatures outside the bounds of what is considered *philosophy,* a range of archaic thinking including Homeric poems, Bakkhylides, Xenophanes, and Herakleitos forms the nexus within which interpretation will move toward disclosing the senses of ἄπειρον as *non*-experience. Pathways to such a disclosure run through the senses of ἄπειρον as a term of relation that refuses the one-many logic and a term that speaks the dynamic of limit-unlimited, both of which situate the term in the region of *experience.*

These interpretive movements constitute crossings, translative and translational motions engaging *more than* what might ordinarily belong to the region of *philosophy.* Such crossings do not unfold as those of *translation* in the narrow sense of choosing from the available words developed by philology that would settle the movements of ἄπειρον—of finding, that is, an equivalent term that would convey "a meaning which transcends its form, circumstances and history, and which could be forever protected from difference and change"[7]—but rather in a way of opening the area for "an abyssal word" and its "unforeseeable meanders" to meander,[8] to address the unforeseeable—in the sense of *non*-experience.

(Col-)Lapsing: ἄπειρον and Relation

Many of the one-many paradigm collapses into a vast array of *ones,* a plurality of entities bound in secure self-identity, so that the notion of unity pervades and determines a logic of one-many. In *Physics,* Aristotle's

---

7. Rosemary Arrojo, "The Revision of the Traditional Gap Between Theory and Practice and the Empowerment of Translation in Postmodern Times," *The Translator* 4, no. 1 (1998): 28, Taylor and Francis Online.

8. *PR,* 21.

discussion of the thinkers he terms *physikoi* and their thinking on ἀρχή (source) develops within the one-many paradigm, so that even those envisioning an ἄπειρον of sources still belong to the way of thinking *many,* while many can be further differentiated on the basis of unity, on the basis of the One (Arist. *Ph.* 184b.18–25). ἄπειρον, insofar as its very meaning (λόγος) makes use of *how much* (ποσόν, 185b.2–3), belongs to the region of *quantity* and enumeration. Accordingly, while ἄπειρον might apply to the enumeration of underlying substances that endure, so that these may be said to be one in kind but different in shape yet not-limited (ἀπείρους) in number (185b.20–21), each such ἀρχή as underlying substance (τῆς οὐσίας ὑπομενούσης, *Metaph.* 983b.9–10) will itself be a one (983b.17–18).

Already in Theano, Pythagoras's wife or apprentice-student (μαθή-τριαν) or both (Diog. Laert. 8.42), a logic other than the one-many makes itself felt in her intervention concerning the received view of Pythagoras's teaching that everything comes to light from number (ἐξ ἀριθμοῦ φύεσθαι, Stob. *Ecl.* 1.11.13).[9] Rather than imposing onto every being in totality a numerically determined identity, where number is understood in the received interpretation as primary order (τάξις πρώτη), "Theano's primary order remains open for beings of a totality to exceed the enumerable identities attached to them in accordance with number not (necessarily) in generation, but in being and in a mode of thinking not bound up with enumerated and enumerable identities."[10] Some abundance exceeds the limitations of enumeration and its one-many categories, provoking a different orientation toward beings as multiplicities; without the determination of unity, multiplicities outspan themselves: "multiplicity multiplies itself."[11]

A look to its early voicings shows that ἄπειρον cannot be reduced to the one-many logic. Unfurling multiplicity, relation joins *opacities* in totality as other than one-many and its determinations according to unity. Xenophanean thinking both joins ἄπειρον with ὕδωρ and γῆ and intimates a collapse of the one-many paradigm by way of this joining:

---

9. For readings of how early Greek thinkers and some Homeric Hymns enact logics beyond the one-many paradigm in terms of binaries, see Decker, "Roots of Life and Death," 87–120.

10. Spitzer, "Archaic Images of Totality," 50; and see the fuller discussion, 48–50.

11. Jung, "Transversality," 426.

of earth, this here at our feet—an upper limit (πεῖρας) is visible, pressing against air (ἠέρι), but that downward (κάτω) reaches into ἄπειρον (Xns. 28 Lesher)

γῆ and ὕδωρ are totality (πάντ'): what is born and rises (φύονται) (29 Lesher)

In the downward movement (κάτω) of ἄπειρον, Xenophanean thinking gestures to the opacities of γῆ and ὕδωρ. This pair forms the generative dynamics of φύσις and totality still pulsing in that name.[12] Such a joining of these energies in the downwardness of their motions already speaks the resonant opacities of each, where receding into ἄπειρον both γῆ and ὕδωρ gather and flow back into the coursing darknesses of φύσις as opening and closing, rising to light from darkness and withdrawing again to darkness. Theirs, that is, moves with the dynamics of ἀλήθεια, a motion between conditions of closure and unclosure or, as John Panteleimon Manoussakis has phrased it (thinking of Heidegger), the movement of light "emerging from darkness, a darkness that it presupposes and, in its emergence, it hides as its utmost secret."[13]

The Xenophanean disclosure of this movement, spoken both in the image that joins limit-unlimited and in the term ἄπειρον, articulates the movement *away from* a limit on the surface opacity of relation—where γῆ meets ἀήρ, Anaximenean name of opacity—*toward* the expansive depths of γῆ. Such expanse both constitutes every being of totality and itself *is constituted* by the con-joining of γῆ and ὕδωρ and the col-lapsing of their downward orientations toward ἄπειρον. Con-joining and col-lapsing here take place according to the joining (*rejoignent*) envisioned by Glissant, a drawing together that does not "merge" (*sans se fonder*) the multiplicities of γῆ and ὕδωρ.[14] Alethetically, the Xenophanean dynamic of γῆ and ὕδωρ, in light of these constitutive and irreducible multiplicities of movements in the direction of ἄπειρον, intimates a withdrawal from a one-many paradigm, with the result that ἀλήθεια, inflected on the energies of opacity, will not

---

12. Heidegger, "Der Spruch des Anaximander," 324.

13. Manoussakis, "Introduction: The Sojourn in the Light," in Hyland and Manoussakis, *Heidegger and the Greeks*, 2.

14. *PR*, 62; *PdR*, 74. This discussion reconfigures Wing's translations of Glissant's terms to give *con-joining* the valence Wing-Glissant give to *joining* (*se rejoignent*).

come to rest in a settled and unified determination, but will continually pulse with the elemental movements of ὕδωρ and γῆ toward multiplicities. The dynamic force of ὕδωρ and γῆ spans multiplicities-of-totality (πάντα), which rise into the limits of their span by the motions of this force (Xns. 27, 29 Lesher). This span extends to γῆ and ὕδωρ, rendering the so-called *elements* multiplicities and not unities, not "original" or "prime elements" unmixed, each inviolate in its being in the manner of a "sufficient entity that would discover its origin [*son commencement*] in itself,"[15] but rather as sites and moments of dynamic opacities in relation. Bound to the opacities of ὕδωρ, the ἄπειρον of γῆ enfolds opacities within opacities in the teeming alethetic motion, the showing-withdrawing movements of ἀλήθεια manifest *as* the relationality of every being-as-multiplicity, constituted in such a way that defies the one-many paradigm.

However, in seeming to rename the force of this dynamic by the term θεός (divinity, Xns. 23 Lesher), Xenophanean thinking elsewhere appears to cast this force as *a being*, settling it and allowing it to harden (*verhärdet*) into mere persistence (*bloße Beharren*), as Heidegger voices the risk associated in the Anaximandros fragment with the naming of the limiting span in the term τὸ χρεών.[16] Yet, the moving force of differing—the force that shakes (κραδαίνει) totality (Xns. 25 Lesher)—does not move or enter and locate itself in any specific place (26 Lesher), since its motions unfurl as *dissimilar* (ὁμοΐος οὔτε, 23 Lesher); not similar, the motions of this force take place as differing, never settling into a condition of sameness. Rather the motion of the dynamic force shakes (κραδαίνει) with and in an activity of relation (νόου φρενί, 25 Lesher), dislodging the dynamic force from a sense of unity by way of differing. This force also surfaces as *among* the gathering of immortals and mortals (ἐν τε θεοῖσι καὶ ἀνθρώποισι, 23 Lesher) and as the whole (οὖλος) in its living perception-as-relation (24 Lesher), such that the unity emerges with the phenomenological bearing both of "always already immediately dwelling among things" and of a perception-as-relation that announces the constitutive "relating itself" of perception.[17] Even as the whole in the theological sayings manifests as an apparently singular unity, as in the name θεός or the voicing of singular verbs (23, 25, 26 Lesher), the force so named also turns within—takes

---

15. *PdR*, 174; *PR*, 160.

16. Heidegger, "Der Spruch des Anaximander," 368.

17. Heidegger, *Basic Problems of Phenomenology*, trans. Albert Hofstadter (University of Indiana Press, 1982), 66.

shape from—the dynamic of ὕδωρ and γῆ whose relations and constitutive opacities animate multiplicities-as-totality (πάντα) and so *include* the force named θεός. Xenophanean thinking raises into view this force as a unity (εἷς θεός) both as unlike and other (οὔτι . . . ὁμοίϊος οὔτε, 23 Lesher) and as already a force of multiplicity, embodying the generative motions of ὕδωρ and γῆ in their relational opacities, opening possibilities for this force to operate as neither unity nor plurality but in a manner *other than* that available within this paradigm: in the manner of *relation* and its dynamic opacities and multiplicities.[18]

In Anaximandrean thinking, ὕδωρ and γῆ seem to form out of and within the *undetermined* opacity of ἄπειρον and its constitutive multiplicities, not, however, as elements, but rather as zones, features, or regions, as bodied dimensions of a multiplicitous *in-which*: early humans develop as an other, fish-like life-form (ἑτέρῳ ζώῳ . . . ἰχθύϊ) within the unspoken life-giving dimension of ὕδωρ (Hippol. *Haer.* 1.6 [Axr. 20 Graham]); γῆ does not appear as emerging, but as a life-sustaining region, figured through an architectural (artifactual) image as a column drum (κίονι λίθῳ, Hippol. *Haer.* 1.6 [Axr. 20 Graham]) or cylinder (κυλινδροειδῆ, Euseb. *Praep. evang.* 1.8.2 [Axr. 19 Graham]), an already present γῆ joined to and encircled by ἀήρ (τῷ περὶ τὴν γὴν ἀέρι), an in-which that, after the γῆ-ἀήρ region is encircled by a sphere of flame like bark around a tree (ὡς τῷ δένδρῳ φλοιόν), would support ὕδωρ and in turn is supported by ἀήρ (Euseb. *Praep. evang.* 1.8.2 [Axr. 19 Graham]). Anaximandrean thinking images ἄπειρον as a dynamic and constitutively undetermined multiplicity that, in order "to pass beyond its own horizon," as Chris Kassam and Robbie Duschinsky put it, "must already contain difference."[19] As *undetermined*, ἄπειρον does not conform to the categories of one or many, which would determine it as unity and/or plurality; Cicero's term *innumerabilis*, seemingly a translation of ἄπειρον embedded within a brief epitome of Anaximandros (Cic. *Nat. D.* 1.25), intimates this nonconformity of Anaximandrean ἄπειρον to categories of number. Because the motion of ἄπειρον causes separation of some kind, it seems to bear within itself some energy of or toward differentiation: arising from what Serge Margel has articulated as a threefold turbine-like motion of ἄπειρον that splits (ἐν τῇ διακρίσει, Simpl. *in Phys.* 1.2, 27.12), separates (ἀποκριθῆναι, Euseb. *Praep. evang.*

---

18. See the related discussion in Spitzer, *Parmenides and Translation,* 24–25.

19. Chris Kassam and Robbie Duschinsky, "Nietzsche and Anaximander on Being and Becoming," *Diacritics* 45, no. 3 (2017): 110, Project Muse.

1.8.2 [Axr. 19 Graham]), and "ejects" (ἐκκρινασθαι, Arist. *Ph.* 187a.20–21 [Axr. 13 Graham]), a generative force (γόνιμον) produces heat and cold, and operates as a regulating and linking force between the extremes.[20]

Such dynamic multiplicity joins Anaximandrean ἄπειρον with the Egyptian Nun and its multiple valences as "infinity," "darkness," "uncertainty" or "hiddenness."[21] This element of infinite indeterminacy forms an in-which and out-of-which for the creative power Re "who came into being by himself," where Nun is that in which Re manifests himself, glossed as "the abysmal waters, in which creation took place,"[22] just as ἄπειρον in Anaximandrean thinking arises as ἀρχή that is both ἀίδιον (temporally expansive) and ἀγήρω (ageless) and moves in continually expansive motion (κίνησιν ἀίδιον, Hippol. *Haer.* 1.6 [Axr., 10 Graham]). The bond joining ἄπειρον and ὕδωρ in Xenophanean thinking has already emerged, and further dimensions of this bond will surface below in a discussion of Homeric πόντος (sea) and ἄπειρον. Overlapping both Xenophanean and Homeric pulse the opacities of ὕδωρ, as the first chapter unfolded. Further, both Nun and ἄπειρον collapse the categories of one and/or many in their multiplicities that do not submit to conceptions of unity or plurality. Nun presents this resistance to unity and/or plurality insofar as its own primordiality already contains an excess not reducible to a unity or a gathering of unities, but rather a teeming multiplicity of creative outpourings, as the *Leiden Hymns* voice, manifold in forth-shinings as Amun rising from "the ur-waters" and as "the god's image" in motion above the primal waters, manifest as both "the Eight of Hermopolis" and as Atum. Even where this hymn sings of the deity as "one alone," it nevertheless constitutes itself in such a way that it defies knowing ("His nature cannot be known," *LH.CC,* 163), which would involve its being apart from the categories of number. ἄπειρον, as multiplicity within Xenophanean thinking, likewise remains apart from and other than the numerical determinations of unity and plurality; Anaximandrean ἄπειρον too refuses a reduction to one-many.

Enuma Elish, too, figures an image of primordial multiplicity. In the moment prior to articulation, when "the heaven had not (yet) been named" and "below the earth had not yet been called by a / name," the text stages the way such a condition resists the categories of numbering

20. Serge Margel, "De la restitution du monde: La nature et le temps dans les fragments d'Anaximandre," *Les études philosophiques* 1, no. 1 (1999): 3–5.

21. Allen, "Celestial Realm," 120–21.

22. Translation by John A. Wilson in Pritchard, *Ancient Near East* 1:3.

in its declaration of this moment of indeterminacy and undetermined equiprimordiality that nevertheless can only come to speech within and as the very names—and their implicit numbering as distinct unities—of a manifold of beings who "mingled their waters together," not discreet entities but multiplicities coursing and streaming within-among-as others (I.1–9).[23] Anaximandrean ἄπειρον swirls in the *tourbillon* of transcultural imaginaries, gathering some of its primary energies from the images of origination in and as undetermined and unavailable, as multiplicities, to the one-many paradigm.

Also associated with ἄπειρον as indeterminate and undetermined and a principle of differing, the figures of Chaos and *Apophis* come forward in some texts as primordial and persisting dimensions of existence, not merely overcome in a single action but dynamically recurring and energizing the cosmos. In *Leiden Hymns,* the nameless deity—the text finding a way to resist at least the singular identification imposed by name/naming—emerges initially as *Ta-tenen,* the "Land-rising" divine manifestation, *from* and *within* chaos (and already "bearing the primal deities") (*LH.LXX*, 157).[24] Originary, primordial, the chaos spoken here forms an in-which for the coming forth of manifestation as Ta-tenen, and the text recognizes that the primordial chaos overflows *being* in its declaration that "before you was no being, no void." The chaos of this hymn recedes even from being, working as a non-being and surplus that dissolves—or overflows—the concepts of unity and plurality.

Similarly, a coffin text from the late third to mid-second millennia BCE narrates the creative deity ("Him-whose-names-are-hidden, the All-Lord") addressing a cohort of divinities as "those who silence the storm." The address begins with the image of the deity's actions taken "in order to silence the strife" out of an originary condition "within the serpent-coil," glossed by Mariam Lichtheim as the "serpent-dragon Apophis who symbolized the lurking dangers of the world."[25] The serpent-coil, as a figure of the primordial chaos, teems as the within-which for any being whatsoever, itself and its motions moving beyond being and identity. While this vision of chaos in τὸ Χάος may not yet be at work explicitly in Hesiodic

---

23. Translation from Heidel, *Babylonian Genesis,* 18.

24. Foster provides the gloss on *Ta-tenen* as "Land-rising." *Ancient Egyptian Literature,* 250.

25. Mariam Lichtheim, *Ancient Egyptian Literature* (University of California Press, 2019), 174–75.

thinking, it already courses in the transcultural imaginaries of the Mediterranean and Near East, eventually voiced, for instance, in Ovid, where the opening image reduces the multiplicities of chaos into a unity (*unus erat toto naturae vultus in orbe, / quem dixere chaos*, Ov. *Meta.* 1.6–7).

Where the rising and falling of beings speaks in the Anaximandrean fragment, ἄπειρον is absent, silent, a shadowing and haunting presence just past the edges of the text: ἐξ ὧν δὲ ἡ γένεσίς ἐστι τοῖς οὖσι, καὶ τὴν φθορὰν εἰς ταῦτα γίνεσθαι κατὰ τὸ χρεών· διδόναι γὰρ αὐτὰ δίκην καὶ τίσιν ἀλλήλοις τῆς ἀδικίας κατὰ τὴν τοῦ χρόνου τάξιν (Simpl. *in Phys.* 1.2.24.18–20 [Axr. 9 Graham]). Whether the antecedent or implied subject of the opening Peripatetic phrase ἐξ ὧν (from those things which) is *elements* or *opposites*, the important dimension of that entire phrase for a poetics of opacity lies in its *multiplicities*: the genitive (ἐξ ὧν) and the dative (τοῖς οὖσι) speak of equiprimordially originary and emerging multiplicities, linking the phrase to the multiplicities of beings-in-relation (αὐτά, ἀλλήλοις) and the multiple terms voicing those relations (δίκην καὶ τίσιν, τὴν τοῦ χρόνου τάξιν).

Although stressing the multiplicities in their irreducible relations that constitute totality, the Anaximandros fragment lets ἄπειρον remain unsaid. Yet, the beings rising and falling in the motion described (or implied) by the fragment also seem to be shadowed by ἄπειρον in its guiding force, a force that Theophrastos—by way of Simplikios—describes as an *other* (ἑτέραν τινά) φύσις (Simpl. *in Phys.* 1.2, 24.17 [Axr. 9 Graham]).[26] By *steering* (κυβερνᾶν) and *encompassing* (περιέχειν), Anaximandrean ἄπειρον *shadows* each of the fourfold as an *other* motion of presencing, even as it also *haunts* as an irreducibly *indeterminate* and *undetermined* dimension of each being (Arist. *Ph.* 203b.11–12 [Axr. 16 Graham]). Both the shadowing and haunting actions of ἄπειρον, in addition to the generative dynamics of the so-called *elements* or the *opposites* constituting them, bring out the constitutive multiplicity of every being. In such shadowing and haunting ἄπειρον bears affinities with Amun of Egyptian thinking in the *Leiden Hymns*, whose shadowing remains in a sense undetermined, "veiled even from the gods" as "a nature that cannot be known" (*LH.CC*, 163).

---

26. Raising into view the differences between the three reports (Simplikios, Diogenes Laertios, Aëtios), Finkelberg opens a gap between a refusal—or failure—to determine the ἄπειρον and a positive assertion of an indeterminate entity as ἀρχή. Aryeh Finkelberg, "Anaximander's Conception of the Apeiron," *Phronesis* 38, 3 (1993): 229–30, Brill Online Journals.

A further association links the shadowing and haunting of Anaximandrean ἄπειρον—its involvement, as encircling and surrounding the living world, the rising-falling movements of φύσις—with the Egyptian vision of Nun and the encircling and pervading nonexistent, "before two things" condition,[27] understood as a moment prior to being, prior to void, initiated by an internal energy toward diversification Obenga has described as "the unity of being, becoming, and effecting."[28] Erik Hornung finds that Egyptian nonexistence can be characterized positively as "limitless waters" (Nun) and as "completely opaque, total darkness."[29] Pervading the living world, the world of manifold existence, nonexistence forms the outermost limit beyond which even the divinities cannot reach, saturates the living world in the dissolution of regularity and order on a cosmic and a local scale to the extent that, as Hornung puts it, "Egyptians encounter the non-existent wherever they go." Nonexistence engenders the limited span of each being as a persisting source of renewal and abundance, opening the circle of each being toward a multiplicity other than one or many.[30]

The Anaximandrean bestowal of ἄπειρον as ἀρχή to beings voices such a shadowing (e.g., Hippol. *Haer.* 1.6 [Axr. 10 Graham]), sounds this register of opacity as a withdrawal and self-concealing of the *other* φύσις and an energy toward relation. As Michel Serres has noted, ἄπειρον resists presence insofar as any *there* forms a determination within limits, but so too would a bare *absence* bind Anaximandrean ἄπειρον to a limited status in the sense of being excluded by or at the limits of those places where it is not.[31] Anaximandrean thinking points toward beings that do not arise as singular, self-identical unities or definitive, determined *elements* into which everything can be resolved, but as figures of continual *tourbillon* and *mixis* from within the motions of ἄπειρον as multiplicity and *relation*.

Insofar as individual entities come to bear themselves toward others in the manner of unities, one against another (one), *forgetting* the

---

27. Allen, "Celestial Realm," 120.

28. Obenga, "Egypt," 39.

29. Erik Hornung, *Conceptions of God in Ancient Egypt*, trans. John Baines (Cornell University Press, 1982), 176–77.

30. Hornung, *Conceptions of God in Ancient Egypt*, 177–82; quotation from 179.

31. Michel Serres, "Anaximander: A Founding Name in History," trans. Roxanne Lapidus, in Jacobs, *Presocratics after Heidegger*, 139. Yet, Serres's attribution of this saturating force, both there and not there, to abstraction narrows the extent of concrete ways such a force inheres to and perhaps conditions experience.

relations of and as multiplicities that constitute them together as totality, the moral-judicial sense of the Anaximandros fragment makes its combative, retributive action felt, as David Michael Kleinberg-Levin has shown, in the ontologically established actors and actions and the subsequent rigid determination of the future that works to "close what cannot be closed."[32] The determination of what cannot be (fully) determined, because shadowed and constituted by the opacities and multiplicities of ἄπειρον, sets in motion the grounding for justice as pay-back (δίκην and ἀδικίας) and "constitutes a system within which difference/time is traversed by and enslaved to the law of identity."[33] As *undetermined*, Anaximandrean ἄπειρον refuses the one-many logic: not, as Nietzsche read it from his insight that ἄπειρον names *indefinite* (*das Unbestimmte*) and final unity (*letzte Einheit*),[34] stationary, immune from change, and a "metaphysical self-identity,"[35] ἄπειρον instead churns in ceaseless motions and with the multiplicities—neither singular nor plural—that continually form in the movements of relation within the undetermined valence of ἄπειρον.

Crossing, Joining: ἄπειρον, Limit-non-limit, and Opacity

Pointing out that in Homeric poetries the related adjective ἀπείρων typically describes earth or sea, both of whose limits also surface in the poems, Charles H. Kahn ranges through several instances of ἄπειρον-related terms before suggesting that the verbal root περ- and its expressions as πείρω (pierce), περάω (pass through), περαίνω (bring to an end, come to an end) should be sought rather than the nominal root πεῖραρ and πέρας (end, limit). From περ- Kahn discloses a basic "literal sense" of ἄπειρον as "what cannot be traversed to the end" and, specifically in the valence(s) the term gains in Anaximandrean expression, as "a huge, inexhaustible mass, stretching away endlessly in every direction."[36] Within these insights made available by Kahn's careful treatment resonate some further overtones of meaning. A frequently recurring Homeric scene of

---

32. David Michael Kleinberg-Levin, "The Court of Justice: Heidegger's Reflections on Anaximander," *Research in Phenomenology* 37, no. 3 (2007): 389, JSTOR.

33. Kassam and Duschinsky, "Nietzsche and Anaximander on Being and Becoming," 107.

34. Nietzsche, *Die Philosophie im tragischen Zeitalter der Griechen*, 170.

35. Kassam and Duschinsky, "Nietzsche and Anaximander on Being and Becoming," 102.

36. Kahn, *Anaximander and the Origins of Greek Cosmology*, 233.

feasting, for instance, runs:

> When the thigh pieces were charred and they had
> Tasted the tripe, they cut the rest into strips,
> Skewered (ἔπειραν) it on spits and roasted it skillfully. (e.g.,
>   Hom. *Il.* 1.464–66)[37]

The feasting warriors of this scene prepare to roast meats by "skewering" or piercing (ἔπειραν) the animal parts with spits. In war the verb bears the hostile sense of driving a weapon all the way through an opponent, as when Patroklos in his battle fury sends a spear straight through (πεῖρεν) the teeth of Thestor (Hom. *Il.* 16.405). Finally, the Homeric poems describe the action of ships cleaving the restless sea. In the *Odyssey*, for example, with the goddess Athene disguised as Mentor Telemakhos sails from Ithaka toward Pylos on the Greek mainland: "The whole night through and unto dawn the ship cut through (πεῖρε) the sea's pathway" (Hom. *Od.* 2.434). All three of these instances of πείρω overlap extensively with the transversal movement spoken in the related verb περάω.

These three registers of the πείρω valences of ἄπειρον voice an action of parting, dividing, and severing within the sense of piercing. Of these, the verb's aspect in the scene of feasting enfolds it in a sphere of ordinary use, survival, daily life. The puncturing action of the spits falls within the activity of living sustenance: piercing the meat in order to roast it protects against starvation and death, the division of the vital principle from the body. This association with death gathers the first two voicings of πείρω: both speak of an action that punctures and that moves in close connection with death—the dead animal being prepared for the feast (and the human beings feasting and thereby avoiding separation, death) and the dying warrior, who, in the simile narrating the death, is pierced "like a fish" (Hom. *Il.* 16.406–08). In a sense, this piercing passes through, opens a channel between human and nonhuman where human vulnerability takes its place on a spectrum of the vulnerabilities joining living beings. Moreover, when Patroklos's spear pierces and drives through Thestor's mouth it causes a separation, a departure of his fighting spirit

---

37. Translation from Stanley Lombardo, *Homer: Iliad* (Hackett, 1997), 15, my interpolation. Other instances and variations of this formula—including the word ἔπειραν—occur at Hom. *Il.* 2.427–29; 7.317–18; 9.210; 24.623–24; and Hom. *Od.* 3.461–62; 12.364–65; 14.75, 430–31; 19.422–23.

(θυμός, 16.410). The parting of θυμός from the lapsing warrior deepens the resonance of separation and severing sounding in the verb πείρω. Such violent punctures are lasting and|or bring about lasting conditions.

In the third example, however, which narrates a ship's movement through the sea, the action of πείρω produces an ephemeral, momentary separation. The ship's movement only momentarily parts the ὕδωρ of sea, whose expansive, ceaseless motion of surge and withdrawal instantly rejoins the cleft hewn by the prow of the ship, closing over and erasing the instant of division. Where the action of πείρω enters the sphere of ὕδωρ the Homeric vision seems to imply a reversal or undoing of the piercing separation spoken by the verb elsewhere. That is, the way the ship carves and pierces the sea both participates in the sense of πείρω as dividing and separating and activates an image that reverses and negates such division and separation.

An image in the Parmenidean poem illustrates the overlapping action of πείρω in Thea's term περάω (περῶντα) during her opening address to the youth, where she unfolds the cryptic final lesson to be learned, and might animate re-readings of δόξα (and ἀλήθεια) in the poem:

> You will learn this, too: how according to involvements (ὡς
> . . . χρῆν)[38]
> meanings (τὰ δοκοῦντα),[39] all manifold specificities (πάντα)
> in their manifestness (δοκίμως), are cutting through (περῶντα)
> a singular totality. (Prm. 1.31–32 Gallop)

The piercing action of πείρω does not destroy the manifold specificities or the singular totality, but passes through and joins all with all as a ship's prow divides and partitions ὕδωρ into cresting wakes that close back into the whole body of ὕδωρ as the ship's movements continue, an instance of

---

38. Translating χρή-χρῆν as *involvements* first appeared in Spitzer, "Being-in-Touch: Touch, Contact, and Bodies in the Poem of Parmenides," *Epoché: A Journal for the History of Philosophy* 29, no. 1 (2024): 16 with notes. A similar translation appears in Spitzer, *Parmenides and Translation*, 75 with notes. For more on this rendering and τὸ χρεών, see below, pp. 80–81, 92–93.

39. In part, this translation of τὰ δοκοῦντα draws on Lombardo's phrase "Interpreted World." Stanley Lombardo, trans., *Parmenides and Empedocles: The Fragments in Verse Translation* (Grey Fox Press, 1982), 12. For a discussion of δόξα/δοκέω/δοκοῦντα as *meanings* in early Greek thinking, see Spitzer, "Trans-philosophy," 577–79.

Parmenidean being as being-in-touch.[40] Hovering between περῶντα and περ ὄντα, the poem's multitext joins such through-passage and (re-)joining spoken in περῶντα with the encompassing sense of περ ὄντα,[41] (similarly) parting and (re-)joining manifold specificities in a dynamic totality wherein "beings in their continual diversifications exceed being."[42] What is more, the image advances a sense of totality in its provisionality—and so subtly endorses its own poetics—since the manifold specificities ever pass through and beyond the reach of any image of totality.

When the valences of πείρω and περάω rise into view within the broad sphere of meanings activated by ἄπειρον, the verb's sense of movement *through* and *across* articulated by Kahn bears with it the image of piercing and severing and an association with (violent) death. Such movement also undergoes transformation when inflected on the living motions of ὕδωρ that seem to undo, erase, reverse the division rendered by the verbal transversal movements of πείρω, περάω, περαίνω. When given the negative complexion of the Anaximandrean word ἄπειρον (ἀ-πείρον), these senses pulse against such negation, such that ἄπειρον trembles from within and reverberates with fissures opened by its internal tremors: ἄπειρον as *not* divided, *not* pierced, *not* severed—*joined*; in this sense the Anaximandrean term looks in the direction of totality, already in the very term speaking a living world in its totality, its differentiated-togetherness. Yet again, in its association with ὕδωρ, ἄπειρον brings to speech an aspect of *not* undivided, *not* closing over itself, *not* reunifying—*un-joined*, differentiated and differing. Anaximandrean ἄπειρον images an open circle, weaving the joined and the unjoined in the manner of Glissant's poetics of relation, not "a circuit, a line of energy curved back on itself," but rather "a circularity with volume,"[43] a circle unclosed, spiraling with the pulse of each opacity in multiple and dynamic relations.

This latter sense lets a vivifying tension echo through the Anaximandrean fragment, reverberating as it does between varying senses activated by key terms in the saying. Piercing and perforating the fabric

---

40. Spitzer, "Being-in-Touch," 4, 10.

41. On multitext specifically related to Homeric poetry, see Casey Dué, " 'Perform Its Song': Translating an Oral Traditional Epic," *Ancient Exchanges* 1, no. 1 (2020), https://wayback.archive-it.org/824/20240707084910/https://exchanges.uiowa.edu/ancient/issues/departures/iliad/.

42. Spitzer, "Archaic Images of Totality," 50–51.

43. *PR*, 32.

of totality, violations and transgressions open divisions that, by the continual movements of their severing actions, keep totality *not* undivided (ἄπειρον), *not* returning in its flow back into itself and seamlessly closing over the rifts generated by the actions of differentiated living motions. That is to say, the violence of δίκη manifests in its continual gestures toward that closure of entities, their ontological stabilization.[44] Even so, another register of δίκη brought into range by Heidegger raises tremors in the very heart of itself: the ordering that lingers within its own span without striving for the disorder of ἀδικία, the disorder of a violent attempt at "sheer persistence" (*der Aufstand in das bloße Andauern*).[45] Δίκη, heard in her female-feminine divine valence (re-)said in the Parmenidean poem (Prm. 1.14, 28), speaks beyond the male-masculine form of retributive justice and in the direction of an earthbound temporality that gathers the movements of φύσις-as-upsurge and ἀλήθεια-as-showing-withdrawing, as well as Hesiodic τὸ Χάος, pulsing with the closings already begun in every opening.[46]

On the other hand, the ἄπειρον implicated in the fragment operates by the variegated agencies of χρεών (need, fate, use, involvement[47]) and χρόνου τάξιν (time's arrangement). Of these, the former speaks with the shrill overtones of prophetic speech and its binding limitations that act, like δίκη, to fix and preserve ontologically determined entities within the horizon of retributive justice and its "logic of usurpation, subsumptive identity and its correlative exclusions, domination and calculated revenge."[48] This would be the voicing of prophecy coopted and violently subordinated to the law of patriarchy, a history figured in the destruction

---

44. See the discussion above and note 32 with reference to Kleinberg-Levin, "The Court of Justice." The relation of justice and ontology disclosed by Kleinberg-Levin informs the discussion of the Anaximandrean fragment.

45. Heidegger, "The Anaximander Fragment," in *Early Greek Thinking: The Dawn of Western Philosophy*, trans. David Farrell Krell (Harper and Row, 1984), 42–44; Heidegger, "Der Spruch des Anaximander," 356.

46. Kleinberg-Levin, "Court of Justice," 405–7.

47. The translation *involvement* takes its bearings from Krell's translation *Use*, which translates *Brauch*, Heidegger's translation of Anaximandrean χρεών. All refer to the engagedness of use. Heidegger, "Anaximander Fragment," trans. Krell, 52–53; "Der Spruch des Anaximander," 367–68. Use/*Brauch* opens the span of a while for what is present, bringing each into the presence within that span that joins each with the twofold absences of arriving and departing.

48. Kleinberg-Levin, "Court of Justice," 393–94.

of Delphi's serpent and the place's colonization by the Arch-Destroyer, Apollo, militant protector of the will of Zeus-the-father.[49] Yet, even as it voices and grounds the repetition of the same required for such justice, χρεών trembles from within itself with the chthonic energies of γῆ-as-Gaia,[50] primordial voice of a radically open and opening futurity coursing in multiple, unforeseeable directions out from the dynamics of female-feminine ways of living resistant to the overmastery of male-masculine forms of thinking and organization.

This dynamics does not deny or negate limits: the oppositional two-fold of establishment and denial of limitations belongs to the metaphysical bearing of Zeus.[51] Rather, it energizes living with the movements of a continual reconfiguration of constellated possibilities opening as expansive and yet-undetermined zones of differently arrayed limitations, even as it also remains open to the radical openness of opening otherwise: the dimension of ἄπειρον in every aspect of totality, the unpredictabilities of opacities in relation. The Anaximandrean χρόνου τάξιν likewise configures limitations in the constitutive array spanning birth—richness-of-living (οὐσία)—collapsing (Hippol. *Haer.* 1.6.1 [Axr. 10 Graham]) while these motion(s) open as an expansive opening of ἄπειρον; as limiting the multiplicities of unclosing arrays (ἀπείρους κόσμους, Euseb. *Praep. evang.* 1.8.2 [Axr. 18 Graham]), the movement of ἄπειρον takes place as ever-expanding-limiting: περιέχειν ἄπαντα καῖ πάντα κυβερνᾶν (Arist. *Ph.* 203b11–12 [Axr. 16 Graham]); πάντας περιέχειν τοὺς κόσμους (Hippol. *Haer.* 1.6.1

---

49. The history of that colonization is given in the *Homeric Hymn to Apollo*, which is also the text where the role as militant protector within the patriarchy comes to speech as Apollo's first words: "*kithara* and the curved bow shall be special to me, and I will establish (χρήσω) for humans the unerring will of Zeus" (*Hom. Hymn Ap.* 3.131–32).

50. Compare Kleinberg-Levin's reading of Heidegger on the justice of earth, whose gender remains unspoken in both sources (Kleinberg-Levin and Heidegger). "Court of Justice," 399–400.

51. Again, the scene of Apollo's birth discloses the transgression of limitation that belongs to the mode of identity asserted by patriarchy: "golden bands cannot bind you nor even cords restrain you as you struggle, but all bonds (πείρατα πάντα) were loosened" (*Hom. Hymn Ap.* 3.128–29). The revelatory scene addresses the association between mother and bonds in resonances—such as dependency and associations with birth and generation as threats to the metaphysics of identity established by Zeus, but also the forms of care, interdependence, and community—that permeate both the patriarchal order and the order beyond its reach. On the metaphysics of Zeus, see the fourth chapter, "Breaking Light, Unclosing Opacity," second section, "Breaking Light: Daybreak on the Continent."

[Axr. 10 Graham]). As a temporality exceeding and overwhelming, though nevertheless mostly concealed by constructions of time as an enumerable and enumerating repetition of the same and of discrete, interchangeable units, the Anaximandrean χρόνου τάξιν carves through the living world as the current of dissolution, erosion, ceaseless decomposition of all risings into and as that living world: this, as Kleinberg-Levin has noted, configures the temporality of nature.[52] Here surges and flows, even beneath a surface of apparently solid ground, the confluence of limited and unlimited and its removal from the one-many paradigm, the expansive openness of possibilities for futures by|as|within variegated and dynamically shifting limitations of the living world.

By the multiple agencies of χρεών and χρόνου τάξιν the Anaximandrean ἄπειρον sustains its futural direction as a totality whose continual spread into that direction exceeds the piercings and transgressions of the living world at any moment of its rendering, its imaging as a totality pierced, severed: just past the edge of horizon, just past the edge of thought, totality teems as a radiant not-yet severed totality, ἄπειρον.

"Infinite," "boundless," or "unlimited" do not translate ἄπειρον in this register of the limits-crossings pair. Rather, something more like *horizoning* or *spanning*, each one a participle, a continual happening: horizoning continually turns the whole beyond the mark of its bound, preserves a past or beyond of the horizon; spanning continually opens a distance, as if measuring, but without the closure that would enable measure. In this sense, Anaximandrean ἄπειρον both resembles and differs from Aristotle's thought of ἄπειρον as a power of a certain type (δυνάμει εἶναι τὸ ἄπειρον, Arist. *Ph.* 206a.18), a power toward always one more (ἀεί γε ἕτερον καὶ ἕτερον, 206a.29). Aristotle's construal of ἄπειρον resonates with Anaximandrean ἄπειρον when he describes ἄπειρον as an ever-one-more, as a spanning (ἀεί) of birth and perishing within limits (πεπερασμένον, 206a.32–33), and as in a certain sense unknowable (207a.25–26[53]). The resonance fades when Aristotle thinks ἄπειρον as an impossible material source (σῶμα αἰσθητόν) because it does not come to light (φαίνεται, 204b.22–35), or when he locates ἄπειρον only in parts, not in totality (207a.8–21), or when he forces a decision between surrounding and being surrounded, finding that ἄπειρον will be surrounded (207a.25)—Anaximandrean ἄπειρον will do both and more,

---

52. Kleinberg-Levin, "Court of Justice," 399.

53. This unknowability, however, is grounded in giving to ἄπειρον the sense of material without form (Arist. *Ph.* 207a.25–26).

otherwise. In surrounding totality (πάντας περιέχειν τοὺς κόσμους, Hipp. *Haer.* 1.4.6 [Axr. 10 Graham]), Anaximandrean ἄπειρον, as an unknowable (ἄγνωστον) and unhorizoned (ἀόριστον) span that surrounds (περιέχειν) and horizons (ὁρίζειν), gains an aura of strangeness (ἄτοπον) and impossibility (ἀδύνατον) for Aristotle (*Ph.* 207a.30–32). The resistance of each differentiation of totality to full comprehension, the outpouring of possibilities and the outspanning and ungatherable ways of showing and withdrawing, shows itself *as opacity* and comes to speech as Anaximandrean ἄπειρον in order to describe each differentiation in its abundances and totality as, in Glissant's terms, "forever totalizing."[54]

As it courses through the other Anaximandrean thinkings ἄπειρον voices a seeming paradox and resonates conceptually with the Egyptian term Atum, which seems to name "Totality" and "undifferentiated."[55] Hornung understood the term as something like "undifferentiated" (*l'indifférencié*) in an unusual sense that compounds non-being and total-being and that has the power to differentiate itself.[56] Throughout the array of diversity the primordial being Atum expresses itself such that "the final product of creation in all its diversity is in one sense nothing more than the ultimate evolution of Atum himself."[57] Atum manifests both in|as limited entities and crosses beyond those entities into an originary condition that is itself at once limited and unlimited, open as the power of differentiating and closed as yet undifferentiated, with no boundaries to define it.

Similarly, the divinity Amun takes place as prior to being and as other than nothing, void, absence. Amun embodies the pair of limits-crossings:

> You began the unfolding of the cosmos,
> before was no being, no void;
> World without end was in you and from you,
> yours on that First Day (*LH*: LXXX, 159).

---

54. Glissant, "Measure, Immeasurability," in *Treatise on the Whole-World*, trans. Celia Britton 137.

55. Atum is glossed as "Totality." Wilson's translation in Pritchard, *Ancient Near East* 1:1n1.

56. The description of "undifferentiated" summarizes Hornung: "L'ancien nom du dieu unique au commencement, Atoum, réunit les sens de 'ne pas être' et 'être complet,' on pourrait également le rendre par 'l'indifférencié." Erik Hornung, "L'Égypte, la philosophie avant les grecs," trans. Gilles Roulin, *Les Études philosophiques* 2/3 (1987): 116, JSTOR.

57. Allen, "Celestial Realm," 122–23.

Unlimited ("world without end") and prior to cosmogonic differentiation, Amun also turns out beyond the limitations of its own condition in order for being to begin as manifold entities.

Anaximandrean ἄπειρον overlaps with both deified concepts Atum and Amun in naming the belonging-together of limits and crossings. Insofar as ἄπειρον remains distinct from the originary entities that arise from it, as the fragment declares, it rests within the limits of that very differentiation. On the other hand, as joined with a ceaselessly expansive motion, ἄπειρον—like Atum and Amun in their restless transfigurations—both outspans itself and takes place as a continually transforming multiplicity, generative of (and haunting) the multiplicity of originary entities and of the openly-expansive orderings (ἀπείρους κόσμους, Euseb. *Praep. evang.* 1.8.2 [Axr. 18 Graham]). In motion, ever-expansive in its opening, ἄπειρον does not produce the limitations on which a metaphysics is founded, but the shimmerings that gleam on the edges of provisional and ever-shifting, transforming, reconstellating limits, "the open-ended, unfolding boundary"—or, *boundaries*.[58]

Joining ἄπειρον and γῆ, Xenophanean thinking also brings to light the gathering of limited and unlimited at the site of opacities:

> of earth, this here at our feet—an upper limit (πεῖρας) is visible,
> pressing against air (ἠέρι), but that downward (κάτω) reaches
>   into ἄπειρον (Xns. 28 Lesher).

γῆ locates a seam joining the light of the upper world, the coming-to-light and the visible, with the lower world's richness of opacities: such riches reverberate in the abundance associated with Hades, called *richly-receiving* (πολυδέγμων) and *rich-in-names* (πολυώνυμος, *Hom. Hymn Dem.* 2.17–18),[59] whose very name Ἀ-ΐδες speaks the unseen and pulses with a sense of opacity. The god and his realm are, as Sallis has put it, "withdrawn, not merely in the way that things are temporarily enclosed in the darkness of night, but rather in such a way that they never admit the light of the sun."[60] The downward orientation (κάτω) of γῆ into ἄπειρον already indicates opacity and abundance and shares with Ἀ-ΐδες the

---

58. Maly, "Echoes at the Edge," 125.

59. Another name of the divinity, Πλούτων, *Pluto*, speaks of riches and abundance.

60. Sallis, "Hades: Heraclitus, Fragment B 98," in *Heraclitean Fragments*, ed. John Sallis and Kenneth Maly (University of Alabama Press, 1980), 63.

negative valence of the alpha privative (ἀ-), lending both the sense of resistance to coming forth into light while naming such resistance. Like opacities of Thalean and Herakleitean ὕδωρ, the speaking (λόγος) of the opacities in ἄπειρον comes to light partially, in contour, shadowed.

On the seam joining the upper and lower regions occurs an aspect of the dynamic force in Xenophanean thinking, a force that by its multiplicity (γῆ and ὕδωρ) animates totality and so haunts and moves within the saying on γῆ as the threshold of limit and non-limit. In the upper world of light and coming-to-light, where beings *manifest* in the while and limited span of their presencing,[61] occurs the limit (πεῖρας) of γῆ conjoined to the opacity of ἀήρ. Joining this upper-limit on the lower dimension of the seam moves a downward energy *away from* the seam and its lighting and *toward* the outspanning open expanse of ἄπειρον in its downward sweep away from the opacities of the upper limit. The Xenophanean saying here discloses the joining of the two, naming the site of limit and non-limit coming-together and belonging in the jointure of earth and ἀήρ, and as constituted as opacities variously spoken: as conjoined with ἀήρ in the upper region of limited span and as ἄπειρον in the lower region. Xenophanean thinking, that is, voices the opacity of ἄπειρον alongside limited span (πεῖρας), letting γῆ arise as both limited and unlimited. How can it be that γῆ—and the dynamic force γῆ embodies—collects limit and non-limit in itself?

Un-joining: ἄπειρον and Experience

Homeric poetries forge connections among and across ἄπειρον, γῆ, and ὕδωρ in the form of πόντος (sea). Kahn argues against the sense of "unlimitedness" precisely on this point: "Neither earth nor sea is devoid of limits, and in fact the poet speaks repeatedly of the πείρατα of both."[62] Yet, the gap between unlimited and limited need not be thought in terms of (in-)consistency. Rather, thinking ἄπειρον as voicing ways of experiencing aspects of the living world that vacillate between unlimited and limited might form a bridge between the two and allow the motions of the unlimited-limited pair to propel new insights toward Anaximandrean ἄπειρον. In what ways do γῆ and πόντος rise into experience as ἄπειρον in the sense of unlimited?

---

61. After Heidegger, "Der Spruch des Anaximander," 354–55, 368.

62. Kahn, *Anaximander and the Origins of Greek Cosmology*, 231.

Attention to the fuller scenes in which ἄπειρον is spoken, and specifically to the characters within each scene and the speakers and narrators involved, opens a way toward the experience of ἄπειρον as unlimited. Turning first to the *Iliad*, as Akhilleus summons Thetis to the shores near Ilion he gazes at the sea, voiced as ἀπείρονα πόντον (Hom. *Il.* 1.350). The messengers from Agamemnon's camp have just taken Briseis, punctuating the dishonor served to Akhilleus by the chief Akhaian warlord. Gazing at the ἀπείρονα πόντον, the swift-footed warrior sits apart and alone, seated on the edge of the gray salt-sea, submerged in grief and bitter anger. In just over ten lines the poem speaks emphatically of Akhilleus's distress: three times the language calls attention to his weeping, the third of which focalizes Akhilleus's weeping through his mother Thetis (1.348, 356, 360); in his cries to Thetis Akhilleus stresses his own mortality and, moreover, the brevity of his life (μινυνθάδιόν περ ἐόντα, 1.352); the summons Akhilleus cries out to Thetis emphasizes lack of honor (1.353–56). Through and within an emotionally charged aperture the scene delivers the phrase ἀπείρονα πόντον. Akhilleus's rising feeling of mortality, his sense of the limits of his own span closing around him, the radical and unshakeable entanglements of his being-in-the-world along with the sense of loss surrounding and permeating his life contrast with the surging expanse of ἀπείρονα πόντον as it stretches out toward unlimitedness. That is, when viewed from the perspective and within the isolation, limitation, anguish, and mortality Akhilleus experiences in the scene, ἄπειρον surges here not as the specific closings and limitings on Akhilleus, but rather as an *other* and *indeterminate* spanning that uncloses to him the situatedness, the *being-in-the-world* laid bear through the breakdown of these specific relations. The scene brings momentarily into view a passing event of uncanniness, of the "not-at-home" connected with anxiety according to which possibilities open, spanning into indeterminacy. Akhilleus, separate from the war camp, aggrieved, in his gazing to the ἀπείρονα πόντον becomes momentarily isolated, "individualized" as he encounters the worldliness of being-as-relation, an isolation enmeshed in being-in-the-world.[63] When heard as one dimension of the character's experience as narrated and illustrated by the entire artistry of the scene, the sense of limitless expanse spreading out before and beyond the isolated warrior echoes in ἀπείρονα πόντον. This is not at all contradictory or inconsistent with a limitation on this same ἀπείρονα πόντον, which comes to an end at the place where

---

63. Drawing on Heidegger's discussion of anxiety and its disclosive force, *Being and Time*, trans. John Macquarrie and Edward Robinson (Harper and Row, 1962), 230–35.

Akhilleus positions himself, that is, on the shore, at each moment moving into and out from varied and shifting limitations as possibilities open and close through his own decisions. Rather, the limitless sweep of ἀπείρονα πόντον begins from that variegated and shifting, while continually limited, position and fans outward to the horizon and the zone(s) beyond the horizon's containment—the way Xenophanean thinking identifies a limit at the uppermost of γῆ *alongside* the unlimited downward motion of γῆ into ἄπειρον. This joining of unlimited with limited the narrative of the *Iliad* embeds in Akhilleus's experience of ἄπειρον.

On the epic's other shore, after the intervening wreckage of a myriad of human lives rendered by plague, rage, and slaughter, an opportunity for mourning Hektor finally opens for the Trojans. The narration that closes Helen's song remembering Hektor expands the sphere of grief and mourning: where following Andromakhe's speech the women vocalized suffering (Hom. *Il.* 24.746), and after Hekabe's lamentation rises a "noise of suffering that does not yield" (γόον δ᾽ ἀλίαστον, 24.760), the wake of Helen's ritual song of grief spreads the whole population into an unlimited condition (ἐπὶ δ᾽ ἔστενε δῆμος ἀπείρων, 24.776). In the phrase, ἀπείρων can be heard hovering between the verb (ἔστενε, *groan*) and the noun (δῆμος, people) so that the crowd itself *and* its profound noise of anguish sweep out away from the limited position of each member of the group and the limited position of the group as a collective body. This hovering draws out the multiple senses of ἔστενε: not only does it speak of groaning, but also of being constricted or pressed by and into narrow limits the force of which generates the noise. The limiting pressures of grief open, through mourning, into a sense of an open expanse experienced as *without limits*. Both the number of the throng and its din begin as limited presences of multiple relations, yet this *ek-static* aspect of mourning, through which the rituals of lamentation transport each mourner—at least momentarily—outside the limits of self and into a wider zone, courses through the experience of being in a vast crowd and sensing the confluence of one's voice into the flood and torrent of myriad other voices. ἀπείρων describes this experience, which begins from, but rapidly not only surpasses, but alters—transfigures—the sense of limitedness. While the expansive ek-static mourning sounded in ἔστενε δῆμος ἀπείρων sweeps away the ordinary sense of a continuity of *nows*, in this way resembling Heideggerian futural *ek-stasis* that discloses the nullity of a self,[64] the ek-stasis of mourning heard in this scene from the *Iliad* also

----

64. Heidegger, *Being and Time*, 379.

bears a Dionysian character and, as such, affectively prefigures the self's futural nullity by the flood and torrent, the sense of being transfigured through merging into the surge of the crowd. That is, ek-static Dionysian mourning is differentiated from Heideggerian ek-static futurity in that, rather than individualizing, its movement converges, merges, flows and overflows, so that the sense of being is not the individualized one whose ownmost death as nullity presents the limited character of being-there and the horizon of responsive possibilities it discloses, but rather the felt sense of being-this-surge in its expansions (ἀπείρων).[65]

This ek-static valence of ἀπείρων in the sound of a multitude may also find expression in the early fifth century BCE lyric poet Bakkhylides. The poem celebrates an athletic victory, Hieron's win in the Olympic chariot race. Voicing the ἀπείρων of a cheering crowd within its narration redu-plicates the poem's celebratory tone: "A crowd roars limitless (ἀπείρων)[66] / 'What a man, threefold blessings upon him! . . .'" (Bacch. Ode 3.9–10). The experience of being drawn beyond the limits of self crosses the limits of specific emotions: where in the scenes from epic ἄπειρον-related terms accompany grief and mourning, in Bakkhylides jubilance and admiration of excellence bear the members of the crowd beyond a sense of their own limits. Again, an ambiguity releases the term's sense of unlimited, an ek-static span beyond the limits of self into the expansive open of a gathered crowd in the surge of an overwhelming emotion. In both cases—profound grief in mourning and exaltation of excellence—the term ἀπείρων describes an *experience* of crossing limits and, further, of being overwhelmed and thrust into a limitless condition, what Nietzsche thought

---

65. In a sense, this Dionysian ekstasis of mourning mirrors (reverses, alters) Heidegger's ekstasis of futurity, where the former releases an existent from individualization, the latter enables an existent to close in upon itself, as Lingis puts it, in the event of authenticity. Alphonso Lingis, "Differance in the Eternal Recurrence of the Same," *Research in Phenomenology* 8, no. 1 (1978): 77–78, JSTOR. The two join perhaps in Heidegger's disclosure of the finite as the primordial and the infinite as the derivative valence of time: Dionysian ek-stasis of mourning prefigures in a felt way the infinite temporal onwardness spreading beyond individuals. From such affective prefiguration the primordiality of temporal finitude, of limit and span, stand out as the possibility of temporal onwardness, its basis in individual demise. Both then share in the disclosure of the transformation whereby everything glows in the shimmer of contingency. "Difference in the Eternal Recurrence of the Same," 78.

66. Campbell notes that the adjective was supplied by an editor and agrees that it is likely "the correct supplement." *Greek Lyric Poetry*, 107, 418.

in *The Birth of Tragedy* as the Dionysian "ecstasy" and its "annihilation of the usual limits and borders."[67] Indeed, Manfred Riedel has brought out the Dionysian resonances of Anaximandrean thinking, specifically in the images of the φλοῖος, tree bark (Euseb. *Praep. evang.* 1.8.2 [Axr. 19 Graham]) and the αὐλός, pipe or flute (Ps.-Plut. 2.20 [Axr. 22 Graham]), both of which also link Anaximandrean thinking to poetry.[68] The surging outspan of the jubilant crowd further relates ἄπειρον to certain modes of consciousness and experience.

ἄπειρον brings to speech a motion beyond, an ek-static movement that sweeps out past the limits of experience opening a sense of an *unlimited* open expanse.[69] Yet, the awareness of this out-spanning, surfacing in retrospect, itself discloses an experience of being outswept: ek-stasis. Such experience enables the possibility of a reflexive turn to awareness of limits of experience and the abundances of the living world with respect to the limits of experience. In this sense, where limits (πείρας) of γῆ constitute an opacity by their constitutive relation with the opacity of ἀήρ, Xenophanean thinking discloses the joining of this limit with the outspanning open expanse of ἄπειρον, the ever-unlimiting dimension always on the edge of a limit in its moment. In the scene of Akhilleus's isolation and sense of the limits of his span, the open expanse manifests as the sea (ἀπείρονα πόντον). The radiance(s) of this constellation of terms—ὕδωρ (as πόντον), γῆ, ἄπειρον—brings to speech an additional and crucial further association. Not only does this constellation of terms illuminate a sense of opacities and the belonging together of limited-unlimited, it also points to another spectrum of radiance out of the term πειράω: *experience.*

---

67. Nietzsche, *The Birth of Tragedy*, trans. Douglas Smith (Oxford University Press, 2000) 46.

68. Manfred Riedel, "ΑΡΧΗ und ΑΠΕΙΡΟΝ: Über das Grundwort des Anaximander," *Archiv für Geschichte der Philosophie* 69, no. 1 (1987): 11. For a discussion of ek-stasis in the performance of early Greek thinking, especially the Parmenidean poem, see Spitzer, *Parmenides and Translation*, 72–73, 78, 113–16, 123–24.

69. With an emphasis on its oneiric dimension, Bachelard explores *immensity* in poetic images, especially Baudelaire, which also bears an ek-static character as it releases a dreamer from the confines of self. Related to ἄπειρον-ἀπείρων, *immense-immensity* in Bachelard's phenomenology names the elsewhere opened by day-dreaming. *Poetics of Space*, 201–13.

Dis-joining: ἄπειρον as (Non-)Experience

From the echoes of ἄπειρον in the opening statement of Herakleitean thinking the sense of πειράω as *experience* makes itself felt and charts a trajectory back to the resonant word ἄπειρον in Anaximandrean thinking. As a starting point for Herakleitean thinking, ἄπειρον emerges as the action of λόγος:

> *Logos* this one being continually humans grow dis-joined (ἀξύνετοι) both before hearing and after having heard at first while multiplicities (πάντων) arising in a way grounded in this *logos*[70] people resemble (ἐοίκασι) the *unexperienced* (ἀπείρου-σιν) experiencing (πειρώμενοι) words and actions of this sort which I go through differentiating each grounded in limits of its spanning (κατὰ φύσιν) and articulating how it holds together. (ὅκως ἔχει, Hct. 1 Robinson)

Listening to *logos* dis-joins, brings about a *disjointure* (ἀξύνετοι) of the settled manner of thinking that guides ordinary experience, opening an openness that resembles a beginning *without* experience (ἀπείρουσιν). Within such an open—the open expanse of ἄπειρον as dis-joined from settled thoughts as if without experience (ἀ-πείρουσιν)—Herakleitean thinking envisions a jointure (ξυνόν) as a mode of thinking (τὸ φρονέειν) that joins totality (πᾶσι) together (ξυνόν, 113 Robinson), an open awareness with which (ξὺν νόῳ) a community sharing in *logos* (λέγοντας) joins itself to what joins totality-of-multiplicities (τῷ ξυνῷ πάντων, 114 Robinson).

In a manner that brings those listening to *logos* into a way of hear-kening like *un*-experience, *logos* comes to pass as a clearing, a region cleared of the debris of what has accumulated and settled in ordinary experience: received opinions, the well-worn pathways (ἦθος) without awareness (γνώμας, Hct. 78 Robinson). Awareness of this sort opens to those who join in readiness with the openness that is *like* (ἐοίκασι) being-without-experience (ἀπείρουσιν, 1 Robinson), a way (ἦθος) guided by the divine (δαίμων, 119 Robinson) toward awareness (78 Robinson), which Herakleitean thinking voices as the one select thing (σοφόν) only partially available to expression and which includes—and emerges (par-

---

70. *In a way grounded in this logos* translates κατὰ τὸν λόγον τόνδε, giving voice to the downward motion of κατά.

tially) as—*logos* (32 Robinson). Opening the way back from ordinary, habitual apprehension of a being to an "understanding of the being of this being (projecting upon the way it is unconcealed),"[71] its φύσις—this is the epochal task of Herakleitean *logos*. Such attention becomes available through the dis-solution of the ordinary pathways, through the awakening of a condition like *non*-experience: ἄπειρον.

At least as it echoes in Herakleitean thinking, Anaximandrean ἄπειρον asks of inquirers that they begin as beginners, as ready with an open awareness for an opening of the living world that diverges from ordinary experience and its sedimented layers. This practice does not exclude ordinary experience, but draws it into heightened attention so that its channels—and ruts—emerge into view. ἄπειρον, that is, does not shear ordinary experience from its territory. Rather, Anaximandrean ἄπειρον takes ordinary experience not as settled pathways on already determined directions, but as open expanse—another valence of the term itself—along|through|across which thinking sweeps from the location(s) brought into view under the practice of ἄπειρον. The radiant words of Anaximandrean thinking unfurl *rather poetically* in this very sense, by an experience like non-experience dis-joining the accepted presuppositions and notions on totality, reconfiguring thought from the imaginary of the *one* (as spoken, for instance, in Hesiodic theogony) and of the *many* (ones) (as in Pherekydean cosmogony) and into the relation of multiplicities. Anaximandrean ἄπειρον names not a withdrawal from experience but a renewal of experiencing, of engaging opacity as a totality of multiplicities in "an insistent presence that we are incapable of not experiencing [*nous ne pouvons pas ne pas vivre*],"[72] incapable of not *living*.

Anaximandros reportedly *ventured* or *dared* (ἐτόλμησε, Agathemeros *Sketch of Geography*, 1.1 [Axr. 6 Graham]) to produce an image of totality—a multimedia projection, sketched on a plank (ἐν πίνακι γράψαι), perhaps incorporating graphic and textual elements—as one moment in the multiplicity of growing and collapsing worlds (Euseb. *Praep. evang.* 1.8.2 [Axr. 18 Graham]). A multimodal projection like this draws attention to the *limits* it inscribes: Diogenes reports that it imaged the limits (περίμετρον) of earth and sea (Diog. Laert. 2.1.2) and Agathemeros that it depicted the inhabited regions (τὴν οἰκουμένην, Agathemeros, *Sketch of Geography*, 1.1 [Axr. 6 Graham]), not merging totality with a closed

71. Heidegger, *Basic Problems of Phenomenology*, 21.

72. *PR*, 111; *PdR*, 125.

whole, but projecting a limited region of totality that exceeds the limits (and limiting) of experience in the manner of ἄπειρον. The projection also brings to light its *poetic* quality, its *having-been-made*: even of the limited region (the inhabited places), the task is a *poetic* one, drawn from imagination, in this case working by way of a visual (and perhaps accompanying textual) image that operates "not," as Heidegger writes of poetic images, in the manner of "mere fantasy and illusions," but instead in a way that generates "visible inclusions of the foreign (*Fremde*) in the view of the familiar (*Vertrauten*)."[73]

Some dimensions of the Anaximandrean projection reconfigure or rearticulate existing images of totality from Mesopotamian sources,[74] but this reconfiguration and rearticulation itself forms the work of thinking: not a beginning from nothing, or a blank slate, but a *beginning again* from what is already there—the ways others have experienced and voiced totality, the accumulated history of this imaginal engagement. In the images of the surrounding fire like bark of a tree (Euseb. *Praep. evang.* 1.8.2 [Axr. 19 Graham]), of the wheel(s) (ἀρματείῳ τροχῷ) of the heavens (Ps.-Plut. *Plac.* 2.20 [Axr. 22 Graham]), and of the column drums (Hippol. *Haer.* 1.6 [Axr. 20 Graham]), as well as the articulation of a beginning and source (ἀρχή) as *non-experience* and *without-experience* (ἀ-πείρον), Anaximandrean thinking urges both a recollection of totality's movements within the span of its while—its rising, dwelling, and collapsing (Hippol. *Haer.* 1.6 [Axr. 10 Graham])—and a radical rethinking and re-envisioning of totality made available by a dis-joining from the ordinary, habitual pathways, an experience like non-experience.

The Anaximandrean poetic image of totality provokes a sense of *being-without-experience*, thinking no longer contained in the limits of the received views conditioning ordinary experience, while its beginning from ἄπειρον as ἀρχή works as a poetic saying to recall the unknown *as* unknown,[75] to preserve the opacities of what continually exceeds the limiting of experience.[76] In this sense does Heidegger's articulation of *Un-Fug* link to ἄπειρον as non-experience by way of the negation (*Un-*, ἀ-), the stress on

---

73. Heidegger, ". . . dichterisch wohnet der Mensch . . . ," 195.

74. Marciano, "East and West," 17–19 and fig. 1.2.

75. Heidegger, ". . . dichterisch wohnet der Mensch . . . ," 194.

76. *PR*, 62.

Un- at the end of Heidegger's discussion connecting τὸ χρεών and ἄπειρον from the Anaximandros fragment.[77] Heidegger writes that to avoid the risk of hardening (*verhärdet*) into mere persistence (*bloße Beharren*), τὸ χρεών keeps itself in a double action of sending the limits within which something comes to presence and of handing over presencing into dis-array (*Un-Fug*). The *Un-* and *dis-* point not so much to τὸ χρεών as to the ἀ- of ἀ-πείρον. What comes to presence in the joint of a while does so in array, and that is the region of presencing as τὸ χρεών, the region of experience in which limiting operates through the familiarity of involvement, use (*Brauch*). The presencing without limits presences in dis-array, the region of ἄπειρον, a region of *non-experience*, itself not bound by its own motions of limiting. ἄπειρον then names an experience-like-non-experience of totality that, in its endless motions and in the continually differentiating *totality* of the coming-to-presences, remains in radical dis-array, open, dis-joined beyond the scope and limiting of experience yet enabling that limiting as and in its movements.

As a beginning and source (ἀρχή), ἄπειρον in Anaximandrean thinking summons this way of *non*-experience. Opening out from the limiting boundaries imposed by sedimented *views*, *habits*, *opinions*, Anaximandrean thinking addresses itself in the direction of what moves without limiting boundaries of experience even as its movements give rise and shape to limiting boundaries. Yet, the joining summoned in the address of ἄπειρον does not reduce totality to a unity or a one, as the multiple worlds indicated in Anaximandrean thinking dissolve a thought of *one* into the open expanses constituting each multiplicity (ἄπειρους κόσμους, Euseb. *Praep. evang.* 1.8.2 [Axr. 18 Graham]); the sense of ἄπειρον as unsevered *and* unclosed into itself—that is, the ways ἄπειρον defies the one-many schema—preserves totality as *multiplicity*. This joining spoken as ἄπειρον con-joins without reducing or merging, so that its movements do not occur *outside* of totality, but *as* its motions: relation, "the knowledge in motion of beings."[78] In this sense ἄπειρον names the visibility or *transparency* of totality's relation while also naming the *opacities* energizing such relation.[79]

---

77. Heidegger, "Der Spruch des Anaximander," 368.

78. *PR*, 187.

79. *PR*, 56, 62.

Spanning: ἄπειρον as (Non-)Experience of Totality

Spanning a threefold range of meanings, ἄπειρον names a way of beginning in a radical transformation of thinking. The span of Anaximandrean ἄπειρον con-joins the relation of opacities in terms of irreducible multiplicities that defy the logic of one-many with an experience of the ek-static open expanse of relation and a manner of thinking that begins by working toward a way of being in relation that resembles *being-without-experience.* Anaximandrean ἄπειρον activates an image of totality straining toward what withdraws from experience (ἀ-πειράω), urging attention to the movement of totality beyond the limits of thinking, a movement unfolding, perhaps, as *horizoning* and *spanning.* Reversing the direction of thinking, Anaximandros gestures toward an opening, a beginning, in its teeming depth and excess registered as a negative, a not, a *dis-*: ἀ-πείρον. This is not the speaking of putting-forward, not a thesis or a position. To initiate thinking, Anaximandrean ἄπειρον begins from *not* (ἀ-), urging primarily—as thinking's beginning—a negation or release of thinking from the familiar and habitual, from received thought.

When brought together with ἄπειρον as collapsing the one-many paradigm, the valences of (non-)experience illuminate the opacity of origination and the lack of emphasis on origination in Anaximandrean thinking. Cosmology seems to overshadow cosmogony, while the image of human beings taking shape out of fish envisions gradual emergence of life from life rather than sudden emergence of first beginnings (Hippol. *Haer.* 1.6 [Axr. 20 Graham]). Anaximandrean thinking, centering ἄπειρον that opens ways away from the logic of one-many, takes place as what Glissant thought as *archipelagic*: a non-atavistic thinking,[80] a movement away from prime elements—unmixed and each inviolate in its being in the manner of a "sufficient entity that would discover its origin (*son commencement*) in itself"[81]—and toward multiplicities in relation.

The span of Anaximandrean ἄπειρον protects against the mode of knowing as domination through reduction to a complete transparency, what Glissant termed *continental* linked to filiation and its obsession with the singular root and origin[82]—an annihilation of the open expanse, named in

---

80. Glissant, "Poetics of the World."

81. *PdR,* 174; *PR,* 160.

82. *PR,* 143–44.

Xenophanean thinking as the generative and constitutive dynamics of γῆ and ὕδωρ. Anaximandrean ἄπειρον urges a poetics of relation, a poetics heard in "the presocratics" by Glissant as sustaining relation of opacities and the imaginaries propelled by them and as guarding (*protège*) diversity,[83] while attending to emerging relations of multiplicities: totality in its movements, *totality totalizing*. Such a way unfurls as poetics, not only speaking poetically so that, as Heidegger writes, "the unknown remains what it is: unknown,"[84] but also making visible its own *poetic* gesture, its capacity to extend, open, imagine. Like Thalean considerations, Anaximandrean thinking brings forth a poetics of opacity. How else to bring to speech the experience of *non-experience*, the limits brought to pass by an unlimited, than in phrases spoken, as Simplikios put it, ποιητικωτέροις, *rather poetically*?

---

83. *PR*, 62; *PdR*, 75.

84. Heidegger, ". . . dichterisch wohnet der Mensch . . . ," 194.

3

Hovering

Anaximenean ἀήρ

Hovering

No birth of ἀήρ. Instead, it comes forward as an event, bound to the event or happening of Tartaros and, in its happening, belongs together with Gaia and Eros: "And Tartaros-full-of-ἀήρ (Τάρταρα ἠερόεντα) in the recess of broad-pathed earth" (Hes. *Theog.* 119). The adjective ἠερόεντα does not add something to the noun Τάρταρά, as if Tartaros—thought here, importantly, in the plural, as a multiplicity—might only incidentally or occasionally come to speech as modified by ἠερόεντα as, for instance, a cloud might be ἠερόεντα *or* it might be κυανέῃσιν ("dark blue,"[1] 757, 745, respectively). Rather, the whole phrase voices the region named in its fullness and manifest (in-)completion, its multiplicity: Τάρταρά ἠερόεντα, Tartaros (multiplicity)-full-of-ἀήρ.[2]

---

1. Translation from Stanley Lombardo, *Hesiod: Works and Days and Theogony* (Hackett, 1993), 82.

2. Of the ten appearances of Tartaros in *Theogony*, six are spoken as some version of the phrase Τάρταρα ἠερόεντα (Hes. *Theog.* 119, 682, 721, 723, 736, 807). Of those expressions that lack ἠερόεντα, most unfold within the narrative of the threat to Zeus posed by the offspring of Gaia and Tartaros (822, 841, 868), implicating the generativity as possible only by way of the elimination of the ἠερόεντα from Tartaros, through a transformation of Tartaros under the sway of the subversive power of Aphrodite. The other voicing of Tartaros without ἠερόεντα comes in the cosmography, where a falling bronze anvil would reach Tartaros on the tenth day (725), though this description

97

Birth of ἀήρ opens as the death of πῦρ. Herakleitean ἀήρ takes place as closely bound with πῦρ and ὕδωρ, where the death of the πῦρ is the beginning (γένεσις) of ἀήρ and its living, while the death of ἀήρ is the beginning of ὕδωρ and its living (Hct. 76a–c Robinson). The Herakleitean sayings address a spanning of each—ἀήρ, πῦρ, ὕδωρ—within which each one shines forth and extinguishes in a cycle of living.

Beginning of ἀήρ: right here, at our feet, a threshold or boundary (πεῖρας) that opens to vision the belonging together of γῆ and ἀήρ (Xns. 28 Lesher). ἀήρ begins at a limit by an action of shaping-pressure toward (προσπλάζον) the density and expansive opacities (ἄπειρον) of γῆ, even as, in Xenophanean thinking, ἀήρ also arises, as with everything else, as a multiplicity, a turbine of opacities from ὕδωρ and γῆ (29 Lesher).

No beginning of ἀήρ: "Anaximenes, son of Eurystratus, of Miletus, was an associate of Anaximander, who says, like him, that the underlying nature (ὑποκειμένην φύσιν) is single and boundless (ἄπειρον), but not indeterminate (οὐκ ἀόριστον) as he says, but determinate (ὡρισμένην), calling it air" (ἀέρα, Simpl. *in Phys.* 1.2.24.26–28 [Axs. 3 Graham]).[3] Anaximenean ἀήρ, said as ἄπειρον, does not begin, for that would determine its span. Anaximenean ἀήρ, as Sallis has written, names "a beginning that has no beginning, a beginning before beginning."[4] Nor does it *not* begin, for *beginning* is its character (ἀρχή, Arist. *Metaph.* A.984a.5–7); as the Xenophanean saying brings to speech, ἀήρ marks the beginning of a delimitation (πεῖρας) that lets the opacity and open expanse (ἄπειρον) of γῆ come into view.

ἀήρ, in Anaximenean thinking, hovers. Hovering between emergence and birth, between limit and open expanse, beginnings and withdrawals, ἀήρ resonates within earlier and other thinkings. Hovering as if echoing the sayings of fellow thinkers, Anaximenean thinking centers ἀήρ in its turnings on the circle of beginnings that is Milesian thinking. In Anaximenean considerations another beginning into the circle of beginnings opens as ἀήρ. Already in Thalean and Anaximandrean thinking ἀήρ has resounded as providing another way toward ὕδωρ and ἄπειρον and their opacities. Even as turning to ἀήρ within the inquiries into ὕδωρ and

---

is bracketed by the fuller, complete expression Τάρταρον ἠερόεντα and with a vivid phrase punctuating the place and its character: ἔνθα θεοὶ Τιτῆνες ὑπὸ ζόφῳ ἠερόεντι / κεκρύφαται βουλῇσι Διὸς νεφεληγερέταο (729–30).

3. Translation by Graham, *Texts of Early Greek Philosophy*, 1:75, my interpolations.

4. Sallis, *Figure of Nature*, 22.

ἄπειρον has already enabled a disclosure of more of what those other terms have to say, the turning itself also works as disclosive of the inseparability, the intricate belonging together of the Milesians and the radiant terms of their sayings. As a *circle of beginnings* constituted, at least in part, by the fellowship of thinking, in the very constellation of thinkers formed in the notion of *Milesians*, Milesian thinking performs the relation—and the opacities charging relation, activating and giving them vital energies—that the figures and images of the sayings address: a *circle* in the sense of a group, a community of thinkers joined in thinking and the togetherness of inquiry, setting out along the polycentric circle of *beginnings* that ever-joins and returns thinking to the "wild link with the world" and the foundational, radically open and bodied perceptivity, the open expanse named in ἄπειρον, the circle that teems with possibilities and meanings as the very structure of its circling.[5]

Thematically, this study of Anaximenean thinking traces the circle in its varied senses as a turning along a circumference shared among the Milesian thinkers, as a continual return to beginning, as a founding togetherness (as if on the same arc) already active in the tasks of thinking. Initially, this chapter turns to the ways ἀήρ circles and spirals into and with ὕδωρ and ἄπειρον within and beyond the Milesian circle. The hovering of ἀήρ also takes place as a *shadowing*. Appearing as accompaniment and as belonging together and alongside, shadowing also manifests an action of ἀήρ as concealing or enclosing, but also as *un-enclosing*, a setting adrift of each living being into its span. Finally, in one dimension of its expansive turnings, ἀήρ addresses itself to the circling itself, the circle of thinkers in the movements of shared inquiry, as the breath and breathing (ἀήρ as πνεῦμα) according to which thought shapes itself in speech as well as the abundance spilling over the edges of speech.

Shadowing

Shadowing of ἀήρ, its primary way of moving, resounds in early Greek thinking as opacity.[6] Where Aphrodite, for instance, sweeps Paris from the

---

5. Anne Freire Ashbaugh, "The Philosophy of Flesh and the Flesh of Philosophy," *Research in Phenomenology* 8 (1978): 223, JSTOR.

6. On ἀήρ as "haze" and dense obscuring mist, see West, *Early Greek Philosophy and the Orient*, 99; Kahn, *Anaximander and the Origins of Greek Cosmology*, 143–45.

jaws of death as they open around him during the duel with Menelaos, the *Iliad* summons the image of the divinity concealing (ἐκάλυψε) the hero in ἠέρι πολλῇ, an abundance of opacity (Hom. *Il.* 3.380–81). This mode of shadowing serves as a beginning, a source and starting point for sounding the varied depths of ἀήρ and its meanings.

The shadowing of ἀήρ sets Anaximenean thinking in motion, propels it toward imaging totality's span and compass: shadowing also calls forth an accompanying. Arising in the word ἀήρ registers similarity, joining. The ancient phrase ἠεροειδὴς Πόντος lets this come to speech: the look of Pontos is ἠέρος—*of* ἀήρ. All the opacity of great Pontos, the vast sea in its sweeping heaves and recedings, its spanning expanse, belongs to ἀήρ with respect to its look. In this valence, ἀήρ holds primacy, its look comes forward in the ὕδωρ of Pontos. Through the reflectivity of ὕδωρ the expansive density of ἀήρ comes into view, in the sense that the great sea collects in its surface the depths of the lower sky, mirroring ἀήρ: the recesses of Pontos mirror the recesses of ἀήρ; both recede into density, opacity. While the collecting and gathering seem to belong most properly to the ὕδωρ of Pontos in the radiant saying ἠεροειδὴς Πόντος, the density and opacity are collected and gathered in Pontos out of their belonging to and in ἀήρ.

Hesiod's *Theogony* accounts Pontos a very ancient being, progeny of Gaia from her own generativity (Hes. *Theog.* 131–32), yet the way of being spoken in ἠερόεντα emerges along with Tartaros (119), one of the primary fourfold of beings, though not a generative being. Its register of ἠερόεντα tells of a fullness, an abundance of ἀήρ that seemingly, in *Theogony*, inhibits generativity.[7] Following this association leads to an edge in the Hesiodic cosmography where a multiplicity of ὕδωρ-related sources (πηγαί) and shimmerings (πείρατ᾽) exist along, or upon, or beside, or even *as* a vast opening (χάσμα μέγ᾽, 740), a reverberation of the originary τὸ Χάος that terrifies the divinities (739) in its constitutive opening-closing action and its bond through that action with ὕδωρ. The shimmerings found at this edge take place as shimmerings on account of the disruption they cause among the divinities, whose own self-forgetting of their span and while this vast opening-closing, in its ownmost motion of opening *and* closing, would be unclosed out of forgetfulness should they ever encounter it. In this sense the shimmering of these limits

---

7. Tartaros gives rise to no other beings in Hesiod's *Theogony* except when Tartaros is spoken *without* ἠερόεντα See above, note 2.

(πείρατ') dissolves the metaphysics of identity enmeshed in the construction of divinity under the reign of Zeus, pulsing instead with the wavering and changeability of unfixed, *not*-immortal, fluid movement that opens and closes. τὸ Χάος resounds as another name for ἀλήθεια and its disclosing movements, an event of opening that occurs at once as a closing, an emergence and a withdrawal; the disclosure of opening *and* closing terrifies divinities insofar as it shows immortals the closing they cannot escape, the limits of their own span concealed by the assertion of their identities as undying (ἀθανάτων, e.g., 21).

Yet, registering the other side of the double genitive, the look of Pontos is also objective, full *of* ἀήρ, full of whatever is spoken in ἀήρ. Returning to the Hesiodic bond with Tartaros, the look of ἀήρ has another dimension, a lower zone—precisely what appears in the reflectivity of Pontos, in which the surface and its depth, reflecting ἀήρ, manifests ἀήρ as the receding depths. The appearing does not deceive, but forecasts, manifests, announces a way of being, the ownmost look of ἀήρ as depth and the lowerness addressed in the imaging of Tartaros. In such a lower zone stir the ὕδωρ-related sources (πηγαί) and the shimmerings, limits that are beginnings and wavering sites that disrupt a metaphysics of stable, perduring, substance-grounded identities. Also in this zone occur the figures connected to Zeus and his suppression or hiding away of opposition, Titans (Those Who Strain in Opposition).

In this lower zone stands a dwelling, itself concealed in deep-blue cloud (νεφέλης κεκαλυμμένα κυανέῃσιν), the dwelling of dark Νύξ, Nyx (Night [Hes. *Theog.* 744–45]). This dwelling is a site of crossings, where in turns the light of Ἡμέρη (*Hemere*, Day), Hemere, and the dark of Nyx turn past one another, crossing the threshold alternately but never sharing the dwelling in common (748–57).[8] This is to say, the zone characterized as an abundance of ἀήρ (ἠερόεντα) contains a site of crossings and uncrossings resonant of Anaximandrean ἄπειρον: the light of Hemere and the darkness of Nyx never cross and dwell together, they never associate and mingle. Rather, the two maintain a separation. Only the threshold signifies a moment of crossing, overlap, temporary convergence when the radical darkness of Nyx enters into the presence of the radical brightness of Hemere, but also when Hemere opens itself to the darkness

---

8. To suspend an overly familiar identification of Νύξ and Ἡμέρη with *Night* and *Day* (understood as calculable spans within the clock-time of earth's rotation), the Greek names are maintained throughout this discussion.

of radically dark Nyx. This crossing marks a site of shimmerings, where the light dims in Nyx's presence and Nyx's darkness gleams in Hemere's presence in such a way that their own (presumed) limits show forth as open, overlapping, converging and transforming in the crossings. This dwelling, site of crossings and shimmerings, belongs to Nyx, who arises from the self-generative power of τὸ Χάος, and who herself, through procreation with Erebos (another creature of τὸ Χάος), gives rise to two luminous beings: Αἰθήρ (Aither), the brightness of sky, and Ἡμέρη, the Shine of Day (123–25), who delivers to earth-dwellers (ἐπιχθονίοισι) the radiance (φάος) and richness of vision (πολυδερκές) of the shining day (755). All these rise from the dwelling of Nyx and her radical darkness in the zone of ἀήρ and its abundance (ἠερόεντα).

In the scene of crossing, Nyx is said to veil herself (κεκαλυμμένη) in a cloud rich in opacity with the look of ἀήρ (νεφέλη . . . ἠεροειδεῖ, 757). Such is the zone of Τάρταρον ἠερόεντα, the Lower-dim full of ἀήρ: a layered depth that shelters in rich darkness a dwelling where crossings unfold, a dwelling and a site of crossing belonging to darkness, to a primary name of opacity: *Nyx*. This is a female-feminine zone, a zone of crossings, shimmerings, and dwelling, in a way beyond or just past the reach of the male-masculine grip of Zeus and his regime of stabilized entities, of metaphysics: Zeus only communicates by way of a female-feminine divinity, Iris (780–86); the whole region, as the Mousai narrate through Hesiod, is hateful (στυγέουσι) to the divinities (810), hateful in part because in that region awaits the disclosure of ἀλήθεια that threatens the stability of Zeus's regime: the limited span of divinities themselves, prefigured in the opening-closing at the site of roots and springs (χάσμα μέγ᾽, 740) and simulated, for those who violate oaths, in a Sleep like death (793–804).[9]

Such, too, is the excess bestowed in the reflectivity of the ὕδωρ of Pontos. While the reflections upon and within this ὕδωρ flow and shift with the daylight's movements and the coming of Dawn and Hemere, Twilight and Nyx, all gathered and shown forth in the showing-forth of ὕδωρ, all these movements turn out from the dwelling that belongs to Nyx and the site of opacities whose opacity comes forward as abundance and fullness of ἀήρ. The look of ἀήρ and its radiant depths and opacities take place as the bestowal of Nyx and, more fundamentally, of the region out of which

---

9. Like death in that the divinities are subject to be concealed by a terrible coma (κακὸν δ᾽ἐπὶ κῶμα καλύπτει, Hes. *Theog.* 798) that is both without breath (ἀνάπνευστος) and without speech (ἄναυδος, 797).

Nyx rises and to which she returns, whose primordial name is ἠερόεντα, full of ἀήρ. This names a source from which the lustrous givings of Nyx pour, in its incipient voicing spoken as a multiplicitous source that delivers or generates otherwise than (re-)productively: Τάρταρα ἠερόεντα, Tartara full of ἀήρ (Hes. *Theog.* 119). The energies of Τάρταρα ἠερόεντα, this site of multiplicity[10] understood as "a bustling city,"[11] open and preserve the zone in and from which arise all the bestowals of Nyx—the light, the darknesses, all in their seasons—without specifically generating anything.

Such sheltering and preserving in darkness that does not generate might be termed a *shadowing* resonant in ἀήρ, a reverberant shadowing in Anaximenean ἀήρ. The opacity of ἀήρ is its primary register already in Anaximenean thinking. Accordingly, the reverberant shadowing of Anaximenean ἀήρ brings forward opacity each time it manifests. The sheltering character of the shadowing of ἀήρ also contours another fold of the radiant term in Anaximenean thinking. For in its compass of totality (ὅλον τὸν κόσμον πνεῦμα καὶ ἀὴρ περιέχει, Stob. *Ecl.* 1.11.12 [Axs. 8 Graham]) and as a beginning-unbegun (ἀρχήν) in open expanse (ἄπειρον, Diog. Laert 2.2.3 [Axs. 1 Graham]) that, *as* ἄπειρον, drifts ceaselessly from whatever limits emerge in the span of generated manifestations from ἀήρ, Anaximenean ἀήρ permeates and extends through and beyond each manifestation, an atmospherically extended dynamics of pressing (πυκνούμενον) and pulling (ἀραιούμενον) in a continual motion (Simpl. *in Phys.* 1.2.24.29–30 [Axs. 3 Graham]), a *tourbillon* (δίνην, Axs. 20 Graham).

By way of such dynamics the Anaximenean totality opens as a radically poetic event, at home and at work in imaginaries and continually generating "unpredictable *tourbillons*"—this is where Glissant locates the "presocratics." As Anaximenean ἀήρ shelters the diversity of totality, it belongs to what Glissant describes as an opacity working against the force of a "reductive transparency" in order to shelter and preserve "the threatened and delicious things joining one another (without conjoining, that is, without merging [*se fondre*]) in the expanse of relation (*l'étendue de la Relation*)."[12] Not only an opacity as sheltering density unavailable to the grasp of a mode of knowing that merges in its grasp (*comprendre*),

---

10. For a reading of Tartaros as such multiplicity, the folded multiple narratives as layers of the region, see David M. Johnson, "Hesiod's Descriptions of Tartarus ('Theogony' 721–819)," *Phoenix* 53, no. 1/2 (1999): 8–28, JSTOR.

11. Lombardo, *Hesiod*, 100nn754–55.

12. *PR*, 62; *PdR*, 74–75.

ἀήρ also emerges as the movement of relation, continually drawing out lines of relay and connection from and into the opacities at each moment of totality's differentiation. Totality does not yield entirely to the grasp of comprehension, and it is the unyielding and diverse opacities that constitute "the threatened beauty of the world" and that motivate a poetics of relation: not driven on a quest for roots or possession, but moving in a movement of "errantry" (*l'errance*) through which takes place a poetic striving "to know [*connaître*] the totality of the world" joined with the knowledge that this cannot be accomplished.[13]

Another aspect of the shadowing of ἀήρ speaks a togetherness, a joining, an accompanying and being-alongside dimension that has already come forward in the joining and accompanying of the phrase ἠεροειδὴς Πόντος:

> Eurustratos's son Anaximenes of Miletos, colleague of Anaximandros, just like Anaximandros calls the underlying force of upsurge-and-downgoing (τὴν ὑποκειμένην φύσιν) ἄπειρον, but not unbounded (ἀόριστον) like Anaximandros. Rather, Anaximenes says it opens as *horizoning* (ὡρισμένην), naming it ἀέρα. And by spreading out (μανότητι) and pressing together (πυκνότητι) according to its abundances (κατὰ τὰς οὐσίας), it differs. So, pulled (ἀραιούμενον) it manifests as fire, when pressed (πυκνούμενον), wind, then cloud, then still more, water, and further, earth, then stones, and the other things from these. (Simpl. *in Phys.* 1.2, 24.26–31 [Axs. 3 Graham])

Such shadowing both joins, in articulating a belonging together and accompanying of ἀήρ and the multiplicities of totality, *and* differentiates, in announcing the way in which each manifestation comes forward as a multiplicity, a *more than itself* that is at once *as itself*. Sallis hears this directly in the Anaximenean sayings, or their echoes: "Wherever anything *is*—be it fire, earth, or stone—there will be not just one, but *two*."[14] More than doubled, multiplied: just as Anaximandrean ἄπειρον refused the one-many paradigm, so the ἄπειρον ἀέρα of Anaximenean thinking surges as

---

13. *PR*, 20; *PdR*, 33. The poetic striving is based on Glissant's statement that "la pensée de l'errance est une poétique" (*PdR*, 31).

14. Sallis, *Figure of Nature*, 22.

multiplicity(-ies), spreading each *this* into an array that is not reducible to one, or a series of ones (many).

This shadowing, indeed, might be meaningfully said of Thalean ὕδωρ and Anaximandrean ἄπειρον, insofar as both have the character of going-alongside and enacting the multiplicity of each manifestation: what Aristotle says of Anaximenean ἀήρ is also said at least of Thalean ὕδωρ, namely, that it bears some resemblance to, or enacts something that Aristotle thinks in the term ὑποκείμενον, an underlying thing (Arist. *Metaph.* A.983b.6–984a.5). Anaximenean ἀήρ, however, manifestly and originarily—that is, in accordance with pre-reflective experience—forms not only this other alongside and spreading-as-multiplicity, but also the atmospheric open expanse (also an opacity in a certain way) that radically joins all in this very opacity: the atmospheric never manifests in a fully present and transparent manner, but always in such a way that its very surrounding character continually, constitutively withdraws, recedes, turns from open awareness as the *behind* and *out of view* of both manifestations in their appearing and the open that opens a region for coming-to-light. In ἀήρ as a surrounding atmospheric open expanse emerges the phenomenon of shadowing, an "obscuring that doubles all manifestation, that shadows it."[15] What shadows and doubles every being in totality registers as *invisible* in the sense of opacity—not as an inaccessible yet stable and definitive core, an essence, but as that which enables relations in its outspanning and withdrawnness, its disclosing-undisclosedness, its moment of ἀλήθεια. ἀήρ is the Anaximenean name for this opacity as an ever-moving and shadowing site of and for relation.

The poetic voicing of similes draws heightened attention to the action of shadowing, where each manifestation spills over itself in relation with others and within itself. Images of manufacture and production, and so too of commerce and trade, bind cosmic-scaled images to the cultural-scale, the level of quotidian human life, and highlight the always-already involvement of humans-in-the-world. The earth is in the shape of a table (τραπεζοειδῆ, Ps.-Plut. 3.10.3 [Axs. 14 Graham]) and takes its flat shape through a process like felting (πιλουμένου, Euseb. *Praep. evang.* 1.8.3 [Axs. 11 Graham]), just as clouds form by felting (κατὰ τὴν πίλησιν, Hippol. *Haer.* 1.7 [Axs. 12 Graham]). Astronomical movements take place as turnings around a flat, circular earth like a felted hat (τὸ πιλίον) turns

---

15. Sallis, "Doubles of Anaximenes," 151.

around the wearer's head (Hippol. *Haer.* 1.7 [Axs. 12 Graham]). Here West has observed a geography drawn from Persian and Mesopotamian sources, in which a central cosmic mountain forms the high point and axis for the revolving heavens:[16] through the many openings of Mount Hara the sun passed, bringing light to one side of the kosmos and night to the other.[17] According to Herodotos, Persian ritual sacrifice involved wrapping a *tiara* with garland prior to the sacrifice and then hearing a theogony performed by a *magos* (Hdt. 1.132). Anaximenean simile, that is, observes and activates both the indissoluble involvement of human-being and a sense of the foreign already active in the familiar.

Similaic relation comes to pass in the Anaximenean vision of the heavens: not only does the opacity of stars come into view, so too does this opacity join at once with images of living beings: "the stars are joined together and secured (καταπεπηγέναι) in an ice-like surface (κρυσταλλοει-δεῖ) just like drawings of living things" (Ps. Plut. 2.14 [Axs. 17 Graham]). Voiced as ice-like (κρυσταλλοειδεῖ), the frozen ἀήρ names the opacity shadowing the stars. The simile embeds likeness in likeness, enacting the torque and multiple possibilities of relations: the frozen condition (κρύος, icy) alters (-αλλο-) by manifesting similarity, likeness (-ειδεῖ). To this whole imaginal cluster the saying joins and steadies or freezes in a momentary, provisional way—the way ice eventually will transform—the stars. This provisional, momentary joining in turn the saying likens to *drawings* of animals, human involvement by way of images that draw on the living motions of animals and steady that movement in a momentary arrangement whose own movement radiates in multiple directions. Human-being as involvement, animal life, the world on a cosmic scale—the saying enmeshes the whole cluster in a dense image of opacity-as-relation.

The momentary, ice-like figuration of stars voices an opacity of thinking's poetic gesture, drawing into view the multiplicity of possibil-ities generated in the meaning-saturated thickness of relations. In the simile linking the opacity of stars to drawn figures of living beings the Anaximenean image announces an extension of opacity in relation and as multiplicity: the stars as drawings of living beings. The way images such as these—the constellations of stars and the drawings of living beings—turn and expand from the profiling or lineality of composition

---

16. West, *Early Greek Philosophy and the Orient*, 106–7.

17. Boyce, *Textual Sources*, 16, and see the useful illustration on 17.

toward an ever-absent-present whole discloses their work of what Sallis termed *imaging* and *profiling,* a through-shimmering of wholeness by what is not whole, also not seen as itself, but as the other (present-absent) whole its imaging images. Profiling, "a specific form of imaging," takes place as unfurling lines and contours "never really discrete" that "shade into one another" in such a way that they remain unfixed, dynamic, unlimited:[18] ἄπειρον. Not even this shading of *one* into another *one;* rather, this form of imaging occurs as neither one nor many ones that might be totted up into the sum of profiles (re-)constituting the ever-absent-present whole, but ἄπειρον and ever in motion, shadowing multiplicities, dynamic as ἀήρ. The constellation, as an enclosing figural composition, that is, has a more primary action of *un-enclosing,* of *disclosing* and *releasing* the images into the rich and mobile network of relations, meanings, tensions—un-enclosing the abundance of world, of beings and things, whose overflow of any one profile shows the way back to a sense of the dynamic mesh of perceptual involvement and the teeming, expansive *beyond* and *other* of the world.[19] In this release Anaximenean thinking becomes a work of art as Glissant has envisioned it, as an encounter and engagement with differents and the offering of differences into the play of relation.[20] Such *un-enclosing* forms in Anaximenean thinking a crucial, central work of ἀήρ and its imaging. As such, Anaximenean thinking summons a primary experience of visual, drawn images as alive and full, as richly dimensional and taking place not as deception or unreality to be measured against the putative reality of their linearity and flatness, but as moments of ἀλήθεια in the ways images are primordially experienced through their ways of opening: expansive in their depths, showing *and* withdrawing, vivid in their relations and in their opening of and into world(s).

Shadowing of ἀήρ: not only darkening, obscuring, veiling, but also *following along and beside, accompanying, doubling-as-enacting-multiplicity.* ἀήρ enacts an enclosing motion that, in its surrounding and sheltering, also *un-encloses,* opens the diverse manifestations of totality.

18. Sallis, "Image and Phenomenon," *Research in Phenomenology* 5 (1975): 73–74, JSTOR.

19. Drawing here on Sallis's encounters with Merleau-Ponty's work toward beginnings of philosophy in *Phenomenology and the Return to Beginnings* (Duquesne University Press, 1973), 39–40.

20. Glissant, "In Praise of the Different and of Difference," 858.

(Un-)Enclosing

As one of its basic actions, Anaximenean ἀήρ encloses totality. Stobaios presents the saying as a direct quotation within his thematic assemblage of philosophic and literary excerpts: " 'Just like soul,' he [sc. Anaximenes] says, 'being our own ἀήρ, governs us, so breath (πνεῦμα) and ἀήρ enclose (περιέχει) the whole kosmos'" (Stob. *Ecl.* 1.11.12 [Axs. 8 Graham]). The simile discloses a resemblance between the way soul-ἀήρ, the breath as ἀήρ, governs every being and the way ἀήρ in its more expansive sense encompasses totality. In such a relation, inner and outer blur, perhaps dissolve: where soul-ἀήρ governs from within an ensouled being, ἀήρ encloses the whole—an image from an outerness, surrounding totality. The simile opens up the relationship it creates, jarring sense and calling poetically for further attention. Since the one is an innerness and the other an outerness, since the one is contained bodily and the other contains and surrounds all bodies, the saying asks: in what ways does soul, as the ἀήρ that governs ensouled beings, resemble the enclosing outerness of ἀήρ? How does being-contained, being-surrounded, being-enclosed resemble containing, surrounding, enclosing? The saying itself both encloses, or joins, the activity of soul and that of ἀήρ, while also un-enclosing the terms of the relation, fraying the limits of inner and outer, pointing to a way of being proper to ἀήρ as unclosing—opening, disclosing, un-enclosing—apparent boundaries or divisions such as inner and outer.

Within and from another motion associated with a boundless determinate or limited thing, ἀέρα ἄπειρον, other simple bodies take shape:[21] through thinning (ἀραιούμενον) fire arises, whereas thickening (πυκνούμενον) molds ἀήρ into wind, cloud, water, earth, and stones. Finally, "the other things arise from these" (Simpl. *in Phys.* 1.2, 24.28–31 [Axs. 3 Graham]). The vocabulary is Homeric and the image of ἀήρ resembles "such mythological principles as Chaos, Tartaros, Nyx or Homichle."[22] In summoning divinities, as it now sounds as *enclosing* the image of the

---

21. This follows Sallis's reading of Aristotle's remark: Ἀναξιμένης δὲ ἀέρα καὶ Διογένης πρότερον ὕδατος καὶ μάλιστ᾽ ἀρχὴν τιθέασι τῶν ἁπλῶν σωμάτων (Arist. *Metaph.* 984a.5–7 [Axs. 2 Graham]); Sallis translates: "Anaximenes posited ἀήρ as the ἀρχή of the other simple bodies." "Doubles of Anaximenes," 148.

22. C. Joachim Classen, "Anaximander and Anaximenes: The Earliest Greek Theories of Change?" *Phronesis* 22 (1977): 100, JSTOR. Classen, however, regards Anaximenean ἀήρ as an "improvement" on the figures from myth he names here.

sevenfold intimates a protective, sheltering aspect. From the elemental sevenfold of Anaximenean thinking, a Zarathustran reverberation sounds, echoed, altered, transformed, translated. In the *Greater Bundahishn*, a collection of Zarathustran thinking gathered from oral traditions of various periods, a divine Heptad composed of Ahura Mazda and "six lesser divinities . . . the great Amesha Spentas, 'Holy Immortals'" together unfold and protect the kosmos: Ahura Mazda, Vohu Manah, Asha, Khshathra take under their protection human beings, animals, fire, and sky (and/or metal), respectively, while the female-feminine beings of the Heptad Armaiti, Haurvatat, Ameretat shelter earth, water, and plants (*GrBdn* 3.11–19).[23] The six Holy Immortals "enter as guardians into their own separate creations," maintaining order throughout their cosmic regions (*GrBdn* 2.3.3.10–19). The resonances change in their vibrations through cultural imaginaries, through thoughtful comportment, through translation; the purpose here is not to suggest correspondence or dependence, borrowing or appropriation, but to give voice to a broader pulsation of a sevenfold in the cultural estuary of archaic Miletos and its community of thinkers, their poetics of *mixis* and the possibilities in its churn. The diverse resonances of divinities in Anaximenean ἀήρ in its sheltering, enclosing aspect suggest both the otherness teeming in the familiar (as in the Thalean saying that all is full of divine-others) and a sense of protective enclosure and care, as when in ἠέρι πολλῇ, an abundance of opacity, Aphrodite and Apollo enfold and protect mortals who are dear to them (Hom. *Il.* 3.380–81 [Paris by Aphrodite]; 20.443–44 [Hektor by Apollo]).[24]

Additionally, the movements of ἀήρ in their associations with τὸ Χάος summon attention. Not only does ἀήρ *enclose*, encircling totality in opacity and shadowing each manifestation with opacities, ἀήρ also opens and closes. Where Anaximenean thinking speaks of ἀραιούμενον and πυκνούμενον it describes the motions of opening and closing, respectively:

---

23. Boyce, *Textual Sources*, 13–14. For a discussion of this Zarathustran image of totality, see Spitzer, "Archaic Images of Totality," 44. *GrBdn* abbreviates *Greater Bundahishn* in the following discussion.

24. In an article that came to my attention years after this project was submitted for review, Folit-Weinberg has articulated this as the "soterial function" of ἀήρ. Benjamin Folit-Weinberg, "Disappearing into Thick Aēr: The Function of Aēr in Homer and Anaximenes," *American Journal of Philology* 144, no. 2 (2023): 191, Project Muse. More generally, Folit-Weinberg's interest in exploring the action of ἀήρ rather than its meaning(s) overlaps with the present discussion, though without Folit-Weinberg's distinction between these two regions.

ἀραιούμενον as opening, insofar as the strain and pull that loosens occurs by way of a pulling, an opening of the span between what pulls; conversely, the density of πυκνούμενον occurs as a result of pressing, of closing the span between what presses. The opening and closing movement of ἀήρ comes forward in its valence as an in-between zone:

> Sleep halted before Zeus could see him,
> Perching in the highest fir tree on Ida
> That rose through mist (δι᾽ ἠέρος) to pure bright air. (αἰθέρ᾽,
>   Hom. *Il.* 14.286–88)[25]

ἀήρ hovers as an in-between region spanning and joining earth and an upper zone, named αἰθέρ᾽, αἰθήρ. As a region, ἀήρ names the span from surface to the upper heights. The passage not only presents ἀήρ as an opening-closing of opacity—as Lombardo's translation "mist" illustrates—but also as in-between, a zone for movement and passage.

The wider scene in which these lines are spoken lets resound the theme of concealment, which saturates the whole passage, and especially the relation of concealment—as a mode of closing—to a way of opening; otherwise said, the passage voices an image of ἀλήθεια in its opening-closing, showing-withdrawing motions, resonant with Anaximenean ἀήρ by way of significant shared vocabulary. For the present inquiry, the scene and its relevant theme may be said to begin with Poseidon appearing among the Greeks disguised as an elder (Hom. *Il.* 14.136). After a brief speech to Agamemnon, Poseidon issues a superhuman battle cry to rally the Greek warriors, which opens possibilities that had momentarily closed in Agamemnon's bleak view of the Greek prospects. In order to open more widely the possibilities for the Greeks, Hera develops a plan to distract Zeus using a combination of the implements of sex borrowed from Aphrodite and the force of Hypnos, "ruler of all divinities and of all humans" (14.233). To prepare herself for the visits, first to Aphrodite and Hypnos, and then especially to Zeus, the narrative shows Hera bathing and anointing herself in her room with a concealed latch (κληῖδι κρυπτῇ, 14.168) before concealing herself with a veil (καλύψατο . . . / καλῷ νηγατέῳ, 14.184–85). Hera's plan involves the concealment from Aphrodite of her plans in order to procure the sex (φιλότητα) and desire (ἵμερον, 14.198), which Aphrodite loans from a pouch that also contains deceptive

---

25. Translation from Lombardo, *Homer: Iliad*, 273.

speech that is said to conceal or occlude (ἔκλεψε) even the dense awareness (νόον πύκα) of those who are especially aware (προνεόντων, 14.217).[26]

The interaction between Hypnos and Hera repeatedly invokes Νύξ, Nyx, "powerful female ruler (δμήτειρα) of divinities and humans" whom Zeus is loath to offend (Hom. *Il.* 14.259–62). Once Hera satisfies Hypnos's request that she swear an oath to Styx, the two depart for Mount Ida, covering and concealing themselves with ἀήρ (ἠέρα ἑσσαμένω, 14.282). Just before the tall fir tree scene, Hypnos has positioned himself in that tall tree in order to escape Zeus's notice. In that place of concealment and shelter, Hypnos is said to compress or make himself compact (πεπυκασμένος, 14.289)—enacting one of the motions through which Anaximenean ἀήρ folds and unfolds manifold differentiation. Indeed, the scene of Hypnos's concealment by self-compression in the tree concludes with a simile joining the divinity to an owl, as if marking the scene with the theme of transformation. When Zeus, given his epithet cloud-gatherer (νεφεληγερέτα) throughout the entire scene in a way that enhances the theme of concealment (14.293, 312, 341), becomes aware of Hera he is totally concealed by lust, "enveloped" in Lombardo's translation:[27] *eros* concealed entirely (ἀμφεκάλυψεν) his compressed awareness (πυκινὰς φρένας, 14.294).[28] Finally for this discussion, Zeus produces a golden cloud that conceals (ἔσσαντο) Hera and himself (14.350).

All told, the concealments narrated in the passage open a zone or region for the divine interventions to be unfolded in favor of the Greeks, but also open a way for Hypnos, owl-like, to become aware, even through the double veil of the enclosing ἀήρ and the cloud Zeus has made, of the proper time for overpowering Zeus (putting him to sleep) and for delivering a message to Poseidon that the way is open for the sea-god to aid the Greeks. Embedded in the scene of concealment, of closing and

---

26. Interestingly, it is at this moment the oft-cited passage in Homer occurs, seeming to voice a cosmological and theogonic vision that involves both an image of the limits of the world (πείρατα γαίης) and a beginning of divinities in a body of ὕδωρ, Ὠκεανός θεῶν γένεσιν (Hom. *Il.* 14.200–01). The theme of deception and concealment so permeates the scene it calls for a reticent reception of this statement, as well as the similar statement—made by Hypnos to Hera in her drive toward concealments—of Okeanos as beginning and source (γένεσις) of all (14.246).

27. Lombardo, *Homer: Iliad*, 274.

28. Terms based on πυκνός also come forward as a theme in the scene, though an exploration of the ways they enhance understanding of the Anaximenean term πυκνούμενον is beyond the present scope.

opening, the narrative deepens the connections joining ἀήρ to the double movement of closing and opening, enclosing and un-enclosing—a way in which the enclosing, concealing force of ἀήρ at once also *opens* along the lines of ἀλήθεια and its continual motions of dis- and en-closure in folded and overlapping ways. In the Homeric scene, that is, the resonant opacities of ἀήρ deepen the linkage of ἀλήθεια and concealment that also-at-once reveals and enables or motivates revelation, while the theme of this interplay of double movement gathered in the term ἀλήθεια enhances the connection of ἀήρ to the opening-closing and its (un-)enclosing.

Additionally, the phrase δι' ἠέρος (through ἀήρ) advances the in-between aspect of ἀήρ: the fir tree rises through ἀήρ. This sense echoes also in the way ἀήρ, through its concealing power, lets Hera and Hypnos pass unobserved in the scene of Zeus's deception, enabling a transition—their passage, their transit—as well as a transformation for such passage to unfold. Taken together with its enclosing—un-enclosing dimension, in bringing out its valence of an in-between the Homeric passage voices ἀήρ as a site of transition and transformation, of passage, as a medium of growth and rising into light. This might be termed a translative dimension of ἀήρ.[29] Enacting this translative dimension, Anaximenean ἀήρ both opens for transit in the image of earth being carried (ὀχουμένην) on ἀήρ (Hippol. *Haer.* 1.7 [Axs. 12 Graham]) and quickens its own transformations through its opening-closing action, spoken as thickening and thinning (Simpl. *in Phys.* 1.2, 24.26–31 [Axs. 3 Graham]). The Homeric scene in this sense recommends Sallis's interpretation that the power of Anaximenean ἀήρ enables the self-showing of things.[30] Importantly, however, the power of ἀήρ in bringing to light does not have the character of transparency into which rising and self-showing unfurl. Rather, the open spoken in the Homeric scene as the region of brightness and light, illumination (αἰθέρ'), when thought in its connection with Anaximenean ἀήρ and its shadowing and doubling-enacting-multiplicity, will not be as purely and homogeneously transparent, but rather as encompassed by and unclosed within the opacity of ἀήρ—a mixing of through-shining transparency and rich opacity. Such mixture, even insofar as whatever appears clear has its clarity, forms the from-, in-, and as-which self-showing occurs. Further, ἀήρ in its unmixed condition does not have the character of transparency

---

29. For more on translative aspects of Milesian thinking, see Spitzer, *Parmenides and Translation*, 9–10 and 17–23.

30. Sallis, *The Figure of Nature*, 24–25.

alone, but also of an opacity closely associated with concealing, even as that concealment and enclosing work also to open, to manifest *as* the multiplicity of opacities.

In, through, and as ἀήρ diverse manifestations in totality come to light as opacities in transit, in passage, in between. Ancient Egyptian thinking imaged two beings whose separation generated, or opened, the regions within which further beings could be differentiated. In the *Leiden Hymns* the pair emerges together in an enactment of the inceptive differentiation quickened by the unnamed, hidden divinity who "sowed the seed of the cosmos as Atum, the Old One, / from whose godhead were moisture and air, / Shu and Tefnut, the primordial couple" (*LH.XC*, 160). Shu and Tefnut are seemingly masculine and feminine powers of emptiness and separation, what Allen calls "void," that also embody two conditions of air (Shu: dry air; Tefnut: moist air).[31] Similar valences may resonate in Anaximenean ἀήρ: both ἀήρ as transparency and as opacity can be heard in Anaximenean thinking. Pavel Hobza locates the different valences in two aspects of Anaximanean thinking, where cosmogony and its stress on *generativity* activates ἀήρ as opacity (he translates "opaque damp mist"), cosmology and the bearing or "*carrying* stuff on which the heavenly bodies float" brings forward the aspect of ἀήρ as transparency—as "transparent atmospheric air," since otherwise the bodies in the sky would not be visible.[32] While these aspects of air are differentiated in the Shu-Tefnut pair, in Anaximenean ἀήρ they are spoken together, letting the term itself undergo transformations within the contexts of its appearance and to remain vivid in its multiplicity. In this way Anaximenean ἀήρ assumes a performative dimension, pressed (πυκνούμενον) into opacity at times, at other times stretched (ἀραιούμενον) into transparency.

Where does the difference arise between *transparency* and *opacity*? Anaximenean thinking may voice both—and more—in its figure of ἀήρ,

---

31. Allen, "Celestial Realm," 122–23; Werner Forman and Stephen Quirke, *Hieroglyphs and the Afterlife in Ancient Egypt* (University of Oklahoma Press, 1996), 8–9 (on the conditions of air); 9 (a tenth c. BCE illustration of Nut separated from an ithyphallic Geb). Hornung describes Shu as an "abstraction" from a term meaning "to be empty." *Conceptions of God in Ancient Egypt*, 77. See also Morenz's derivation of both divine names from verbs having to do with spitting. Siegfried Morenz, *Egyptian Religion*, trans. Ann E. Keep (Routledge, 2004), 163, and, for a discussion of two modes of creation by sexual and verbal means, 162–65, EBSCOhost.

32. Hobza, "Anaximenes' ἀήρ as Generating Mist and Generated Air," 108, 107, respectively.

and these seemingly opposite aspects of ἀήρ may say something more about such opposition and the underlying notion of fixity. Transparency allows light and vision to cross, to shine *through*, to permeate, a way of saying *un-en-closing*, while what is transparent remains unseen, the medium withdrawn, concealed, *enclosed* when considered in the movements of emergence, of manifestation. In this sense Sallis reads Anaximenean thinking as sounding the movement of coming to presence *and* withdrawing from presence, the alethetic double movement of revealing and concealing that Anaximenean ἀήρ enacts in its "very invisibility, its transparency, its never showing itself as itself," its power to open "the site where things can come forth and be manifest."[33] One might say that transparency shares a certain opacity of its own, insofar as its constitutive movement *withdraws* and also names a kind of abundance spilling beyond apparent boundaries and limits.

Furthermore, sense gathers the presence of transparency from its absence, from its non-showing. All these are also said of opacity. So, too, has the withdrawing that makes possible any presencing been said of opacity. No longer opposite to transparency, still opacity arises initially as opposite: where transparency allows crossing of vision and light, opacity obstructs such crossings and permeations. Yet, insofar as opacity arises *as* what does not yield to knowing and/or sight, it bears its own transparency—its very appearing *as* opacity. Glissant's mention of "the Pre-Socratics" brings out the entanglements of the two, or certain valences of the two in contrast to other valences that stress the same: in contrast to a "reductive transparency" that resolves into a single origin and fixed identity from which an assault on otherness can be mounted, once unfolded as an opacity that concealed "the sacred mystery of the root" and its establishment of a purified identity and sameness, another opacity emerges, one that protects and shelters diversity "in the expanse of Relation" and that nevertheless comes to pass as "Relation's imaginary," a form of transparency associated with early Greek thinking and others in which Relation, as the relay of opacity and diversity, guides thinking.[34]

A differentiation of opacity and transparency comes forward as direc-tional, a matter of vantage or approach in the experience of the motions they name: attuned to the sites of relation, emphasis falls on *opacity*; attuned rather to the relations of those sites (that they are related), the stress falls on *transparency*. While the non-filiational, non-root—which is to say, relational

---

33. Sallis, *The Figure of Nature*, 24.

34. *PR*, 61–62.

and archipelagic[35]—opacity preserves diversity by sustaining its otherness in the face of another's approach, gaze, thought, inquiry, knowing, this form of transparency lets appear *the span of relations*, totality's totalizing and its "gush forth in chaos,"[36] the spanning multiplicities and opacities in and as relation. The apparent opposition emerges now as an interplay of letting the abundant withdrawals show themselves in the transparency of their relations while preserving the differences enclosed in-as-by opacities: transparent-*opacity*, opaque-*transparency*, and the movements between them. This would bring into view a certain erosion of binarity in Anaximenean thinking, where apparent oppositionality teeming in the very name ἀήρ becomes reconfigured as moments of a dynamic, fluid, textured multiplicity of relations and possibilities.[37]

Along similar lines, Shu in particular arises as a differentiating power that, in its primordial opening and preservation of the span between earth and sky, opens the expanse in which any manifestation can come to light: from Shu and Tefnut are born Geb and Nut and, from these and their offspring, further generations of the remaining divinities of the Ennead.[38] In iconography, Shu appears—adorned with ankhs on every limb and so emphasizing the life-enabling power Shu enacts[39]—as the in-between deity actively supporting the separation of Geb and Nut, while the *Book of Going Forth by Day* refers to the opening made by Shu's separation of the two as "the holy gate."[40] The differentiation enacted by Shu lets emerge all further manifestations, opens the zone in which such differentiation can unfold—not as sky, an upper limit in the cosmology, but as the in-between, the expansive air.

---

35. Glissant brings together the "root" and the "continental" in contrast to the "relation" and "archipelagic" forms of identity. "The Poetics of the World"; see also *PR*, 143–44.

36. Glissant, "Measure, Immeasurability," 137, 139.

37. Decker, reading early Greek thinking and Homeric Hymns, has opened pathways for rethinking apparent oppositions in archaic Greek texts through "a reading sensitive to the liminality of borders and the permeability of apparent oppositions." "The Roots of Life and Death in the Homeric Hymns and Presocratic Philosophy," 90.

38. Hornung, *Conceptions of God in Ancient Egypt*, 146.

39. Hornung, *Conceptions of God in Ancient Egypt*, 68, fig. 4, and 269, n. 4 (Hornung's sources). See also the figure in Marinatos from the tenth c. BCE or so that may show the Shu-Tefnut pair as the in-between opening. "The Cosmic Journey of Odysseus," 385, fig. 3.

40. Translation from Raymond O. Faulkner et al., *The Egyptian Book of the Dead: the Book of Going Forth by Day* [. . .], 3rd rev. ed. (Chronicle Books, 2015), 17, pl. 8b.

In one way, Shu's own manifesting seems to coincide with the differing it opens, as in the emergence of Shu and Tefnut from Atum. In another way, the differentiation Shu embodies and inaugurates takes place prior to that very embodiment and enactment, as in the way Atum transforms itself to Re and differs from what it has made:

> I was Atum when I was alone in the Primordial Waters; I was Re
> in his glorious appearings when he began to rule what he
>   had made.
> *What does it mean?* It means Re when he began to rule
> what he had made, when he began to appear as king,
> before the Supports of Shu had come into being . . .[41]

Differing forms a primary facet of the unfolding of being in the Re-Atum-Shu constellation. Similarly, in the Memphite Theology of the Shabaka Stone, Ptah gives rise to Atum, from whom Shu and Tefnut emerge through a combination of sexually-generative power and speech.[42] Here, the differentiations that eventually Shu and Tefnut embody already activate diversification in and from Ptah and its self-differentiating manifestations. This is to say, differing precedes its own identification, its own identity.

Like Anaximenean ἀήρ, the Shu-Tefnut pair emerges as a force of un-enclosing, releasing the possibilities for multiplicity through their differentiation out of Atum, their differentiating generativity, and their separation of Geb and Nut to open—un-enclose—a zone in which further differentiation can unfold. Shu performs the un-enclosing of earth and sky through its being *air*, an in-between that transforms. ἀήρ, too, forms a site of transformation. The differing of resemblance manifests in the reflections of ἀήρ in ὕδωρ that appear *as* reflections: the clouds, for instance, hovering both in and as ἀήρ, as in the cloud cover (ἠέρα πουλύν) Cloud-Gathering Zeus renders for himself on his withdrawal from Olympos to Ida following his threat of violence to any other deities who would oppose him (Hom. *Il.* 8.50). The reflective surface and manifest depths of ὕδωρ, whose downwardness points upward and away from itself by way of the reflected ἀήρ, intimate this very movement outward, toward another and others, into the expansive network of meanings that links and relinks totality-in-motion in continual transformations. Directing away

---

41. Translation from Faulkner et al., *The Egyptian Book of the Dead*, 17, pl. 7a.

42. Translation from Lichtheim, *Ancient Egyptian Literature*, 88–89.

and toward others, the transforming and transformative character of this expansive ἀήρ takes place as shadowing and as a kind of in-between, a zone of transit for (and of) transformation. This is the movement of the signs made by Delphi's master (Hct. 93 Robinson), as well as of the many signs (σήματ' ἔασι / πολλὰ μάλ') along the one way articulated by the Parmenidean Thea (Prm. 8.2–3 Gallop), both of which chart this course into the manifold layers of meaning churning as totality.[43]

The work of the sign, while enclosing thought within the apparently limited terms of similes and images, also and at once un-encloses, releases thinking into the multiplicities of relation, urging further thinking on the possibilities of the radiant terms. Possibilities and relations activated in this manner also gesture to live engagement, to the living circle of Milesian thinking, the members of its circle and the continual expansion and opening of that circle. The circle itself occupies Anaximenean ἀήρ and its connections, voiced in the saying on ἀήρ, ψυχή, and πνεῦμα, to the circle of speaking and thinking, to λόγος and its intimate, inextricable relation with breathing.

Breathing

Returning to the beginnings summoned by the Anaximenean simile joining the (enclosed) ἀήρ of each being with the (enclosing) ἀήρ of totality, the simile's image of breathing and its indissoluble linkages to the opacity of ἀήρ come into view: "'Just like the soul (ψυχή),' he says, 'being our ἀήρ governs us, so also πνεῦμα and ἀήρ enclose (περιέχει) the whole kosmos'" (Stob. *Ecl.* 1.11.12 [Axs. 8 Graham]). The saying's un-enclosure of resemblance points to something of totality's relation as opening the sense of identity through the very pivot between ἀήρ and πνεῦμα, *breath*. ἀήρ comes forward as an active element suffusing and forming totality, enmeshed in-and-as the relational weave of totality and its differentiations.

With respect to the action of ἀήρ as a governing principle West has suggested linkages to the identity of Brahman and Atman and their

---

43. Pointing away and toward, the Parmenidean signs not only depend on negating patterns of experience that would seem to lead *away* from the one way of being (such as its character of ἀγνητον, unborn, and ἀνώλεθρον, indestructible), but also on images—like the bonds and limits that prevent being's movement (Prm. 8.26–31)—that direct attention to difference and a tendency toward movement.

connections to breath, "the basic doctrine of all the Upanishads."[44] Resonant with the Anaximenean saying on ἀήρ-ψυχή-πνεῦμα as circulating throughout totality, a passage from *Taíttíríya Upanishad* voices in air-as-breathing a dynamic image of totality according to which sounds both a "unity of being in-as Brahman" and "a dynamic of variation and substitution . . . that reperforms the ever-shifting and even aleatory aspects of the totality."[45] Inquiring of his father into the meanings and identities of Brahman, Bhṛigu investigates a sixfold articulation of Brahman. In the second fold of the six, which also includes food, sight, hearing, mind, and speech, the seeker arrives at the insight that "life-breath is Brahman." The narrator then develops and articulates Bhṛigu's understanding:

> For truly, from life-breath these beings are born,
> by life-breath they are sustained,
> and to life-breath they go and merge again. (*TU* BV.3)[46]

Beyond the resonance of this passage with the Peripatetic phrasing used to summarize Milesian thinking,[47] the overlap with the Anaximenean constellation of ἀήρ-ψυχή-πνεῦμα emerges in the way Brahman fills and overflows each differentiated manifestation and totality—a power suffusing, animating, and exceeding totality.[48] Like Anaximenean ἀήρ, Brahman as life-breath announces the pulse of breathing as a circulation of air within and beyond each differentiated manifestation. Elsewhere in *Taíttíríya Upanishad* the circulation itself comes directly to speech:

> Lifebreath—gods breathe along with it
> as do men and beasts.

---

44. West, *Early Greek Philosophy and the Orient*, 105. But note Olivelle's word of caution to any attempt to encapsulate the rich spread of *Upanishads* within "a single doctrine or philosophy." Introduction to *Upaniṣads*, xxiv.

45. Spitzer, "Archaic Images of Totality," 47.

46. Translation from Vernon Katz and Thomas Egenes, *The Upanishads: A New Translation* (Penguin, 2015), 128. Abbreviations of *Upanishads* follow Olivelle's table. *Upaniṣads*, xii–xiii.

47. On Alexandros's expedition into India (327–26 BCE), the Cynic Onesikritos (ca. 380–305 BCE) is reported to have interacted, through translators, with the Indian thinkers the Greeks called *gymnosophists*.

48. Katz and Egenes, *The Upanishads*, 10–11.

> For lifebreath is the life of beings,
> so it's called "all life." (*TU* 2.3)[49]

The *Upanishadic* identity of atman and brahman resounds throughout the texts, declaring that the "Self of the individual is identical to the Self of the universe (*brahman*)."[50] In *Bṛhadāraṇyaka Upanishad*, for instance, a cosmogonic vision begins with a thinking that unfolds as differing: "In the beginning, this world was only *brahman*, and it knew itself (*ātman*), thinking, 'I am brahman'" (*BU* 1.4.10).[51] This identity occurs as difference, differentiation, as in the Anaximenean ἀήρ-πνεῦμα scheme: the Anaximenean saying quoted by Stobaios does not collapse each soul in an undifferentiated unity of ἀήρ, but lets the language disclose contours in the variegated aeroscape or atmosphere. The manner in which ἀήρ as soul governs from within, while ἀήρ as πνεῦμα surrounds and so exceeds totality resembles the way breath comes forward in *Bṛhadāraṇyaka Upanishad* as both a unity and a difference with(-in) and *as* itself:

> "Who is the one god?"
> "Breath. He is called 'Brahman' and 'Tyad.'" (*BU* 3.9.9)[52]

As with Herakleitean thinking, the apparent unity voiced here circulates through multiple names, unsealing its own unity as already a multiplicity differing with itself. As Brahman, breath undergoes totality's dynamic reconfigurations in the span of living opened as each differentiation, while as Tyad breath remains withdrawn, "the indistinct," "never resting," and "non-perceived" (*TU* 2.6.), an abundance uncontained—unenclosed—by the manifestations of totality.[53] Along similar lines, *Kena Upanishad* voices Brahman as the moving force making possible a fivefold of speech, thought, sight, hearing, and breath (*KeU* 1.5–8). Developing valences of brahman linked closely in earlier Vedic literature to the power of speech as manifest

---

49. Translation from Olivelle, *Upaniṣads*, 186.

50. Katz and Egenes, *The Upanishads*, 7.

51. Translation from Olivelle, *Upaniṣads*, 15.

52. Translation from Olivelle, *Upaniṣads*, 47.

53. Based on Olivelle's helpful notes. *Upaniṣads*, 187 (translation), 312n9.9 (notes).

in prayer,[54] *Kena Upanishad* opens the fivefold through which Brahman echoes in repetition with its statement on Brahman as a power that "is not uttered by speech, / but by which speech is uttered" (*KeU* 1.4).[55]

By its circulation into a governing force from within ensouled beings and as an abundance permeating and enclosing totality, Anaximenean ἀήρ would also intimate both speech's power and that which powers speech: the shaped breathing of ἀήρ. As with the *Upanishadic* thinking of air-as-breath and breathing that works as the joining-parting element spanning totality—that is, differentiating by rhythmic pulsation and permeations—Anaximenean ἀήρ in this sense prefigures the action of Herakleitean λόγος that both joins and parts (e.g., Hct. 1, 2, 51 Robinson) and the Herakleitean disclosure of totality as this very double motion: "gatherings whole and not whole joining parting concord / discord from all one and from one all" (Hct. 10 Robinson). The outspan of each gathering from itself—of *whole* into *not-whole*—at each moment of totality's differentiation occurs not as a deficiency in human perception, not an epistemological problem, but as the continual, constitutive movements (withdrawals, outpourings, foldings and unfoldings) of each moment of totality, a "knower" and the "known" as woven together as-in the world in its tangible and intangible forms, its mesh of visibles and invisibles,[56] the "dimensional belonging-together of visibility and invisibility" spoken as "in-visibility."[57]

Such motion figures also in Herakleitean thinking explicitly in its cosmic spread as the movements of πῦρ, the kosmos a life-spanning (ἀείζωον) πῦρ alternately flaring into life and dimming into embers, ash, and darkness (Hct. 30 Robinson). Herakleitean thinking binds the life-spanning πῦρ to ἀήρ in the cycle of death and genesis that unfolds a patterned reconfiguration of opacities:

- the downward motion of γῆ into its recessed opacity gives way to the upward luminosity of πῦρ whose opacities flash on the shimmering edges its movements generate;

---

54. Signe Cohen, *Text and Authority in the Older Upaniṣads* (Brill, 2008), 46–48, ProQuest.

55. Translation from Katz and Egenes, *The Upanishads*, 36.

56. This discussion is inspired by Maurice Merleau-Ponty's thinking on the weave of the visible and the invisible in "The Intertwining—The Chiasm," in *The Visible and the Invisible*, trans. Alphonso Lingis (Routledge, 1968), 149–51; also Ashbaugh, "Philosophy of Flesh and the Flesh of Philosophy," 217.

57. Spitzer, "Envisioning In-Visibility," 232, with discussion on 230–31.

- a hovering and deepening of opacity of ἀήρ emerges in its moment of transition and transformation as the luminous opacity of πῦρ fades, dies;

- the transformational hovering and in-between of ἀήρ dies as the downward motion into depths and reflectivity emerges as the moving currents of opacity of ὕδωρ;

- finally, the currents of ὕδωρ and its opacity slow and continue the downwardness towards movements so gradual as to resemble stillness in γῆ. (Hct. 76a–c Robinson)

Each moment on the cycle trembles with the energies of the others—since at times γῆ, too, springs upward, πῦρ downward, and so on—so that each apparently distinct moment is quickened by the stirring presences of the others in their opacities. Here the Herakleitean sayings on the clashing of πόλεμος (war; e.g., Hct. 53, 80 Robinson) and the gatherings and mixing of so-called opposites (e.g., 67, 88 Robinson) give voice to multiplicities active and teeming in what will have come to be determined as *elements*.[58] Instead of radically pure and irreducible substances and identities arrayed in a sequence of fundamentally discrete units, the so-called elements—as with Xenophanean totality collapsing the one-many logic—emerge in Herakleitean thinking as bodied multiplicities, enmeshed and abundant opacities-in-relation. Similarly, identity in Herkaleitean thinking, as Decker has articulated, unfolds not as an independent, isolated, self-contained entity that remains in a condition of sameness with itself, but as active and "dynamic" according to which "a thing's identity is constituted through its motion," such that "each thing is both identical to itself and simultaneously *not* identical to itself."[59] Through the simile reported by Stobaios, Anaximenean ἀήρ both *joins* the nexus of totality as a dynamic relay of opacities,

---

58. On the problematic translation of early Greek thinking into thinking of στοιχεῖα-*elements*, see Sallis, *Figure of Nature*, 16–17, 36–37.

59. Decker, "Roots of Life and Death," 91. Decker's stress, however, falls on the presence of tensions within each being, where here the accent lies more on the *mixing* of otherness within each, on the being-multiple of each apparent unity. This insight on identity can be heard in a different register in the short, early *Aítareya Upanishad* (sixth–fifth c. BCE), encapsulated in the question "Which of these is the self?," to which an answer eventually arises in a multiplicity where the self differentiates (from) itself (*AU* 3.1–3; trans. and Egenes, *The Upanishads*, 142–43). Dating is based on Olivelle, *Upaniṣads*, xxxvi–xxxvii.

where the opacity of ἀήρ in each being is relayed into a span of relations with totality enclosed by the opacity of ἀήρ, and *parts* totality at each of its nodes of opacity, each differentiated manifestation. In this twofold manner ἀήρ enacts a differentiation along those threads of totality's relation where each being in its differentiation opens in its while into the intricacies of totality-as-dynamic-relations, relations of totality's ceaseless totalizing.[60]

The poetic saying given in Stobaios says more. Since what is sur- rounded and enclosed is said to be like what surrounds and encloses, does the saying gesture in a circle, indicate circularity and permeating as a way of being that, along with governing and enclosing, describes ἀήρ? And would this permeating circularity not also include a differing that somehow belongs to its way—a differing spoken in the distance opened by likeness (οἷον), not sameness? If, as Silvia Benso has observed, πνεῦμα in the saying articulates an aspect of ἀήρ, differentiated as a "life-force," that "enlivens the soul, makes it mobile, pulsating, active, verbal and not substantive,"[61] and if πνεῦμα and ἀήρ are indeed synonymous as the commentary states (λέγεται δὲ συνωνύμως ἀὴρ καὶ πωεῦμα, Stob. *Ecl.* 1.11.12 [Axs. 8 Graham]), this breathing action called πνεῦμα will man- ifest throughout totality in degrees of opacity, undergoing the motions of thickening and thinning along with ἀήρ and concretely joining each manifestation by way of circulation in a "moving contiguity of difference" to be called later, by Anaximenes's pupil Parmenides (Diog. Laert. 2.2.3), τὸ ἐόν and αἰθήρ.[62] Anaximenean ἀήρ quickens totality and the expansive abundance overflowing totality, ventilating and circulating throughout all manifestations, diversely translating the movement of ἀήρ that joins and differentiates like Herakleitean λόγος. Joining ἀήρ and breathing (πνεῦμα), the simile's image pulses with a continual motion of breathing that brings into view the living movement of totality in its totalizing, the motion of breathing that grants vitality. Such breathing names the ceaseless motion(s) of ἀήρ ensouling totality in a manner resembling the partial disclosure of unilluminated opacities in Thalean considerations, and such

---

60. Glissant, "Measure, Immeasurability," 137.

61. Silvia Benso, "The Breathing of the Air: Presocratic Echoes in Levinas," in *Levinas and the Ancients,* ed. Brian Schroeder and Silvia Benso (Indiana University Press, 2008), 14, ProQuest. Benso, situating the Anaximenean insight prior to the division of nature and spirit, shows that Anaximenean ἀήρ results in spiritualized nature and naturalized spirit, an infusion and circulation (14–15).

62. Spitzer, "Being-in-Touch," 16.

ensoulment bears the mark of the divine, not transparency but an opacity of multiplicity, of *mixis*.

Heard as *breathing*, ἀήρ addresses the possibilities of both voicing and exceeding λόγος in its narrower sense. Anaximenean ἀήρ arises not merely as a power to bring essences to light so as to lay emphasis on the same joining each similar, but rather as the differing constitutive of λόγος in Herakleitean thinking. Yet, in its shadowing action ἀήρ summons the λόγος into both a differing with itself as well as a pivoting movement of saying-and-hearkening. Differing with itself, Anaximenean thinking of ἀήρ spreads and contracts along the voiced plumes of synonyms—ἀήρ, ψυχή, πνεῦμα (Stob. *Ecl.* 1.11.12 [Axs. 8 Graham]), ἀέρα ἄπειρον (Simpl. *in Cael.* 1.5, 202.13–14 [Axs. 4 Graham])—as each voicing addresses differently the differing of ἀήρ and its resistance to the singular, to the paradigm of one-many. As breathing, ἀήρ is not subject to the one or many ones, but widens and narrows throughout multiplicities, totality, and again in excess of totality—ever beyond the singular aspect that haunts *the* totality (as ἕν and as πάντα). So too, as poeticized—crafted, shaped, made—ἀήρ, λόγος recoils, en-in-un-folds in giving voice to the shadowing action of ἀήρ, the other-than-itself multiplicity of each manifestation. To accomplish this, Anaximenean thinking activates what Simplikios described as an emerging (φύσιν) that both encloses itself as horizoning (ὡρισμένην) and un-encloses or opens itself as ἄπειρον (Simpl. *in Phys.* 1.2, 24.27–28 [Axs. 3 Graham])—a shimmering, the horizon of boundary ever-opening by the expanse of ἄπειρον, which in turn animates and inhabits the span of each horizon *in its motion of horizoning.* As the voiced breathing of speech, ἀήρ takes place as an advance to "harmoniously embrace the other," as Irigaray has phrased it, *and* the complementary "withdrawal into oneself," such that those joined in the λόγος form horizonal shimmerings never fully enclosed and never fully merged.[63]

ἀήρ, as the shaped breathing of speech, curls onto itself as the shaping intake of hearing made possible by the breathing of speaker, of hearer, and of the atmosphere in which speaker and hearer participate.[64] This does

---

63. Irigaray, *In the Beginning, She Was*, 26.

64. Where Merleau-Ponty seems to suggest an internality of the coiled reflexivity of speaking and hearing, this vision of Anaximenean ἀήρ opens up the "within" as the site of hearing-oneself to include not only the *also without* of self-hearing—the coil of vibrations recoiling from mouth to ear in addition to that from throat to throat. A circulation of this expanded sense may be included in the thought likening touch

not describe a fog of undifferentiated unity to which all can be reduced, but instead a relay from opacity to opacity through the bivalent, hovering in-between of ἀήρ as it resounds in the phrase echoed in Hippolytos: in its moment of self-sameness when it is most smooth and even (ὁμαλώτατος),[65] ἀήρ hovers in the between voiced in the term ἄδηλον (Hippol. *Haer.* 1.7 [Axs. 12 Graham]): an opacity (not-clear) *and* a transparency (not-visible). Here again appears in-visibility, the interplay or weave of opacity and transparency. Since Anaximenean ἀήρ is said in the same statement to be moving ceaselessly along a span of life (κινεῖσθαι δὲ ἀεί), and since motion activates the span of transparency or clarity (δηλοῦσθαι . . . τῷ κινουμένῳ) of ἀήρ, its moment of self-same repose or quietus (ὁμαλώτατος), and so of being ἄδηλον, never occurs. Not enclosing itself in itself so as to be a quietus of ἄδηλον—an absolute opacity or absolute transparency that would amount, as Glissant put it, to something like "Being-as-Being" that "is not opaque but self-important (*suffisant*)," an emptiness (*vacuité*) in its separateness from relation[66]—ἀήρ continuously moves as in-visibility, the vibrant weave of transparencies and opacities, of differences differing.

The speaking of λόγος takes place as twofold, gaining itself through not only the sounding of words but through a speaking that already involves hearing.[67] The poet's investiture early in *Theogony* enacts the twofold and the circulatory aspect of ἀήρ, resonant in the passage's figure of the shaped breathing of ἀήρ into speech, πνεῦμα. After voicing to the poet their alethic power to veil the differences between veiling and unveiling by way of similes of genuine things (ἐτύμοισιν ὁμοῖα, Hes. *Theog.* 27), a power that activates tremors through the entire poem, the Mousai bestow on the mortal singer a staff, a garland, and then the most special bestowal of ἀήρ as πνεῦμα:

---

and visibility to hearing, that, as with those other senses, "there is a reflexivity of the movements of phonation and of hearing." "The Intertwining—The Chiasm," 144–45.

65. Duncker and Schneidewin translate ὁμαλώτατος as *maxime aequalis*. Ludwig Duncker and F. G. Schneidewin, eds., *Hippolyti Refutationis omnium haeresium librorum decem quae supersunt* (Göttingen, 1859), 19. Graham gives "most uniform." *The Texts of Early Greek Philosophy*, 1:79.

66. *PdR*, 199; *PR*, 185. In its separateness, its self-withdrawal from relation, being-as-being merges with non-being. *PR*, 186–87.

67. On the twofold of speaking and hearing, see Spitzer, *Parmenides and Translation*, 19–23 (on Milesians and the *already-there*), 27–28 (on Empedoklean thinking and hearkening-speaking), and 75–80 and 115–16 (on this cluster in the Parmenidean poem).

And they breathed into me (ἐνέπνευσαν δέ μοι)
A voice divine, so I might celebrate past and future. (τά τ᾽
ἐσσόμενα πρό τ᾽ ἐόντα, Hes. *Theog.* 31–32)[68]

With its stress on the circulation of ἀήρ as breathing—as πνεῦμα—as a condition for the speaker's speech (the Mousai's πνεῦμα enables the poet's song), the expression brings out the speaking and hearkening twofold of λόγος. This twofold does not occur as mere repetition of the same, but as a speaking-and-listening that opens a difference. A great difference emerges in the temporal range of the mortal and immortal songs: even as the ἀήρ-as-breathing-πνεῦμα joins in togetherness immortals (Mousai) and mortals (the poet), the mortal song unveils the chasm of the present (Hesiod declares his song will unfold future and past [τά τ᾽ ἐσσόμενα πρό τ᾽ ἐόντα, 32], eliding present), while the song of the Mousai performed among the immortals covers such a chasm (theirs includes the present [τά τ᾽ ἐόντα τά τ᾽ ἐσσόμενα πρό τ᾽ ἐόντα, 37–39]).

"To try to speak with the other," as Irigaray has written, "represents a means of approaching them without ever adapting them to or into a world of one's own."[69] This movement between, and the between-us of speaking that sustains diversity while connecting differents, resounds in the Anaximenean voicing of ἀήρ as enclosing—un-enclosing, as joining-differing, as a gesture toward the loosening (ἀραιούμενον) and tightening (πυκνούμενον) embodied mesh of ἀήρ-πνεῦμα-breathing that en-in-un-folds in saying and hearkening as differing. Dramatized later in the Parmenidean poem, this mode of relaying opacities in the relations of saying and hearkening emerges when Thea, after welcoming the narrator, announces the fittingness (χρεώ) of his inquiring (πυθέσθαι) into totality (πάντα, Prm. 1.28 Gallop), then urges him to learn the enmeshed enfoldings of appearings and meanings (τὰ δοκοῦντα) as the perforating movements (περῶντα) of totality beyond itself (1.31–32 Gallop).[70]

---

68. Lombardo, *Hesiod*, 62; my interpolations.

69. Irigaray, *In the Beginning, She Was*, 47–48.

70. Compare the scene of expanse in *Bṛhadāraṇyaka Upanishad*, where "the one and a half" that manifests as "the purifying wind" is explained as not only one, but more than one (less than two) on account of its relation to totality's self-increase in that wind (*BU* 3.9.9; trans. Olivelle, *Upaniṣads*, 47).

Circling

Circulating from their own breathing, through their shaped breath of song into the mortal poet, the Mousai recirculate ἀήρ as πνεῦμα in a way that both encloses totality—figured in the way ἀήρ links and binds mortals and immortals in its circulation—and un-encloses totality in its work of disclosing totality in poetic speech. The narrative binds the Mousai to all the opacities of ἀήρ and its resonant associations with Nyx, Tartaros, and Χάος through the reduplication of their own sheltering opacities as they are said to move *within night's darkness* (ἐννύχιαι) veiled in the abundant opacity of ἀήρ (κεκαλυμμέναι ἠέρι πολλῷ, Hes. *Theog.* 9–10). The very breathing of ἀήρ-as-πνεῦμα, which the Mousai shape into their tremulous, shimmering speech, bears the character of their own movements and self-concealments that also reveal. Mousaic ἀήρ encloses and un-encloses, enacting the movements of ἀλήθεια. A major tremor shaking the entire song of *Theogony* surfaces here: the song of totality that is *Theogony* will unfold and refold according to the circulating pulse of the Mousai's ἀήρ-πνεῦμα and its veiling-unveiling-re-veiling, its opacities. In both its joining-differing and its enclosing—un-enclosing aspects, Anaximenean ἀήρ reflects the opacities already spoken in the ἀήρ-πνεῦμα and the Nyx-Tartaros-Χάος clusters in the Hesiodic theogony.

As if recommencing the circle of Milesian philosophy, Anaximenean thinking enacts a repetition that, like the circulatory relations joining the Mousai and the mortal poet, opens the circle, adding torque and dimension in the manner of a spiral or helix, the circle's curve opening into more numerous planes. Circulation—the circling of early Greek thinking—performs a repetition that takes place as a "flux of convergences," a "mode of knowing (*connaissance*)" beyond itself, at once "here and elsewhere" and, with Glissant, saying again, "relentlessly" rebeginning:[71] Anaximenean thinking cycles through Thalean ὕδωρ and Anaximandrean ἄπειρον, transforms them while returning them to the moment of thinking, reverberates the earlier thinkings in such a way that generates a reimagining and regeneration of the earlier Milesian images.[72] In focalizing ἀήρ, Anaximenean thinking registers the depths of opacity sounded in Thalean

---

71. *PdR*, 57; *PR*, 45.

72. An image's reverberation "involves," as Bachelard writes, "bringing about a veritable awakening of poetic creation, even in the soul of the reader"—or, hearer. *The Poetics of Space*, 7–8.

ὕδωρ while reorienting the view toward what appears in human-being as indissoluble involvement, as the ἀήρ reflected in ὕδωρ that resounds in the ancient phrase ἠεροειδὴς Πόντος. Similarly, voicing ἀήρ as joined with ἄπειρον, Anaximenean thinking of ἄπειρον ἀέρα sets in motion the multiplicity sounded in Anaximandrean ἄπειρον—the self-as-more-than-itself and no longer subject to the one-many(ones) paradigm. Making explicit the opacities of ἄπειρον in the figure of ἀήρ and pointing to its circulating, enclosing—un-enclosing character, Anaximenean ἀήρ thickens and thins the ἄπειρον of Anaximandrean thinking, opening up its bodied and atmospheric pulse. The quickening of ἀήρ transforms the apparent oppositions of inner and outer, closed and unclosed, transparency and opacity, gesturing toward an experience of being as bodied-enmeshment brought to light in the sign of a chiasmus, a recoil of circulation: a circling.

Perhaps more than Thalean ὕδωρ and Anaximandrean ἄπειρον, Anaximenean ἀήρ figures a circularity. Yet, insofar as what circulates—ἀήρ—also spans beyond the circle, its action as un-enclosing reconfigures the circle. What later comes—or has already come—to speech in the poetic sayings of Parmenidean thinking as τὸ ἐόν also tremors within Anaximenean ἀήρ as beyond totality, ever-outspanning itself, exceeding itself:

> You will learn this, too: how according to involvements
> surfacing meanings in their manifestness
> all manifold specificities (πάντα)
> are permeating a singular totality. (Prm. 1.31–32 Gallop)

Especially with respect to the challenges of speaking opacity, the risks, that is, of allowing a reductive transparency to dissolve the opacity of opacity, the closing-disclosing transformative work of Anaximenean ἀήρ (re-)directs thinking to its task of letting a distance open between the saying and what is said (or *unsaid*[73])—the translative engaged-distance and distancing of ἀήρ as in-between of-for-as transition and transformation that preserves respectful hesitance toward what withdraws from and exceeds any saying, any said: *opacities.*

---

73. Elements of this discussion are inspired by Levinas's thinking of "the unsayable," specifically the question as to "whether one can at the same time know and free the known from the marks which thematization leaves on it by subordinating it to ontology." Emmanuel Levinas, *Otherwise Than Being*, trans. Alphonso Lingis (Duquesne University Press, 1981), 7.

Conclusion

Breaking Light, Unclosing Opacity

Breaking Light: Unclosing

All that remains is the dark urn of
words

—Glissant, "Acclamation"

Opacity saturates Milesian thinking, overwhelmingly resonates through the radiant terms of their sayings: ὕδωρ, ἄπειρον, ἀήρ. Sayings, to be said—that is, to unfold in the dynamics of λόγος as speaking and hearkening—circulate within the atmosphere(s) and imaginaries of the saying: Anaximenean thinking bestows interrelated names for this circulation, πνεῦμα and ἀήρ, pulsing in the enclosing—un-enclosing rhythms of breathing, of the atmospheric λόγος as shaped breath forming the "unspoken whole that surrounds everything we say or write."[1] Even as the Milesian sayings circulate in the richly diverse imaginary of the wide eastern Aegean and Near Eastern archaic cultural matrix, activating meanings already pulsing within that imaginary, those sayings also produce torque on the imaginary and its predominant meaning network, opening possibilities for different extensions and variously relayed meanings. For Milesian thinking, the plasticity and resources of poetic language and, specifically, of simile, generate this torque from which new meanings flow.

---

1. David W. Johnson, "The Limits of Language: Philosophical Hermeneutics and the Task of Comparative Philosophy," *Journal of Speculative Philosophy* 34, no. 3 (2020): 380, Project Muse.

Some of the torque generating new meanings has been articulated in the chapters. Now, a view specifically onto the parts in torsion—the early poetries and the early Milesians—becomes available. From the tensions developed in terms of two modes of thinking and being—the *continental,* aligned in the archaic Greek imaginary with the figure of Zeus, and the *archipelagic,* enacted by the Milesian circle, the Milesian *archipelago*—begins to resonate a newness of early Greek thinking. In what follows the continental mode unfurls from the figure of Zeus into a tradition of philosophic thinking, while the archipelagic Milesian thinking works poetically against the lineage of Zeus. The breaking light of Milesian thinking enacts not a revolution in the sense of a fundamentally different mode characterized by clarity and intelligibility, one that turns away from the obscure and inchoate mythic and poetic imaginary in the direction of a fully rational explanation, but a breaking light as a revolution that develops a different mode of poetic thinking animated by other dimensions of the mythic and poetic imaginary in the direction of opacity. At least, not *exclusively* does Milesian thinking constitute such a revolution toward the clear and intelligible rationality that will have become not only a tradition but a primary mode of philosophic inquiry; for that trajectory can be read and traced from antiquity and highlights the multiplicity of selves the Milesians manifest in the diverse span of their activities and inquiries. Another trajectory, a subterranean line, a faultline, courses also;[2] thinking the Milesians through a poetics of opacity does not seek to replace or erase the traditional narrative, but to suggest that a plurality of modes—including the rational and in excess of it—from the outset constitutes what comes to be called philosophy. In this sense, Nietzsche's discussion of Thales resonates, where something other than the calculating (*rechnenden*) and measuring (*abmessenden*) way of thinking enables Thalean considerations, a "strange, illogical power, *Phantasie*" elevates thinking across possibilities[3]—possibilities like stones in a mountain stream, such as those that figure, for Glissant, the archipelagic mode.[4] Already at the beginnings, philosophy exceeds itself, or what it will have become.

---

2. The image of *faultlines* related to traditions is drawn from Lorna Hardwick, "Singing Across the Faultlines: Cultural Shifts in Twentieth-Century Receptions of Homer," in *Homer in the Twentieth Century: Between World Literature and the Western Canon,* ed. Barbara Graziosi and Emily Greenwood (Oxford University Press, 2007), 62.

3. Nietzsche, *Die Philosophie im tragischen Zeitalter der Griechen,* 164.

4. Glissant, *Philosophie de la relation,* 45.

Philosophy's narrative tends to align the early Greeks with the continental mode figured in the storm god Zeus, father of gods and men, prioritizing and pursuing unity along two entwined pathways Jussi Backman has articulated in terms of metaphysics: one, a unity of knowledge, a "unified grasp" of totality; two, a unity as a joining principle, a grounding one, a *"unity of being."*[5] Aristotle's influential treatment of Thales and Anaximenes in *Metaphysics* A identifies them as thinkers of unity (*Metaph.* 983b.17–984a.11), and in this Nietzsche's likewise influential work on early Greek thinking converge. In Nietzsche's study, too, the emphasis on unity defines philosophy. Of the three reasons to take seriously what Nietzsche regards as Thales's proclamation "All is water," the third grants the saying its philosophic complexion: not that the saying declares the origin (*Ursprung*) of all things, nor that it does so—in Nietzsche's presentation in this passage—without image (*Bild*) or myth (*Fabelei*), but decisively because it contains the stirrings of something that will hatch into a different form (*Verpuppung*): "Alles ist Eins," *All is One.*[6] Zeus reigns over the continent, embodies the way of being that belongs to the *continental mode*: attempt at mastery by way of an assertion of stable, fixed identities and the emphatic concentration of and on *unity*.

Breaking Light: Daybreak on the Continent

Continental thought is thought of the one . . .

> —Glissant, "Poetics of the World"

This Ἕν, however, is twofold. For one thing, it is the unifying One in the sense of what is everywhere primal and the most universal; and at the same time it is the unifying One in the sense of the All-Highest (Zeus).

> —Heidegger, "Onto-theo-logical Constitution of Metaphysics"[7]

---

5. Jussi Backman, *Complicated Presence: Heidegger and the Postmetaphysical Unity of Being* (State University of New York Press, 2015), 1, EBSCOHost.

6. Nietzsche, *Die Philosophie im tragischen Zeitalter der Griechen*, 163–64.

7. Heidegger, "The Onto-theo-logical Constitution of Metaphysics," translated by Joan Stambaugh, in *Identity and Difference* (University of Chicago Press, 1969), 69.

Storm god—master of the light, as lightning-wielder, and of the darkness, as cloud-gatherer, the One who grips the all in his overpowering grip—Zeus embodies the One and the drive toward unity. Zeus: the god destined to be a name for the One and its commander, leader-source of all that emerges (φύσεως ἀρχηγέ) and the One governing and steering all (κυβερνῶν, Kleanthes *Hymn to Zeus* 2). Zeus: a continent, a name for the *continental*.

Continental mode, the thinking of the One, as one of its basic maneuvers involves assimilation and-or annihilation of others.[8] Through violence and the persistent threat of harm, Zeus establishes and maintains power over others, a power constituted by the dual actions of *assimilation* and *annihilation*. "The One," writes Irigaray, "is founded through suspending or reversing the bond of dependence upon the other. Man henceforth pretends to give birth to what is, accepting to receive the revelation of this ability from a master."[9] The myth of the Hesiodic *Theogony* names that master *Zeus*. Assimilating and annihilating, Zeus devours the female-feminine divine being Metis and gathers unto himself the powers she embodies, including the power to give birth (Hes. *Theog.* 886–900). The tale of this assault, concretizing Zeus's assertion of his role as ultimate patriarch through the assimilation of the female powers of generation, presents the myth-history of both the replacement of living relations with a logic of final, absolute, unitary, male-masculine source and the violent, reductive assimilation of all humanity—of female-feminine beings and others—into the gendered universal *man* to stand for all humans while erasing the female-feminine, or rendering the female-feminine an instance of "inferior specifications" subordinated to the human essence *man*.[10]

Zeus, father of gods and men (*sic*: θεῶν πατέρ᾽ ἠδὲ καὶ ἀνδρῶν e.g., Hes. *Theog.* 47), stands at once *behind* and *before* all in the manner of the ἀρχή, both from which and to which, Aristotle associates with Milesian thinking (Arist. *Metaph.* 983b6–10). A deity whose birth from Kronos and Rheia *Theogony* sings and punctuates with his identity as the father and source, Zeus in that very song asserts himself as father of gods and

---

8. *PR,* 49.

9. Irigaray, *In the Beginning, She Was,* 54.

10. Adriana Cavarero, *In Spite of Plato: A Feminist Rewriting of Ancient Philosophy,* trans. Serena Anderlini-D'Onofrio and Áine O'Healy (Polity Press, 1995), 53; and see wider discussion 50–53.

men, exerting mastery by reshaping history into the story of his own supremacy and, impossibly, of himself as source (πατήρ):[11] in the account of his birth Zeus is already called "father of gods and men" (Hes. *Theog.* 457). The great god storms over and through the entire poem, the will of Zeus raises tremors even on the narrative preceding his birth, extending its reach into the time prior to himself, universalizing the power of the god's will. When Rheia consults Gaia and Ouranos as to how to protect her offspring, for instance, the foretelling of his own destiny to overthrow father Kronos unfurls "according to the will of Zeus the great" (465). As father of gods and men whose will precedes his own coming forth and determines totality, Zeus takes a double stand, at once behind and before all others: behind in his identity as source (πατήρ), before in the determinative force of his will and the double sense of both temporally *before* (preceding) and spatially *before* (in the fore), in front of all others.

In ordering (διέταξεν) the honors and powers among the divinities in the new regime (Hes. *Theog.* 73–74), and in distributing (διεδάσσατο) the honors and powers formerly belonging to the earlier divinities following the defeat of the Titans and Typhoeus (885), Zeus's *behind* and *before* character further emerges. The behind and before converge in a sense of being-outside: Zeus's authority fixes from without the powers and honors due to each divinity, and those powers and honors are in Zeus's control, available to his grasp for itemization, distribution, assignment. *Grasping* (*comprendre*) is the basic gesture of this mode, involving "the movement of hands that grab their surroundings and bring them back to themselves. A gesture of enclosure if not appropriation."[12] Assertion of fixed identity prevails in Zeus's ascendance and his regime of the continent, the One.

The position of being-outside, his behind and before position, in *Iliad* Book 8 Zeus himself brings to speech as a threat to all other divinities. After assembling the many divinities into a unity (θεῶν ἀγορὴν ποιήσατο, Hom. *Il.* 8.2), Zeus issues his command that they remain in this condition

---

11. The implicature of paternity, as in the Okeanos-Tethys passage (Hom. *Il.* 14.200–201, 246), involves being a source, the generative power prior to and behind all others. Where Tethys is called the Mother of the divinities, Okeanos is called the source (γένεσις, 14.201), pointing to a schema of generation according to which the male delivers the seed of reproduction that will germinate and develop within the female; source (γένεσις) and father according to that schema are synonymous.

12. *PR*, 191–92.

of unity and no longer give aid to the warring humans (8.10).[13] To punctuate the restriction, first Zeus explicitly threatens violence to the other divinities—to cast them into Tartaros (8.13–17)—and then he presents a challenge to prove his superiority (εἰμὶ θεῶν κάρτιστος ἁπάντων, 8.17) in a way that reveals his being-outside:

> Come on. Hang a gold cable down from the sky.
> All you gods and goddesses holding the end
> Couldn't drag down from sky to earth
> Zeus the Master (Ζῆν᾽ ὕπατον μήστωρ: *Zeus, highest master*),
>   no matter how hard you tried.
> But if I wanted to I could haul up all of you,
> With the earth itself and the very sea,
> Then loop the cable around a spur of Olympus,
> And the totality (πάντα) would hang suspended in space.
> That's how superior I am to gods and men. (8.18–27)[14]

The address takes its continental bearing from the gathering that reduces the diversity of the others on Olympos to a gathered unity under the sway of Zeus the Master. In this passage, Zeus continues to establish his position as a being-outside with respect not only to the gathered unity of other immortals—expanded here to include mortals, as if leveling immortals and mortals in their relation to Zeus—but also to totality. Projecting himself to a position apart from (outside of) totality, Zeus can take hold of totality, *bind it* (δησαίμην, 8.26). Zeus, lightning-wielder, master of totality, the continent and continental, the One that remains immobile while being capable of causing motion. In this sense, the Zeus imaged here prefigures the primary being of metaphysics, the divine being set apart, self-sufficient, a cause and source of motion and of being while itself remaining unbegun, unsourced, motionless.

Another dimension of the continental mode as embodied by Zeus involves a reconfiguration of the twofold of λόγος as speaking-and-hearkening. Zeus the Master reduces this twofold as a passage into a

---

13. In this line Zeus has begun his threat more directly, telling the other divinities not to separate themselves from the assembled unity: ὃν δ᾽ ἂν ἐγὼν ἀπάνευθε θεῶν ἐθέλοντα νοήσω (Hom. *Il.* 8.10). Lombardo translates: "If I catch anyone of you with a private plan." *Homer: Iliad*, 143.

14. Translation is from Lombardo, *Homer: Iliad*, 143–44; my interpolations.

unity, the unity of the speaker-as-commander. As in the scene from the *Iliad* staging Zeus's being-outside, where Zeus's speech begins with the injunction "Listen to me (κέκλὖτε μευ), divine ones, / So that I can tell you what I want" (Hom. *Il.* 8.5–6),[15] in *Theogony* Zeus's first words spoken to the Hundred-Handers begin with the phrase that reduces the twofold of the λόγος:

> Hearken unto me (κέκλὖτε μευ), glorious children of Gaia
>   and Ouranos,
> so that I might speak those things which the spirit in my breast
>   urges. (Hes. *Theog.* 644–45)

The imperative mode of Zeus's address, with its accent on gathering the attention of others to the speaker for the purpose of asserting and realizing his will, collapses the dynamic twofold speaking-and-hearkening of λόγος. Not opening toward the relay of differences in λόγος and its differing, as in the interaction between the Mousai and Hesiod on Mount Helikon (21–35), the λόγος of the One ceaselessly pursues its own establishment as authority and overmastery of any other, beginning with those whose listening no longer occurs as differing but instead as being-assimilated. Such a λόγος moves ever in the direction of the same, of repetition.[16]

In the scene from *Iliad* 8, following the delivery of his "masterful speech" (κρατερῶς ἀγόρευσεν, Hom. *Il.* 8.29),[17] Zeus withdraws from Olympus to the peak of Gargaros, situating himself at a distance—apart from and above—the assembled Olympian host. As the scene progresses the narrative voices another epithet of Zeus, νεφεληγερέτα, cloud-gatherer (Hom. *Il.* 8.38), pivoting toward the closing moment when the great god encloses himself in ἠέρα πουλύν, dense ἀήρ (8.50). Not only does Zeus commandeer and transform the differing relay of opacities in λόγος, converting it to an expression and exercise of power-over-others that reduces the other(s) to the role of functionary within the master's scheme, in the scene from the *Iliad* the lightning-wielder also reconfigures the opacity of ἀήρ according to a similar aim. In *Poetics of Relation*, Glissant articulated this assimilative and hostile opacity in terms of continental philosophies, that is, thinking of the One and the linkage to filiation—"the absolute

---

15. Translation is from Lombardo, *Homer: Iliad*, 143–44; my interpolations.

16. Irigaray, *In the Beginning, She Was*, 55.

17. Translation is from Lombardo, *Homer: Iliad*, 144.

exclusion of the other" (*PR*, 52)—and its violences. Grounding itself in a root identity, the continental "senses Being only as in-itself, because it never conceives of it as relation" (*PR*, 50). Each member of the relation constitutes itself as transparent for itself and "threateningly opaque for the other" (*PR*, 49). Relation would disrupt the imagined transparency of purity, pure lineage and filiation that both roots identity and projects it into any relation as self-enclosed and hostile to whatever other opposes it in such relation; the oppositional character of this relation flows from the thought of the One, the unity developed in and as the lines of filiation. Such oppositionality springing from the root Glissant reads as undergirding the narrative of the *Iliad*, where protection of filiation's legitimacy, or retribution for its disruption, motivates the epic's action: "it is legitimacy that is disrupted by the abduction of Helen" (*PR*, 50). In the passage from the *Iliad*, when Zeus withdraws and conceals himself in thick ἀήρ, it takes place as a projection of power-over-others, an assertion and amplification of Zeus's before and behind position relative to the other divinities and totality; indeed, the lightning-wielder's superiority forms a refrain throughout *Iliad* Book 8. From his position of concealment above the field of action (Hom. *Il.* 8.50–52), Zeus as the One adopts the aerial view characteristic of the continental mode.[18]

The passage also brings out the annihilating aspect of illumination as part of the overall continental character Zeus embodies and prefigures in the scene on Mount Olympos. Emblematic of Zeus, the lightning bolt reinforces the great god's readiness for violence in the form of annihilation and/or assimilation—characteristics of the continental mode. Accordingly, the scene of Zeus's threat to the other divinities, his assertion of supremacy and his departure emphasizing his being-outside, begins by introducing the storm god with the epithet τερψικέραυνος, delights-in-lightning (Hom. *Il.* 8.2). The great god wields the lightning bolt, annihilates by means of fiercely relentless illumination, irradiation. Exhumed from the folds of Gaia (Hes. *Theog.* 505), Zeus's weaponized light destroys and portends destruction: in the Hesiodic *Theogony* the lightning bolt is the weapon of mass destruction that annihilates-assimilates both Typhoeus (853–68) and the Titans (687–700)—where the text merges the weapon with Zeus's own force (πᾶσαν . . . βίην) that he brings to light (ἐκ . . . φαῖνε, 688–89). In the scene from the *Iliad*, the blazing lightning flash announces the coming

---

18. Glissant, *Philosophie de la relation*, 45.

doom Zeus has weighed out on his golden scales (Hom. *Il.* 8.75–77).[19] As if heralding this destructive valence of lightning's illumination, the scene on Olympos begins with the rising Dawn spreading over the whole earth (8.1), laying bare and exposing totality just as Zeus lightning-wielder will lay bare and expose to the other divinities as a gathered whole the threat of illumination in the speech that follows. In Zeus, a figure of continental thinking, light and illumination not only disclose, but destroy, annihilate.

Light of day breaks over the continent, the One. In a sense, this lighting radiates from and as One in its unity, a potent symbol of its drive toward conquest, toward reduction of difference into its own self-sameness. The light, weaponized, becomes the lightning hurled by Zeus the father, source and ultimate end whose will extends beyond his own coming-into-being, irradiating the myth-history of *Theogony* with something like an extended and universal *being*. From behind and before, Zeus governs and directs, annihilates and assimilates: the lightning renders all transparent; all is laid bare in the clear light of clarity, stripped of all opacity so that light can pierce and penetrate, reduce to the general, the universal to which all things, as *particulars,* are subordinated in the assimilating and annihilating movements of the "process of generalization."[20] The continental mode seeks domination, equating knowing and mastery: the reductive, transparent continental mode and its universal endows the one who knows an authority over others, to command (ἐπιτάττειν) and not be commanded, not to obey but to be obeyed (Arist. *Metaph.* 982a.17–19). In *Metaphysics* A, Aristotle aligns the Milesians with this continental mode, the thought of the One and of the light and clarity through which everything becomes transparent, which is to say intelligible and accessible to the λόγος, emblem and instance of Zeus's lightning. The essence available for full expression in the brilliant λόγος of clarity and light makes visible the intelligible core that most truly defines each manifestation by rending differences from it, reducing it to the One, the single cause (μίαν . . . αἰτίαν) that forms the substance (οὐσίαν)-essence (τὸ τί ἦν εἶναι) leading to the last word (τὸν λόγον ἔσχατον) on every manifestation. As essence that is source (ἀρχή), the One encircles as first (πρῶτον) and last (983a.27–29).

---

19. In *Iliad* 8 Zeus's lightning bolt becomes thematic, delivering threats that halt both mortal (Diomedes on his chariot, Zeus sends the lightning flash; Hom. *Il.* 8.130–35) and divine going forth (Athene on her chariot, Zeus threatens annihilation by lightning; 8.381–408), while fire in a primarily destructive valence laces the whole book.

20. *PdR,* 61–62; *PR,* 49.

Zeus names the continental. For Milesian thinking, however, opacity works to protect diversity and to voice the continually mobile abundances that do not answer to the thought of unity, of the One. As a site of relations, Milesian thinking opens the expansive opacities as multiplicities not subject to the One. With the theme of ὕδωρ that has emerged throughout the chapters as relaying each member of the Milesian circle while granting the diversity of each, early Greek thinking figures an archipelago.

Breaking Light: Opacities, an Archipelago

We have suggested that Relation is an open totality evolving upon itself. That means that, thought of in this manner, it is the principle of unity that we subtract from this idea.

—Glissant, *Poetics of Relation*

If truth is a continent over which we purpose dominion, an appropriate mode of expression will be the tract. But suppose it is an archipelago. Suppose to know is more like to visit or to cohabit than to own.

—Jan Zwicky, "What Is Lyric Philosophy? An Introduction"[21]

Archipelago: a beginning (ἀρχή), the sea (πέλαγος).

Not *Zeus*, not even isolated regions or certain beings such as those immortals whose being is said to be ἀεί (typically translated: eternal) and that, through translation, come forward as "eternal Immortals" (ἀθανάτων ἱερὸν γένος αἰὲν ἐόντων, Hes. *Theog.* 21),[22] Milesian thinking images *totality* inspired, quickened by breathing (ἔμψυχον) and by ἀήρ-πνεῦμα (Stob. *Ecl.* 1.3.28, 1.11.12 [Axs. 8 Graham]), overflowing (πλήρες) with the opacities of divinities (Stob. *Ecl.* 1.3.28 [Ths. 37 Graham]), expansively opening as worlds of divinized opacities (τοὺς ἀπείρους οὐρανοὺς θεούς, Ps.-Plut. *Plac.* 1.7 [Axr. 42 Graham]), open awareness shimmering with the opacity of divinity (νοῦν τοῦ κοσμοῦ θεόν, Ps.-Plut. *Plac.* 1.7, Stob. *Ecl.* 1.3.28 [Ths. 37 Graham]).

---

21. Jan Zwicky, "What Is Lyric Philosophy? An Introduction," *Common Knowledge* 20, no. 1 (2013): 26, Project Muse.

22. Translation from Lombardo, *Hesiod*, 61.

Archipelago: a beginning (ἀρχή), the sea (πέλαγος).

Breaking light of its force to assimilate and annihilate in the service of the One, Zeus the Master, the great god and lightning-wielder, would involve recalling Gaia as the umber darkness out of which that light was seized. Gaia: in Xenophanean thinking, joined with both ὕδωρ and ἄπειρον, Gaia (γῆ) enacts and quickens multiplicities and the spread of opacities. For Thalean considerations, a jointure of ὕδωρ and Gaia makes itself felt in the irreducible overlap of opacities, the dark waters from dark springs that flow out from dark recesses of earth. Drawn from poetries that link Gaia and bodies of ὕδωρ through their character as ἄπειρον, Anaximandrean ἄπειρον also activates multiplicities and their opacities as ever-relating complexes of relation. Anaximenean ἀήρ, similarly echoing archaic poetries, voices both Gaia and bodies of ὕδωρ as ἠερόεντα in the sheltering depths and opacities resonant in upper and lower registers. This twofold of ὕδωρ and γῆ already names a configuration of differences, their dynamic relations of opacities; otherwise said: an *archipelago*.

Already a return to Thalean considerations and the very ancient and first thinkers of the divine (θεολογήσαντας) for whom ὕδωρ in variegated manifestations activates beginnings (Arist. *Metaph.* 983b.28–29), the thought of archipelago—*archipelagic thinking*—resonates with the thematic relations of ὕδωρ-ἄπειρον-ἀήρ that have emerged in the chapters. In turn, the thematic return to Thalean considerations announced by *archipelagic* thinking in its very naming of ὕδωρ-as-πέλαγος—joining the three Milesians in variously thinking ὕδωρ—reveals the span of Thalean considerations beyond themselves, constituted not as a system developed by an identifiable, individual philosopher advancing a theory in competition with other theories,[23] not, that is, as a continent, but rather as an archipelago: connected, in relation, differing, an open circle of thinking continually opening in relations.

Archipelagic, Thalean considerations already sound the relation(s) with Anaximandrean and Anaximenean thinking as an archipelago, the

---

23. See Wians's articulation of a conventional distinction between philosophy (as *logos*) and myth—a distinction he uses as preliminary and representative rather than final or exhaustive—based on grounds that philosophy issues from an identifiable person who posits in writing a theory in competition with others of which "at most only one can be true." William Robert Wians, "From *Logos* and *Muthos* to . . . ," introduction to *Logoi and Muthoi: Further Essays in Greek Philosophy and Literature*, ed. William Robert Wians (State University of New York Press, 2019), 11, EBSCOhost.

Milesian archipelago. As such, the Milesians form indissoluble networks of meaning and thinking, a community of thinking resistant to the strain of the One, the continental grasp of Zeus toward unity, *a community beyond unity*. The open community in its opening movements finds itself animated by the constitutive relations forming it: *communities beyond the One*. Milesian thinking surges in the archipelagic communities of diverse imaginaries as a poetics unbound by the principles of clarity and intelligibility that will have become (part of) its legacy.

Archipelagic: Community Beyond Unity

Archipelagic opposes continental.[24] A current of the relations between the Milesian archipelagic and earlier continental thinking runs in the direction of Zeus and the continental mode voiced in that divinity's character in Homeric and Hesiodic poetries. The relation, intimated in Aristotle's discussion of the earlier theologians who seemed to have identified ὕδωρ as an ἀρχή, when understood as bringing to light and clarity (ἀποφήνασθαι, Arist. *Metaph.* 984a.3) the ancient thought through a practice characterized by grasping (λαβὼν ἴσως τὴν ὑπόληψιν, 983b.22, 25), extends the continental mode through Homeric and Hesiodic poetries and Milesian thinking, joins and merges both the earlier poet-theologians and the later philosophers in the continental mode: even the earlier poet-theologians are said to have believed (οἴονται) to have grasped (ὑπολαβεῖν) the ἀρχή of φύσις (983b.29–984a.2). Some of Aristotle's thinking on ἄπειρον, if taken in the direction of Anaximandrean ἄπειρον, would attempt to assimilate the latter into the grasping mode, the continental mode and its grounding unity. Where a resonance sounds between Anaximandrean thinking and Aristotle in understanding ἄπειρον as a spanning-beyond (ἀεί τι ἔξω ἐστί, Arist. *Ph.* 207a.1), Aristotle brings this spanning into the mode of grasping, for that spanning-beyond constitutes a something more for seizing into a grasp (λαμβάνειν, 207a.3, 7–8). With the earlier theologians and the archaic philosophers striving for a grasp on knowledge of the first cause and source by means of the lightning rationality of Zeus that assimilates and annihilates, a lineage makes itself felt wherein a latecomer succeeds where the former failed. This, too, replays the Hesiodic narrative of filiation-through-overmastery according to which Kronos overthrows Ouranos and Zeus overthrows Kronos, deepening the underlying reduction of both to

---

24. Glissant, "Poetics of the World."

the continental mode of thinking. The overthrow narrative persists, though without the sense of filiation, typically by assigning a certain rationality as the decisive weapon—like Zeus's lightning bolt—to accomplish the succession, a rationality that eliminates divine agency from the workings of natural phenomena, a "purely naturalistic theory" in the manner of "a sort of proto-scientific explanation of events that hitherto had been viewed as marvelous and prodigious."[25] Yet they join in the reductive drive and its establishment of a root identity, the drive and identity Glissant associated with conquest.[26] Just as Zeus conceals (annihilates, assimilates) the Titans within Gaia's depths (Hes. *Theog.* 717–20), the continental mode conceals its lineage running down into the grasping orientation of Zeus in the earlier poetries.

Not merely *against* the unifying grasp (*con-tinere*) of the continental mode figured in Zeus, the fluidities of Milesian archipelagic thinking course differently, flow otherwise. As the chapters illustrate, the different character of the Milesian archipelagic does not lie in a rejection of mythic figures; indeed, their thinkings activate some poignant dynamics within the mythic imaginaries of archaic Mediterranean and Mesopotamian regions. Beyond just the opposing term in a twofold relation of one-many through which the One nevertheless persists in the unity of each member of the many, archipelagic in the Milesian voicings resists the unifying action of the continental, releases opacities into their multiplicities.

Not one, not many *ones*, Milesian archipelagic thinking takes place as fluid, mobile, seeking not dominion but relation, voyaging, engaging, learning with others. Rethinking the Milesian circle will involve breaking the spell that aligns a continental mode of thinking to their own sayings, making room for their thinking to spread in numerous directions of multiplicities, diversities, opacities in the manner of what Glissant termed the *archipelagic*, understood as "diffracté,"[27] "the thought of the many, of the multiple," thinkings that unfold as " 'composite,' which are born of the mingling of cultures," "meandering," "swollen,"[28] toward and as "the dispersion of non-Being, which brings together the being of the world";[29]

---

25. Graham, *Texts of Early Greek Philosophy*, 1:17.

26. *PR*, 56–57. See also Glissant's discussion of "invading" and "arrowlike" "nomadism" and its associations with universalizing thought (*PR*, 11–22).

27. Glissant, *Philosophie de la relation*, 47.

28. Glissant, "Poetics of the World."

29. Glissant, "Measure, Immeasurability," 148.

a scape of "rivers and stones," of "holes of shadow that unclose (*ouvrent*) and reclose (*recouvrent*)."[30]

 Archi-pelago takes its name and its shapes from the differentiations of-between-on earth and sea, γῆ and ὕδωρ. So, too, Milesian thinking occurs in such differentiations of earth and sea, mobile, in an archipelagic relation spreading through differences without assimilating or effacing them.

Multiple Imaginaries

Archaic Miletos formed an archipelago, "a system of relation, as an aptitude for 'giving-on-and-with' [*donner-avec*]" contravening on the violent striving toward "undifferentiated conglomerations,"[31] the grasp of the continental, the One. In the cultural archipelago of Miletos, Milesian thinking activates a diverse network of mythic imaginaries, not discrete units of belief that might occasionally and incidentally enter into relations, but a *tourbillon* of meanings as relations. The relations unfurled throughout the chapters articulate an archipelago of Milesian thinking. From the Greek poetic traditions, ancient Egyptian archives, Hebrew and Mesopotamian cosmogonies, ancient Persian cosmology, and the Indian *Upanishadic* sources, Milesian thinking expands and multiplies, a *creolization* in Glissant's sense, in which relations form of "several cultures or at least several elements of distinct cultures, in a particular place in the world" and generate "something new, completely unpredictable in relation to the sum or the simple synthesis of these elements."[32] Diffusing and diffracting into a complex and diverse meaning network of the broad and variegated eastern Aegean cultural matrix, the Thalean image of an originary opacity named ὕδωρ and the Anaximandrean and Anaximenean similes and images build out the relations and poetics of *mixis, creolization*, an archipelagics of Milesian thinking.

Multiplicities, Not Unities

Thalean ὕδωρ

Teeming depths of opacity, each differentiation in the Thalean hydroscape surges as a multiplicity not reducible to a single explanation, not available

---

30. Glissant, *Philosophie de la relation*, 45.

31. *PR*, 142.

32. Glissant, "Repetitions," in *Treatise on the Whole-World*, trans. Celia Britton, 22.

to the continental grasp of the One. Each manifestation in this sense always summons something more than itself in thinking and thoughtful naming. As Thalean divine-opacities fill totality (θεῶν and-or δαιμόνων, Arist. *de anim.* 411a.7–8, Stob. *Ecl.* 1.3.28 [Ths. 35 Graham]; Diog. Laert. 1.1.27 [Ths. 1 Graham]), divine-opacities *and* ὕδωρ compose each differentiation of totality in a slippage of identity determined as unity by the One of the continental mode, a sluice beyond singularity and plurality, the logic of One-many(ones). Thalean ὕδωρ and divinities swirl so that each manifestation comes forward as a multiplicity.

Anaximandrean ἄπειρον

Anaximandrean ἄπειρον offers a name for such multiplicities outside the grasp of the continental mode, the male-masculine grasp of Zeus, the One. A dense conglomeration of not-yet separated forces—called by Aristotle opposites (Arist. *Ph.* 187a.20–21 [Axr. 13 Graham]), ἄπειρον teems with the energies of multiplicities indissolubly and originarily in relation (μίγμα, 187a.23). ἄπειρον, an energy of already active relations, comes forward as a certain φύσις, a surging and growing that manifests as each differentiated being (Hippol. *Haer.* 1.6 [Axr. 10 Graham]). Each differentiation within totality arises as the φύσις of multiplicity, of relations and possibilities called ἄπειρον.

Anaximenean ἀήρ

Insofar as Anaximenean ἀήρ spreads out as both ἄπειρον and opening within its own spanned horizon (ὡρισμένην, Simpl. *in Phys.* 1.2, 24.28 [Axs. 3 Graham]), multiplicity already describes it: as ἄπειρον, because its opening takes place as an open expanse of possibilities named by ἄπειρον itself; as ὡρισμένην, because a kind of folding takes place in that action that enables the difference between ἀήρ in its outspan (ἄπειρον) and ἀήρ in its in-span horizon (ὡρισμένην).

Archipelagic: Horizons

Thalean ὕδωρ

Not only do the divinities of Thalean considerations teeming in each manifestation name a multiplicity of opacities, they also open each manifestation with the open awareness (νοῦν τοῦ κοσμοῦ θεόν, Ps.-Plut. *Plac.* 1.7, Stob.

Ecl. 1.3.28 [Ths. 37 Graham]) that opens beings as already-in-relation. Such opening animates the kosmos, totality. Taken together with the saying that the source and beginning (ἀρχή) of everything is ὕδωρ (Stob. *Ecl.* 1.11.12 [Ths. 16 Graham]), the articulation of opacities as the continual beginnings everywhere, in and as every differentiation, Thalean considerations open totality along a horizonal-horizontal spread. Everything lives fluidly and with opacities that open relations as a constitutive opening (νοῦς): animals and plants, the growing things of earth and earth in its multiplicity—stone and soil, metal and dust; the fish of the waters and the waters in their multiplicity—turbulent and still, murky and clear; the birds of the air and the air in its multiplicity—clouds and wind, fog and clarity; the lights of the kosmos and the light in its multiplicity—steady and wavering, white and multicolored; awareness and thinking in their ceaseless alethetic turnings, opening and closing, revealing and concealing so that a self appears reflexively as "a thick cloud of knowledge."[33] Open-expanse, as νοῦς-θεῶν πλῆρες-ὕδωρ, spreads across and through totality, a horizontal opening as a horizon always shimmering, drifting as a dynamic site where showing and withdrawing mingle. Thalean ὕδωρ speaks an experience of mobile depths in their lustrous gatherings of showing-forth and in their dark recedings, the sense of abundance ever-opening a world of horizons *beyond* knowing.

Anaximandrean ἄπειρον

ἄπειρον voices the horizoning drift in the gesture toward the ways identities diversify, continue in motion torqued with the fixity language threatens to impose—and, especially, the language and logic of the continental mode and its assertion of identity-as-unity, stability. Irigaray, looking initially to the ways plant life unfolds "according to the hour, the day, the season, the year" in a motion that might be called *bordering*, sees this temporally dynamic *bordering* or *forming* also in the lives of human beings.[34] Anaximandrean thinking calls forth such horizoning (ὡρισμένης) of living beings as the meaning of temporality (χρόνον, Hippol. *Haer.* 1.6

---

33. *PR*, 186. Compare Sallis's discussion of the opacity ("opaqueness") of a subject rising from the always-already situated-relation in a world, with the result that this involvement "cannot be absorbed into the relation of the subject to itself." *Phenomenology and the Return to Beginnings*, 30.

34. Irigaray, *In the Beginning, She Was*, 57–58.

[Axr. 10 Graham]). Language—and in Irigaray's discussion, specifically ἄπειρον—risks petrifying the variegated temporality spanning life forms. Yet, where an assertoric or argumentative λόγος would be unable to reach such a temporality and accompanying way(s) of being on account of its own rigid conceptual-linguistic determinations, Anaximandean thinking speaks a pliable, supple λόγος, a poetic language and its open expanse of possibilities. Voicing an experience of multiplicity outside of the one-many paradigm (of unity), an experience of an irreconcilable dimension exceeding each perspective, Anaximandrean ἄπειρον names those movements as like *non-experience*, the newness and expansiveness teeming past the edges of habitual encounters.

Anaximenean ἀήρ

Anaximenean ἀήρ moves *horizontally* as the thickening (πύκνωσιν) and thinning (ἀραίωσιν), the motion through which totality is born (γεννᾶσθαι,[35] Euseb. *Praep. evang.* 1.8.3 [Axs. 11 Graham]). The double motion takes place as the span of ἀήρ (κίνησιν ἐξ αἰῶνος, Euseb. *Praep. evang.* 1.8.3 [Axs. 11 Graham]); ἀήρ moves throughout its ownmost temporal span (κινεῖσθαι δὲ ἀεί, Hippol. *Haer.* 1.7 [Axs. 12 Graham]). As ἄπειρον the dual motion, the birthing movement of ἀήρ spans and spreads as an open expanse, while as ὡρισμένον, the birthing movement of ἀήρ takes place as emerging horizons everywhere as each differentiation of totality thickens or thins into its momentary and seasonal *howness* or *whatness* (ποιότησιν, Euseb. *Praep. evang.* 1.8.3 [Axs. 11 Graham]). Anaximenean ἀήρ names a shifting, quickened location on which join ἄπειρον, as an open of expansive possibilities according to birthing, and *horizoning* (ὡρισμένον), the limning—in a double sense of *illuminating* or letting appear and of tracing the liminal, the harbor or threshold as site of differing—of each differentiation of ἀήρ. This motion of thickening and thinning, as Anaximenean horizoning and birthing, continually moves, infusing totality with a pulse, a fluxion of opening and closing on and as liminalities,

---

35. The variants in the text of this passage in Eusebios are γένει (kind according to birth) and μεγέθει (size). In light of the passage's ambience of birthing (γεννᾶσθαι, γεγενῆσθαι, γενέσεως), the former seems more consonant. Graham presents μεγέθει in the main text and gives γένει in a note. *The Texts of Early Greek Philosophy*, 1:78 and 78n2. Dinsdorf's edition of Eusebios gives only γένει. Wilhelm Dinsdorf, ed. *Praeparationis Evangelicae*, I–X, in *Eusebii Caesariensis Opera* (Leipzig, 1867), 1:26.

boundaries where—in the manner of a *horizon*—the visible and the invisible touch in-as-on a ceaselessly turning edge. The sites where visible and invisible touch Anaximenean thinking calls ἀήρ and its *open-expansive-horizoning*. Totality is born in and as such expansive-opening-horizoning, such that this moving touch comes to experience and brought to speech in Anaximenean ἀήρ *everywhere manifesting occurs*: the sense of shadowing—being-shadowed, encompassing—being-encompassed, the embodied mesh of being-in-the-world.

Horizoning: Archipelagic

Horizon: a span-across, elongation and widening, an ever-moving threshold.

Horizoning: a continual happening, horizoning continually turns the world beyond the mark of its bound, preserves a past or beyond of the horizon.

Thinking totality in its open-expanse of multiplicities opens Milesian thinking not as a grasping, a taking hold from a position of behind-and-before, the position of Zeus and the orientation of the continental mode, but as a being-with and a togetherness in the manner of an archipelago, shaped by formations of earth and the waters that shape those formations. "In Relation," writes Glissant, "the whole is not the finality of its parts: for multiplicity in totality is totally diversity (*totalement une diversité*)."[36] Milesian thinking opens a horizon—a movement *across*, a spreading, a drift.

Unlike the λόγος of Zeus and the continental mode, ever-seeking repetition of the same on the grounds of unity, the way of λόγος at work in the Milesians opens the circle, produces a "circularity with volume,"[37] dimensionalizes it in the manner of the Mousaic speaking in *Theogony*—whose movement and dwelling speaks of this very dimensionalizing, the spiraled *helix* of Mount *Helikon* (Spiral Mountain) where their dance whirls *around* (περί) the sacred spring (Hes. *Theog.* 3). Differing orients Milesian λόγος, both in the open circle of the diverse imaginary in which their thinkings sound and in the interactions of each joining without merging. Emphasis falls on expanse and extension in the manner of Glissantian baroque that "exalts the quantity repeated to infinity, the

____

36. *PR,* 192; *PdR,* 206.
37. *PR,* 32.

eternally re-beginning (*recommencée*) totality."[38] Anaximandrean ἄπειρον points to such baroque repetitions through its infinitely ceaseless motions and continual beginnings spoken in the expansive openness of worlds (ἀπείρους κόσμους) in their churning outspan (ἀποκεκρίσθαι, Euseb. *Praep. evang.* 1.8.2 [Axr. 19 Graham]), folds of possibilities thickening the kosmos into a multiplicity, a *manifold* of dense layerings.

In the sayings of totality as continually recomposing through and as the movements of opacities in relation—in locating opacity every-where—the Milesian poetics *horizontalizes*, spreads and opens. Thalean ὕδωρ "runs," as Krell has put it, "through our fingers when we try to grasp it," and as it flows "without external boundaries or internal limits" it joins in the open-expansive character of Anaximandrean ἄπειρον,[39] a character set adrift and aloft in Anaximenean ἀήρ, which likewise eludes the grasp.

No grasp—in terms of the grasping of knowledge as *seizing* (*comprendre*, ὑπόληψις)—can be made, not only because the fluidities these radiant terms announce pour through even the firmest grip, but also because of the vast array of multiplicities in relation, where no single differentiation elevates to a continentally oriented position of before and behind all—the position for grasping is not available.

A poetics of opacity joins without con-joining, without reducing, without grasping, as in an archipelago in relation over and from the opacities of each overlap and span of γῆ and ὕδωρ. Belonging to this spread: humans *among* others, not above and behind others. Such overlappings, the sites of permeable, shifting contours, summon a shift in human comportment and belonging as being-in-the-world, calling forth, as Allen has phrased a similar turning, "a volatile reorientation, which impacts and reposi-tions the horizonal narrowness of anthropocentric certainty and unravels anthropocentrism of the human as discretely bounded center."[40] Milesian archipelagics, voicing opacities that energize each differing-multiplicity in totality, *decenters*, continually reconfiguring into *variable* and *multiple* centers; in de- or multi-centering totality, archipelagic likewise decenters

---

38. Glissant, "Brève philosophie d'un baroque mondial," *Le Courrier de l'UNESCO: une fenêtre ouverte sur le monde* 40, no. 9 (1987): 18, UNESCO Digital Library.

39. Krell, *Sea*, 137.

40. Allen, "Philosophy and Porous Imagination: Between Coral Reefs," *South African Journal of Philosophy* 27, no. 4 (2008): 430, EBSCOhost.

humans and the human-shaped divinities through whom totality becomes a *something* to grasp as if available from a (non-)position of before and behind, joining these perspectives and ways of being in the horizonal multiplicity, its multi-centers spreading numerous, shimmering, abundant.

Against the male-masculine grasping figured in Zeus of the earlier mythic-poetic tradition Milesian thinking sets in motion an expanse of horizonal relations of being-together and being-with in which humans come late and open into the already opening openness (νοῦς) of totality's expansive horizoning: a network of quickening, reconfiguring multiplicities joining by way of opacities.

Breaking Light: A Poetics of Opacity

> A poetics that is latent, open, multilingual in intention, directly in contact with everything possible.
>
> —Glissant, *Poetics of Relation*

Clarity of opacity, of opacities *as* opacities, a non-reductive transparency operates as the imaginary of relation. Glissant thinks this also as an "insurrection of the imaginary"[41] and a weave of "invariants" that describes neither absolutes nor static, fixed points, but a nexus of relations where differences weave invariantly as "fleeting encounters."[42] On this very locus—the transparency of opacities *as* opacities—the "presocratics" surface in Glissant's thinking in opposition to the reductive transparency and clarity embodied in the figure of Zeus and his continental mode of *grasping* that "evaporates" an "initial density that difference presents" to arrive at a mirrorlike transparency:[43]

> Against this reductive transparency, a force of opacity is at work. No longer the opacity that enveloped and reactivated the mystery of filiation but another, considerate of all the threatened

---

41. Glissant, "Poetics of the World."

42. Glissant, "What Was Us, What Is Us," 100.

43. Simek, "Stubborn Shadows," 366. For Glissant's image of the mirrorlike transparency of the continental mode, see *PR*, 111.

and delicious things joining one another (without conjoining, that is, without merging) in the expanse of Relation.

Thus, that which protects the Diverse we call opacity. And henceforth we shall call Relation's imaginary a transparency, one that for ages (ever since the Pre-Socratics? or the Mayans? in Timbuktu already? ever since the pre-Islamic poets and the Indian storytellers?) has had premonitions of its unforeseeable whirl [*les tourbillons imprévisibles*].[44]

That opacities join in various and varying configurations—this brings forth a certain clarity or transparency. Yet, in order to avoid spilling over this limited insight—fluid, reticent, since the thought of opacity inhibits rashness of thought, checks the impulse toward "unequivocal courses and irreversible choices"[45]—the phrasings themselves do not sound into and through the mode of clarity or transparency, the reductive transparency of Zeus and the continental mode.

Reenacting this mode, the Aristotelean formulation and the epitomists' renderings preceding and underlying it—that early Greek thinking sought that out of which all things emerge and that into which at last they perish (ἐξ οὗ γάρ ἐστιν ἅπαντα τὰ ὄντα καὶ ἐξ οὗ γίγνεται πρῶτου καὶ εἰς ὃ φθείρεται τελευταῖον, Arist. *Metaph.* 983b.8–9)—take transparency's clarity to be the principal methodological distinction of philosophy, the guiding force that distinguishes philosophic from non-philosophic thinking. The sayings themselves, the radiant terms animating them, all voice an overwhelming *opacity.* Instead of releasing philosophers from the embrace and stirrings of wonder from which they begin—where wonder names a condition of unknowing (ἀγνοεῖν, 982b.18), dissolving wonder into unknowing and fleeing from it into the stability of a knowledge freed from all relation (982b.24–28), effectively "putting an end to wonder"[46]—Milesian thinking urges a continual return to the moments of such wonderment as the open expanse of totality in motion.

Knowing such expanse in its motions Glissant terms a way of knowing relation, a dynamic involvement in totality's expansions, its pulse, its

---

44. *PR,* 62; *PdR,* 74–75.

45. *PR,* 192.

46. Sallis, ". . . A Wonder That One Could Never Aspire to Surpass," in Maly, *Path of Archaic Thinking,* 247.

tides.[47] Milesian thinking opens, in a "gesture of giving-on-and-with that opens finally on totality,"[48] to such expanse as the ὕδωρ opening from the harbors in the relay of its moving opacities, as the ἄπειρον of such movements as an ek-static outspanning that undoes a one-many(ones) paradigm, as the (un-)enclosing of ἀήρ in its ever-togetherness with the faces and depths of ὕδωρ and the differing enabling that togetherness. Streaming into and within the *tourbillons* of broader Mediterranean and Near Eastern cultural imaginaries, early Greek thinking makes this gesture of opening and openness. Their motions open *transversally*, horizontally through relation. If the Milesians signal the coming-to-be of *philosophy*, as tradition holds, such emergence takes place as a reconfiguration of multiple traditions and images, such that at the supposed beginning philosophy already diffracts, its "center everywhere and its circumference nowhere," multicentered and transversal.[49]

Milesian thinking begins at the moment of an experience that ruptures, disrupts, *opens* and *breaks* both the vertical-hierarchical light of clarity and intelligibility, under the sway of Zeus, that subordinates particulars to universals by the force of its grasp—a mode based on "reducing and hierarchizing" by way of "universal models and categories"[50]—and the flat light of ordinariness and familiarity that flattens the world through the pressures of habit and received thought. Such moments and their horizon(s) open not as a retreat from the living world, not what Nietzsche identified as the essence of philosophy's way (*Wesen der großen philosophischen Natur*), a "lack of consideration for what is here and now,"[51] a core Cavarero reads—at least in the afterlife of Milesian thinking, specifically Thalean considerations, as formulated in Plato (*Tht.* 174a.4–b.1)—as the "de-realization" constitutive of philosophy, a commitment to the "disavowing of the reality of the world" by which "the things of the world are hidden from philosophical thought."[52] Rather, the moment of such an experience as the very *now* of experience—an ek-static *now* that remains open to the opening and withdrawing of each manifestation, that opens in the

------

47. *PR,* 187.

48. *PR,* 192.

49. Jung, "Transversality," 423.

50. Simek, "Stubborn Shadows," 366.

51. Nietzsche, *Philosophy in the Tragic Age,* 66; *Die Philosophie im tragischen Zeitalter der Griechen,* 184.

52. Cavarero, *In Spite of Plato,* 54.

moment of *not*-knowing and not seeking to arrest the shimmering and hovering—opens into a condition *like* non-experience, full of newness and alertness in dynamic open-relation with the world. As Bernasconi has observed, Thales's fall into the well does not occur from self-involvement, from an isolated soul gathered as itself into itself (e.g., Pl. *Phd.* 83a.8–b.2), but from star-gazing,[53] opening awareness to the shimmering dome of the night sky in its weave of familiarity and strangeness—that wonder which sets philosophy in motion (Arist. *Metaph.* 982b.12–19).

The *now* of experience like non-experience lets opacities pulse and lets thinking remain unclosed, alert to the strange permeating the familiar in a kind of suddenness, a passing. Where the impulse to articulate to another the *what*, to assign a whatness to the motions of vision that would unfurl toward a conceptual determination—where such an impulse instead yields to a voicing of the effervescence, the momentarity of experiencing the *non-* as *non-*, here arises a need for "the poetic—that which in its thickness and creative mutability cannot be reduced to calculable transactions,"[54] a need for poetic words (such as those of the Milesians), radiant words that activate multiple registers and valences in their own shimmering, their flickering between luminosity and obscurity. These words, poetic, elusive, depart and (re-)figure the ek-static expansiveness called forth in Anaximandrean ἄπειρον; the poetic language "suddenly moves away into the distance, it leaves us, doubtless to reach other poems, rejoin and designate other common places, other invariants"[55]—a name Glissant activates for these very motions of relation and opacities—and it moves on as a passing, fading, a *breaking away* from those who sounded it. Breaking the light of grasping, a name for such words is: *opacity*.

For the Milesian circle, those words of opacity gesture in various directions without the grasp to enclose: ὕδωρ, ἄπειρον, ἀήρ. The force of these terms uncloses rather than closes, energizing renewed attention to everything we thought we knew, and everything missed by the concealing action of that certainty.[56] As with Glissantian thinking, Milesians

---

53. Bernasconi, "Almost Always More Than Philosophy Proper," 5.

54. Simek, "Stubborn Shadows," 368. Simek is developing a line opened by Patrick Chamoiseau in an interview she quotes, a line articulating the need for a poetic dimension or voice within political discourses.

55. Glissant, "What Was Us, What Is Us," 104.

56. "The thought of opacity distracts me from absolute truths whose guardian I might believe myself to be" (*PR*, 192).

let sound a manifold language, a language full of tensions—later to be articulated in Herakleitean thinking in the figure of the bow and lyre (Hct. 51 Robinson) or, in Glissant's translation of another Herakleitean saying, "en se transformant il demeure"[57] (Hct. 83 Robinson)—and advancing "by derivation and extension" as a poetic language "and its creative force (*puissance créatrice*)," but also disclosing that this poetic language constitutes a foundation and origin of philosophic language.[58] But unlike Glissant, early Milesian thinking takes place on the cusp of this distinction, on its fold, where and when, perhaps, the language is *folding* into these two folds but not yet folded.

The suddenness of the *now* happens not as sudden illumination—what Glissant thought as the "lightning flashes" of personal revelation, a dream "of totality that is impossible or yet to come"[59]—but as a break-through, a translative break through the light of familiarity and its clarity into the darkness of suspense and vivid opacities. No longer closing the edged circle of particular and universal, this poetics releases each into the darkness of a night pierced with stars, with shimmering constellations and their possibilities.

Opacity intervenes on the movement away from sense and experience and into the region of universal judgments, the very movement of conquest figured in Zeus, master, emblem of the continental mode. The sense of opacity already pulses in awareness, the awareness of depths, layeredness, the richness and thickness of beings, of world. A shadow of this phenomenon arises in Athene's theophany in *Iliad* 1, where in her engagement with Akhilleus the divinity clutches (ἔλε) and shines forth (φαινωμένη)—without being seen—as behind and out of view (στῆ δ'ὄ-πιθεν, Hom. *Il.* 1.197), akin, perhaps, to what Faulkner voiced in his novel *Intruder in the Dust* as a "sense feeling" of "a massed adjacence," in that case an unseen human presence.[60] In the universal-particular scheme, a movement away from so-called particulars forms the way toward wisdom and involves, as a step along that way, the compression of many memories

---

57. Glissant, *La terre le feu l'eau les vents* (Galaade Éditions, 2010), 68.

58. Raphaël Lauro, "Édouard Glissant: L'extension Poétique," *Contemporary French and Francophone Studies* 20, no. 4–5 (2016): 545, Taylor and Francis online.

59. *PR*, 33.

60. William Faulkner, *Intruder in the Dust* (Random House, 1948), 95. In Faulkner's tale the experience comes to the boy Chick as he rides through night's darkness on his way to aid, through unearthing, disclosing, a wrongfully accused Black man in 1940's Mississippi.

of the same thing into a single experience (Arist. *Metaph.* 980b.9–10). The movement continues along a pathway of knowledge that diverges from art (τέχνη) toward a wisdom that is knowledge of causes and sources (981b.30–982a.6) freed from use (981b.18–20), a knowledge of the one, the universal-set-down-over-the-whole (τὴν καθόλου ἐπιστήμην, 982a.22), that stands most remote from experience and particulars (982a.24–25) and that bears the force of command and power-over-others (982a.17–19). Attention to diversities characteristic of the senses, and chiefly of vision (980a.1–7), gives way to increased attention to *similarities* in a way that emphasizes *sameness,* the unity of the universal.

Opacity in the early Milesian thinkers works as a *poetics* insofar as the universal knowledge—the transparency of opacity: that opacity animates diversities—becomes the turning point around which such knowledge reconfigures itself as an art, a poetics, that reawakens the openness toward so-called particulars in their opacities, as multiplicities, in short, in their resistances to the universalizing mode and its "oppressive gaze of transparency that demands the right to assimilate the Other with the Same."[61] As a "double-thrust [*double portée*]," a poetics of opacity works as "a theory that tries to conclude" and as "a presence that concludes (presumes) nothing."[62] The "force" of such a poetics, a poetics of opacity, pulses in Glissant's thinking "as radiant—replacing the absorbing concept of unity; it is the opacity of the diverse animating the imagined transparency of Relation. The imaginary does not bear with it the coercive requirements of idea. It prefigures reality, without determining it a priori."[63]

A poetics of opacity bears along with it its own transparency—or clarity—that relation relays opacities and that opacities quicken relation. This releases things and beings from their status as particulars[64]—since particularity belongs to universality—and into the openness of possibilities,

---

61. Headley, "Glissant's Existential Ontology of Difference," 77.

62. *PR*, 183; *PdR*, 197.

63. *PR*, 192.

64. Such a release does not erase the universal-particular scheme, since that scheme remains on a horizon that both precedes the Milesians, in the genealogical, filiational mode figured in Zeus, and antecedes them, in the development of this scheme within the history of philosophy still on the horizon of the not-yet with respect to the Milesians. Glissant may move in a between on the universal-particular scheme. For an insightful discussion of the latter where attention is given to cultural and historical specificity as it relates to the universal-particular scheme, see Headley, "Glissant's Existential Ontology of Difference," 64–67.

of multiplicities and their opacities. A reconfiguration of Polos's wisdom cited by Aristotle unfolds, a "radical reversal" according to which philosophy imbued with the resources of an imaginary and the poetic leading to a profound sensitivity for the diversities in their concreteness:[65] where the statement of Polos declares that "experience (ἐμπειρία) makes art (τέχνη), but non-experience (ἀπειρία) makes chance" (τύχη, Arist. *Metaph.* 981a.3–5), the reconfiguration brought about by opacity into an opening diversity of possibilities says: *experience makes an art that returns engagement to an openness like non-experience* (ἄπειρον) *in which unpredictabilities, the unforeseeable tourbillon of opacities in relation, quicken as the multiplicities of what experience closed.* Put differently, the one centers similarity and sameness, the other centers difference and diversity. If the concept cuts away the distinguishing aspects of this and that on the way to its formation of universal applicability, a poetry energized by and as opacity sounds the resonant possibilities, filaments and tendrils linking and relaying differents in their differences, not their similarities (on the way to a sameness), shifting the emphasis of *similar* to *differing*.

Voicing the resonant names ὕδωρ, ἄπειρον, ἀήρ, Milesian thinking summons a poetics at the very heart of thinking, a way of voicing—or writing—and being-in-the-world that unseals the borders closed by the habitually determined manner of experience and its elision of differences.[66] If he wrote anything, Thales may have composed dactylic hexameters (Diog. Laert. 1.1.34; Plut. *De Pyth. or.* 402f);[67] Theophrastos and Simplikios regarded the language of the Anaximandros fragment ποιητικωτέροις, *rather poetic* (Simp. *in Phys.* 1.2.24.20–21 [Axr. 9 Graham]), while the other attributed phrases are rich in poetic resonance by way of simile, as in the movement of the cosmic circles turning as wagon wheels (ἁρματείῳ τροχῷ, Ps. Plut. *Plac.* 2.20 [Axr. 22 Graham]); Anaximenean thinking, phrasing characterized as *simply* (ἁπλῇ) and *plainly* (ἀπερίττῳ, Diog. Laert. 2.2.3 [Axs. 1 Graham]), likewise frequently resounds in and as similes, such as the comparison of the pushing-pulling, opening-closing action as like felting (πίλησιν, Hipp. *Haer.* 1.7 [Axs. 12 Graham]). A poetics of opacity not only speaks such poetic words and phrases, it strains toward

---

65. Leupin, *Édouard Glissant, Philosopher,* 76.

66. Compare Decker's thinking on the erotics of poetic language, which likewise operates to release what it names from the fixed determinations of binaries and to keep in view that "boundaries are permeable and fluid." "Roots of Life and Death," 110.

67. On this topic, see Kirk and Raven's discussion in *The Presocratic Philosophers,* 85–86.

how thinking and speaking might preserve the shimmering opacities restlessly teeming in an experience like non-experience: in poetic words, in similes, *poetically*.

The Milesians issue reminders of such a poetics by calling attention to the unassimilable, the open, the abundance animating others: ὕδωρ, ἄπειρον, ἀήρ. These terms, when naming not only totality but an experience of each differentiated manifestation joined in the span of totality including thinking, ask for a renewal of alertness to those very differentiations by the similaic turning of attention between each thing or being and the terms ὕδωρ, ἄπειρον, ἀήρ. The summons calls for thinking to pivot between how these manifest in experience and then the range of ways their manifesting also addresses the ways each differentiation manifests. Where, for instance, ordinary experience involves wholes—the visible stone, for instance, is experienced as a whole even as totality of its manifestations never rise into view, never becomes available to experience—the Milesian call is toward a thinking that returns into alert engagements with each manifestation through a reconfigured way of experiencing them according to the ways they exceed and withdraw from the wholeness of the ordinary encounter with them, and the ways those exceedings and withdrawals form an aspect of their very appearing.

Rather than describing a deficit or limitation embedded in human knowing, such renewed experience on the pivot of the simile both propels thinking into the relationality in which, as Oppen wrote of the daylight, "things explain each other, / Not themselves,"[68] but also discloses the exceedings and withdrawals as descriptive of things themselves, of the world itself and thinking in the diversity of their appearings: even the continental itself, the One and its universality, would be archipelagized, set adrift into more and further relations already teeming within it.[69]

Dissolving the oppositional character of *continental* and *archipelagic* by way of archipelagic thinking, multiplicities expand beyond and yet include such a binary relation, while not reducing either to a self-enclosed

---

68. George Oppen, "A Narrative," in *New Collected Poems*, ed. Michael Davidson (New Directions, 2002), 151.

69. Inspired by Allen's thinking of and with Hampâté Ba, envisioning the drying up of oceans and the "slow and persistent mobile process" still at work on continents, imagining the connections with totality of shifting contours and relations beneath the ocean's waters. "Philosophy and Porous Imagination," 430–31.

unity but "of oneness in and through multiplicity."[70] And, with Glissant,[71] such a pivot, such a renewal that disrupts the speed and swift passage of thought in rapid progress toward enclosing each manifestation within a mode of knowing in which each differentiation becomes stabilized and arrested like Daidalos's chained sculptures (Pl. *Meno* 97d.6–7) or the unmoving heart of ἀλήθεια (Prm. 1.29 Gallop), the work of poetry—of poems, poetry's work—slows the pace, sounds forth an invitation to a reticent engagement that seeks "to tarry with uncertainty—with that which trembles, wavers and ceaselessly becomes all over again,"[72] turning attention and thinking toward

        differentiations in the motions
             of their differing and protecting   that diversity.

Towards a poetics of opacity:
a poetics of Milesian

    thinking, voiced
      in the radiant terms that keep thought in motion, on the *between*

of the simile's pivot—like the openings of an
      archipelago, their   relations—emphasizes

                 not identity
               or sameness, but

    the action of similarity that sustains difference, relays
    differences into mobile relations

        on the shifting currents and shores, on
        churning in the moments
        of their opacities

---

70. Wiedorn, *Think Like an Archipelago*, 109.

71. *PR*, 192: "the thought of opacity saves me from unequivocal courses and irreversible choices."

72. This is part of the opening passage of Glissant's first book of poems, *Riveted Blood* (*Le Sang rivé*, 1961), quoted in Leupin, *Édouard Glissant, Philosopher*, 5–6, trans. Andrew Brown.

Bibliography

Allen, Danielle S. "The Flux of Time in Ancient Greece." *Daedalus* 132, no. 2 (2003): 62–73. Gale Literature Resource Center.

Allen, James P. "The Celestial Realm." In *Ancient Egypt*, edited by David P. Silverman. Oxford University Press, 1997.

Allen, Jeffner. *Lesbian Philosophy: Explorations*. Institute of Lesbian Studies, 1986.

———. "Philosophy and Porous Imagination: Between Coral Reefs." *South African Journal of Philosophy* 27, no. 4 (2008): 429–35. EBSCOhost.

Arrojo, Rosemary. "The Revision of the Traditional Gap Between Theory and Practice and the Empowerment of Translation in Postmodern Times." *Translator* 4, no. 1 (1998): 25–48. Taylor and Francis Online.

Ashbaugh, Anne Freire. "The Philosophy of Flesh and the Flesh of Philosophy." *Research in Phenomenology* 8 (1978): 217–23. JSTOR.

Astrachan, Isabel. "Language and Being(s): Édouard Glissant and Martin Heidegger." *CLR James Journal* 26, no. 1 (2020): 163–76. JSTOR.

Bachelard, Gaston. *The Poetics of Space*. Translated by Maria Jolas. Penguin, 1964.

Backman, Jussi. *Complicated Presence: Heidegger and the Postmetaphysical Unity of Being*. State University of New York Press, 2015. EBSCOhost.

Baracchi, Claudia. "Contributions to the Coming-to-Be of Greek Beginnings: Heidegger's Inceptive Thinking." In Hyland and Manoussakis, *Heidegger and the Greeks*.

———. "Looking at the Sky: On Nature and Contemplation." *Research in Phenomenology* 39, no. 1 (2009): 13–28. JSTOR.

———. "The ΠΟΛΕΜΟΣ That Gathers All: Heraclitus on War." *Research in Phenomenology* 45, no. 2 (2015): 267–87. JSTOR.

Benso, Silvia. "The Breathing of the Air: Presocratic Echoes in Levinas." In *Levinas and the Ancients,* edited by Brian Schroeder and Silvia Benso. Indiana University Press, 2008. ProQuest.

Bernasconi, Robert. "Almost Always More Than Philosophy Proper." *Research in Phenomenology* 30, no. 1 (2000): 1–11. JSTOR.

Blakeney, E. H., ed. *The Hymn of Cleanthes*. Macmillan, 1921.

Boyce, Mary, ed. and trans. *Textual Sources for the Study of Zoroastrianism*. University of Chicago Press, 1990.

Brogan, Walter. "Heraclitus, Philosopher of the Sign." In Jacobs, *Presocratics after Heidegger*.

Bryan, Jenny. "The Pursuit of Parmenidean Clarity." *Rhizomata* 8, no. 2 (2021): 218–38. EBSCOhost.

Campbell, David A., ed. *Greek Lyric Poetry: A Selection of Early Greek Lyric, Elegiac, and Iambic Poetry*. Bristol Classical Press, 1982.

Cassin, Barbara. "The Energy of the Untranslatables: Translation as a Paradigm for the Human Sciences." *Paragraph* 38, no. 2 (2015): 145–58. EBSCOhost.

———. "Philosophising in Languages." Translated by Yves Gilonne. *Nottingham French Studies* 49, no. 2 (2010): 17–28. EUP Publishing.

———. "Translation as Paradigm for Human Sciences." *Journal of Speculative Philosophy* 30, no. 3 (2016): 242–66. Project Muse.

———. " 'Whole' and 'Ensemble': *Pan* Open / *Holon* Closed." In *Dictionary of Untranslatables: A Philosophical Lexicon*, edited by Barbara Cassin, Steven Rendall, and Emily S. Apter. Princeton University Press, 2014. ProQuest.

Cavarero, Adriana. *In Spite of Plato: A Feminist Rewriting of Ancient Philosophy*. Translated by Serena Anderlini-D'Onofrio and Áine O'Healy. Polity Press, 1995.

Chandler, Mielle, and Astrida Neimanis. "Water and Gestationality: What Flows beneath Ethics." In *Thinking with Water*, edited by Cecilia Chen, Janine MacLeod, Astrida Neimanis, and Elab Gis†e Trudel. McGill-Queen's University Press, 2013. ProQuest.

Classen, C. Joachim. "Anaximander and Anaximenes: The Earliest Greek Theories of Change?" *Phronesis* 22 (1977): 89–102. JSTOR.

Cockle, Walter Eric Harold. "Naucratis." In *The Oxford Classical Dictionary*. 3rd rev. ed. Edited by Simon Hornblower and Antony Spawforth. Oxford University Press, 2003.

Cohen, Signe. *Text and Authority in the Older Upaniṣads*. Brill, 2008. ProQuest.

Coldstream, J. N. "Prospectors and Pioneers: Pithekoussai, Kyme and Central Italy." In *The Archaeology of Greek Colonisation: Essays Dedicated to Sir John Boardman*, edited by Gocha Tsetskhladze and Franco De Angelis. Oxford Committee for Archaeology, 1994.

Decker, Jessica Elbert. "The Roots of Life and Death in the Homeric Hymns and Presocratic Philosophy." In *Otherwise than the Binary: New Feminist Readings in Ancient Philosophy and Culture*, edited by Jessica Elbert Decker, Danielle A. Layne, and Monica Vilhauer. State University of New York Press, 2022.

Diels, Hermann, ed. *Simplicii in Aristotelis Physicorum libros quattuor priores commentaria*. Berlin, 1882.

Dinsdorf, Wilhelm, ed. *Praeparationis Evangelicae, I–X. Eusebii Caesariensis Opera*. Vol. 1. Leipzig, 1867.

Dué, Casey. "'Perform Its Song': Translating an Oral Traditional Epic." *Ancient Exchanges* 1, no. 1 (2020). https://wayback.archive-it.org/824/20240707084910/https://exchanges.uiowa.edu/ancient/issues/departures/iliad/.

Duncker, Ludwig, and F. G. Schneidewin, eds. *Hippolyti Refutationis omnium haeresium librorum decem quae supersunt.* Göttingen, 1859.

Edmonds, J. M. *Lyra Graeca.* Vol. 2. Rev. ed. Harvard University Press / William Heinemann, 1979.

Faulkner, Raymond O., Ogden Goelet, Eva Von Dassow, and Carol Andrews. *The Egyptian Book of the Dead: the Book of Going Forth by Day* [. . .]. 3rd rev. ed. Chronicle Books, 2015.

Faulkner, William. *Intruder in the Dust.* Random House, 1948.

Finkelberg, Aryeh. "Anaximander's Conception of the Apeiron." *Phronesis* 38, no. 3 (1993): 229–56. Brill Online Journals.

Folit-Weinberg, Benjamin. "Disappearing into Thick Aēr: The Function of Aēr in Homer and Anaximenes." *American Journal of Philology* 144, no. 2 (2023): 183–219. Project Muse.

Forman, Werner, and Stephen Quirke. *Hieroglyphs and the Afterlife in Ancient Egypt.* University of Oklahoma Press, 1996.

Foster, John L., trans. *Ancient Egyptian Literature: An Anthology.* University of Texas Press, 2001.

Furlong, Iris. "The Mythology of the Ancient Near East." In *The Feminist Companion to Mythology*, edited by Carolyne Larrington. Pandora, 1992.

Gadamer, Hans-Georg. *Der Anfang der Philosophie.* Translated by Joachim Schulte. Philipp Reclam, 1996.

———. "Mythos und Vernunft." In *Kleine Schriften.* Vol. 4, *Variationen.* J. C. B. Mohr, 1977.

Gallop, David, ed. and trans. *Parmenides of Elea: Fragments: A Text and Translation and Introduction.* University of Toronto Press, 1984.

Gerber, Douglas E., trans. and ed. *Greek Elegiac Poetry from the Seventh to the Fifth Centuries BC.* Harvard University Press, 1999.

Gibson, John C. *Canaanite Myths and Legends.* Bloomsbury, 1978. EBSCOhost.

Glissant, Édouard. "Acclamation." Translated by Mary Ann Caws. *Callaloo* 36, no. 4 (2013): 854.

———. "Brève philosophie d'un baroque mondial." *Le Courrier de l'UNESCO: une fenêtre ouverte sur le monde* 40, no. 9 (1987): 18. UNESCO Digital Library.

———. *The Collected Poems of Édouard Glissant.* Edited by Jefferson Humphries, translated by Melissa Manolas. University of Minnesota Press, 2005.

———. "Cross-Cultural Poetics." In *Caribbean Discourse: Selected Essays,* translated by J. Michael Dash. University Press of Virginia, 1989.

———. *Philosophie de la relation: Poésie en etendue.* Gallimard, 2009.

———. *Poetics of Relation.* Translated by Betsy Wing. University of Michigan Press, 1997. Originally published as *Poétique de la Relation.* Gallimard, 1990.

———. "Poetics of the World: Global Thinking and Unforeseeable Events." Translated by Kate Cooper Leupin. Chancellor's Distinguished Lectureship Series, Louisiana State University, Baton Rouge, April 19, 2002. Published online October 20, 2017, https://sites01.lsu.edu/wp/theglissanttranslationproject/2017/10/20/the-poetics-of-the-world-global-thinking-and-unforeseeable-events/.

———. "In Praise of the Different and of Difference." Translated by Celia Britton. *Callaloo* 36, no. 4 (2013): 855–62. JSTOR.

———. *La terre le feu l'eau les vents*. Galaade Éditions, 2010.

———. *Treatise on the Whole-World*. Translated by Celia Britton. Liverpool University Press, 2020. ProQuest.

Graham, Daniel, ed. *The Texts of Early Greek Philosophy: The Complete Fragments and Selected Testimonies of the Major Presocratics*. Vol. 1. Cambridge University Press, 2010.

Greaves, Alan M. *Miletos: Archaeology and History*. Taylor and Francis, 2002. ProQuest.

Guirand, Felix, ed. *Larousse Encyclopedia of Mythology*. Translated by Richard Aldington and Delano Ames. Prometheus Press, 1959.

Hardwick, Lorna. "Singing across the Faultlines: Cultural Shifts in Twentieth-Century Receptions of Homer." In *Homer in the Twentieth Century: Between World Literature and the Western Canon*, edited by Barbara Graziosi and Emily Greenwood. Oxford University Press, 2007.

Headley, Clevis. "Glissant's Existential Ontology of Difference." In *Theorizing Glissant: Sites and Citations*, edited by John E. Drabinski and Marisa Parham. Rowman and Littlefield International, 2015. ProQuest.

Heeren, A. H. L., ed. *Ioannis Stobaei Eclogarum Physicarum et Ethicarum*. Göttingen, 1792. HathiTrust.

Hegel, Georg Wilhelm Friedrich. *Vorlesungen über die Geschichte der Philosophie*. Edited by G. J. P. J. Bolland. A. H. Adriani, 1908. HathiTrust. Translated by E. S. Haldane as *Greek Philosophy to Plato*. Vol. 1 of *Lectures on the History of Philosophy*. Lincoln, 1892.

Heidegger, Martin. "ALETHEIA: (Heraklit, Fragment 16)." In *Vorträge und Aufsätze*.

———. *Basic Problems of Phenomenology*. Translated by Albert Hofstadter. University of Indiana Press, 1982.

———. *Being and Time*. Translated by John Macquarrie and Edward Robinson. Harper and Row, 1962.

———. ". . . dichterisch wohnet der Mensch . . . ." In *Vorträge und Aufsätze*. Translated by Albert Hofstadter as ". . . Poetically Man Dwells." In *Poetry, Language, Thought*. Harper and Row, 1971.

———. *Early Greek Thinking: The Dawn of Western Philosophy*. Translated by David Farrell Krell. Harper and Row, 1984.

———. "The Inception of Occidental Thinking." In *Heraclitus: The Inception of Occidental Thinking and Logic: Heraclitus's Doctrine of the Logos*, translated by Julia Goesser Assaiante and S. Montgomery Ewegen. Bloomsbury, 2018.

———. "Logos (Heraklit, fragment 50)." In *Vorträge und Aufsätze*.

———. "The Onto-theo-logical Constitution of Metaphysics." In *Identity and Difference*, translated by Joan Stambaugh. University of Chicago Press, 1969.

———. *Parmenides*. Translated by André Schuwer and Richard Rojcewicz. Indiana University Press, 1992.

———. "Der Spruch des Anaximander." In *Holzwege*. Klostermann, 1950.

———. *Vorträge und Aufsätze*. Klett-Cotta, 1954.

Heidel, Alexander. *The Babylonian Genesis: The Story of Creation*, 2nd ed. University of Chicago Press, 1951.

Heyd, Thomas. "And Yet She Moves!—The Earth Rests on Water: Thales on the Role of Water in Earth's Mobility and in Nature's Transformations." *Apeiron* 47, no. 4 (2014): 485–512. De Gruyter.

Hix, H. L. "Fire at Night: A Version of Herakleitos." *Yale Review* 103, no. 2 (2015): 1–15. Project Muse.

———. "A 'Sneaky' Form of Non-Translation." On Non-Translation and Translation Panel, Annual Conference, American Literary Translators Association, Rochester, New York, November 20, 2019.

Hobza, Pavel. "Anaximenes' ἀήρ as Generating Mist and Generated Air." *Apeiron* 53, no. 2 (2020): 97–122. De Gruyter Journals.

Hornung, Erik. *Conceptions of God in Ancient Egypt*. Translated by John Baines. Cornell University Press, 1982.

———. "L'Égypte, la philosophie avant les grecs." Translated by Gilles Roulin. *Les Études philosophiques* 2/3 (1987): 113–25. JSTOR.

Hyland, Drew A. "First of all Came Chaos." In Hyland and Manoussakis, *Heidegger and the Greeks*.

———. *The Origins of Philosophy: Its Rise in Myth and the Pre-Socratics: A Collection of Early Writings*. Humanities Press, 1973.

Hyland, Drew A., and John Panteleimon Manoussakis, eds. *Heidegger and the Greeks: Interpretive Essays*. Indiana University Press, 2006.

Irigaray, Luce. *In the Beginning, She Was*. Bloomsbury, 2013.

Jacobs, David C., ed. *The Presocratics after Heidegger*. State University of New York Press, 1999.

Johnson, David M. "Hesiod's Descriptions of Tartarus ('Theogony' 721–819)." *Phoenix* 53, no. 1/2 (1999): 8–28. JSTOR.

Johnson, David W. "The Limits of Language: Philosophical Hermeneutics and the Task of Comparative Philosophy." *Journal of Speculative Philosophy* 34, no. 3 (2020): 378–89. Project Muse.

Jung, Hwa Yol. "Transversality and the Philosophical Politics of Multiculturalism in the Age of Globalization." *Research in Phenomenology* 39, no. 3 (2009): 416–37. JSTOR.

Kahn, Charles H. *Anaximander and the Origins of Greek Cosmology*. Hackett, 1985.

Kassam, Chris, and Robbie Duschinsky. "Nietzsche and Anaximander on Being and Becoming." *Diacritics* 45, no. 3 (2017): 100–16. Project Muse.

Katz, Vernon, and Thomas Egenes, trans. *The Upanishads: A New Translation.* Penguin, 2015.

Kirk, G. S., and J. E. Raven, eds. *The Presocratic Philosophers: A Critical History with a Selection of Texts.* Cambridge University Press, 1957.

Kirkland, Sean D. "Nietzsche and Drawing Near to the Personalities of the Pre-Platonic Greeks." *Continental Philosophy Review* 44, no. 4 (2011): 417–37. Springer Nature Link.

Kleinberg-Levin, David Michael. "The Court of Justice: Heidegger's Reflections on Anaximander." *Research in Phenomenology* 37, no. 3 (2007): 385–416. JSTOR.

Krell, David Farrell. "Kalypso: Homeric Concealments after Nietzsche, Heidegger, Derrida, and Lacan." In Jacobs, *Presocratics after Heidegger.*

———. *The Sea: A Philosophical Encounter.* Bloomsbury, 2019.

Laks, André, and Glenn W. Most, eds. *Early Greek Philosophy.* Vol. 2, part 1, *Beginnings and Early Ionian Thinkers.* Harvard University Press, 2016.

Lauro, Raphaël. "Édouard Glissant: L'extension Poétique." *Contemporary French and Francophone Studies* 20, no. 4–5 (2016): 542–49. Taylor and Francis online.

le Nourry, Nicolai, ed. *Clement of Alexandria, Stromata.* Vol. 2. Paris, 1857. Google Books.

Lesher, J. H., ed. and trans. *Xenophanes of Colophon: Fragments: A Text and Translation and Introduction.* University of Toronto Press, 1992.

Leupin, Alexandre. *Édouard Glissant, Philosopher: Heraclitus and Hegel in the Whole-World.* Translated by Andrew Brown. State University of New York Press, 2021.

Levinas, Emmanuel. *Otherwise Than Being.* Translated by Alphonso Lingis. Duquesne University Press, 1981.

Lichtheim, Mariam. *Ancient Egyptian Literature.* University of California Press, 2019.

Lingis, Alphonso. "Differance in the Eternal Recurrence of the Same." *Research in Phenomenology* 8, no. 1 (1978): 77–91. JSTOR.

Lombardo, Stanley, trans. *Hesiod: Works and Days and Theogony.* Indianapolis, 1993.

———. *Homer: Iliad.* Hackett, 1997.

———. *Parmenides and Empedocles: The Fragments in Verse Translation.* Grey Fox Press, 1982.

López-Ruiz, Carolina. "Near Eastern Precedents of the 'Orphic' Gold Tablets: The Phoenician Missing Link." *Journal of Ancient Near Eastern Religions* 15, no. 1 (2015): 52–91. EBSCOhost.

Malkin, Irad. "Postcolonial Concepts and Ancient Greek Colonization." *MLQ: Modern Language Quarterly* 65, no. 3 (2004): 341–64. Project Muse.

Maly, Kenneth. "Echoes at the Edge: Shimmering Images in *Delimitations.*" In Maly, *Path of Archaic Thinking.*

———, ed. *The Path of Archaic Thinking: Unfolding the Work of John Sallis.* State University of New York Press, 1995. EBSCOhost.

Manoussakis, John Panteleimon. "Introduction: The Sojourn in the Light." In Hyland and Manoussakis, *Heidegger and the Greeks.*

Mansfeld, Jaap. "Aristotle and Others on Thales, or the Beginnings of Natural Philosophy." *Mnemosyne* 38, 1–2 (1985): 109–29. JSTOR.

———. "Aristotle, Plato, and the Preplatonic Doxography and Chronography." In *Storiografia e dossografia nella filosofia antica*, edited by Giuseppe Cambiano. Tirrenia, 1986.

———. "Insight by Hindsight: Intentional Unclarity in Presocratic Proems." *Bulletin of the Institute of Classical Studies* 40 (1995): 225–32. JSTOR.

Marciano, M. Laura Gemelli. "East and West." In *Ancient Philosophy: Textual Pathways and Historical Explorations*, edited by Lorenzo Perilli and Daniela P. Taormina. Routledge, 2018.

Margel, Serge. "De la restitution du monde: La nature et le temps dans les fragments d'Anaximandre." *Les études philosophiques* 1, no. 1 (1999): 1–8.

Marinatos, Nanno. "The Cosmic Journey of Odysseus." *Numen* 48, no. 4 (2001): 381–416. JSTOR.

Merkelbach, Reinhold, and M. L. West, eds. *Hesiodi Theogonia, Opera et Dies, Scutum*. 3rd ed. Oxford University Press, 1990.

Merleau-Ponty, Maurice. "The Intertwining—The Chiasm." In *The Visible and the Invisible*, translated by Alphonso Lingis. Routledge, 1968.

Monro, David B., and Thomas W. Allen, eds. *Homeri Opera*. 3rd ed. Clarendon, 1920–25.

Morano, Donald V. "Thales and the Dawn of Western Philosophy." *Journal of Thought* 10, no. 3 (1975): 200–205. JSTOR.

Morenz, Siegfried. *Egyptian Religion*. Translated by Ann E. Keep. Routledge, 2004. EBSCOhost.

Most, Glenn W. "Alcman's 'Cosmogonic' Fragment (fr. 5 Page, 81 Calame)." *Classical Quarterly* 37, no. 1 (1987): 1–19. JSTOR.

———. "The Poetics of Early Greek Philosophy." In *The Cambridge Companion to Early Greek Philosophy*, edited by A. A. Long. Cambridge University Press, 1999.

Munn, Mark. "Earth and Water: The Foundations of Sovereignty in Ancient Thought." In Scott and Kosso, *Nature and Function of Water*.

Naas, Michael. "Keeping Homer's Word: Heidegger and the Epic of Truth." In Jacobs, *Presocratics after Heidegger*.

Naddaf, Gerard. "Anthropogony and Politogony in Anaximander of Miletus." In *Anaximander in Context: New Studies in the Origins of Greek Philosophy*. State University of New York Press, 2003.

Neimanis, Astrida. "feminist subjectivity, watered." *Feminist Review*, no. 103 (2013): 23–41. JSTOR.

Nietzsche, Friedrich. *The Birth of Tragedy*. Translated by Douglas Smith. Oxford University Press, 2000.

———. *Die Philosophie im tragischen Zeitalter der Griechen*. In *Die Geburt der Tragödie und weitere Schriften zur griechischen Literatur und Philosophie*, edited by Bernhard Greiner. Alfred Kröner Verlag, 2014. Translated by

Marianne Cowan as *Philosophy in the Tragic Age of the Greeks*. Regnery, 1962.

Oakley, Seanna Sumalee. "Commonplaces: Rhetorical Figures of Difference in Heidegger and Glissant." *Philosophy and Rhetoric* 41, no. 1 (2008): 1–21. Project Muse.

Obenga, Théophile. "Egypt: Ancient History of African Philosophy." In *A Companion to African Philosophy*, edited by Kwasi Wiredu. John Wiley and Sons, 2004. ProQuest.

Olivelle, Patrick, trans. *Upaniṣads*. Oxford University Press, 1996.

Oppen, George. *New Collected Poems*. Edited by Michael Davidson. New Directions, 2002.

Palladino, Chiara, ed. The Text of *The Sketch of Geography* [Agathermos]. http://www.digitalagathemerus.org/text.html. Last accessed March 6, 2023.

Pritchard, James B., ed. *The Ancient Near East*. Vol. 1, *An Anthology of Texts and Pictures*. Princeton University Press, 1958.

Riedel, Manfred. "ΑΡΧΗ und ΑΠΕΙΡΟΝ: Über das Grundwort des Anaximander." *Archiv für Geschichte der Philosophie* 69, no. 1 (1987): 1–17.

Robinson, T. M. *Heraclitus: Fragments: A Text and Translation with a Commentary*. University of Toronto Press, 1987.

Rojcewicz, Richard. "Everything Is Water." *Research in Phenomenology* 44, no. 2 (2014): 194–211. JSTOR.

Ross, W. D. ed. *Aristotelis Physica*. Oxford University Press, 1950.

Russon, John. "To Account for the Appearances: Phenomenology and Existential Change in Aristotle and Plato." *Journal of the British Society for Phenomenology* 52, no. 2 (2021): 155–68. Taylor and Francis Journals.

Sallis, John. *Chorology: On Beginning in Plato's Timaeus*. Indiana University Press, 1999.

———. "Doubles of Anaximenes." In Jacobs, *Presocratics after Heidegger*.

———. *The Figure of Nature: On Greek Origins*. Indiana University Press, 2016.

———. "Hades: Heraclitus, Fragment B 98." In *Heraclitean Fragments*, edited by John Sallis and Kenneth Maly. University of Alabama Press, 1980.

———. "Image and Phenomenon." *Research in Phenomenology* 5 (1975): 61–75. JSTOR.

———. *Phenomenology and the Return to Beginnings*. Duquesne University Press, 1973.

———. ". . . A Wonder That One Could Never Aspire to Surpass." In Maly, *Path of Archaic Thinking*.

Sassi, Maria Michela. *The Beginnings of Philosophy in Greece*. Translated by Michele Asuni. Princeton University Press, 2018.

Schofield, Martin. "ΑΡΧΗ." *Hyperboreus* 3 (1997): 218–36.

Scott, Anne, and Cynthia Kosso, eds. *The Nature and Function of Water, Baths, Bathing, and Hygiene from Antiquity through the Renaissance*. Brill, 2009. EBSCOhost.

Scott, John C. "The Phoenicians and the Formation of the Western World." *Comparative Civilizations Review* 78 (2018): 25–40.

Serres, Michel. "Anaximander: A Founding Name in History." Translated by Roxanne Lapidus. In Jacobs, *Presocratics after Heidegger.*

Simek, Nicole Jenette. "Stubborn Shadows." *Symploke* 23, no. 1–2 (2015): 363–73. Project Muse.

Skjaervo, Prods Oktor. *Spirit of Zoroastrianism.* Yale University Press, 2011.

Snell, Bruno. "Die Nachrichten über die Lehren des Thales und die Anfänge der griechischen Philosophie- und Literaturgeschichte." *Philologus* 96 (1944): 170–82.

Spitzer, D. M. "Archaic Images of Totality." In *Studies in Ancient Greek Philosophy in Honor of Professor Anthony Preus*, edited by D. M. Spitzer. Routledge, 2023.

———. "Being-in-Touch: Touch, Contact, and Bodies in the Poem of Parmenides." *Epoché: A Journal for the History of Philosophy* 29, no. 1 (2024): 1–22.

———. "Envisioning In-Visibility." In *The Translator's Visibility*, edited by Larisa Cercel and Alice Leal. Routledge, 2025.

———. "Figures of Motion, Figures of Being: On the Textualization of the Parmenidean Poem." *Ancient Philosophy* 40, no. 1 (2020): 1–18.

———. "Images in Archaic Thinking." *Epoché: A Journal for the History of Philosophy* 26, no. 1 (2021): 1–19.

———. "Introduction: Bordering Approaches and Trans-bordering Themes in Dialogue with the Work of Rosemary Arrojo." In *Transfiction and Bordering Approaches to Theorizing Translation: Essays in Dialogue with the Work of Rosemary Arrojo*, edited by D. M. Spitzer and Paulo Oliveira. Routledge: 2023.

———. *Parmenides and Translation: Figures of Motion, Figures of Being.* Peter Lang Verlag, 2025.

———. "Trans-philosophy: Translating Philosophy on and beyond the Boundaries." *Journal of Speculative Philosophy*, 37, no. 3 (2023): 564–83. Project Muse.

Taylor, Rabun. "River Raptures: Containment and Control of Water in Greek and Roman Constructions of Identity." In Scott and Kosso, *Nature and Function of Water.*

Tejera, Victorino. "Listening to Herakleitos." *Monist* 74, no. 4 (1991): 491–516. JSTOR.

Tessier, Linda. "Boundary Crossing: The Chaos-Cosmos Dynamic in Cosmogonic Myth (Egypt; Japan; Babylonia)." PhD diss., Claremont Graduate School, 1987. ProQuest.

West, M. L. *Early Greek Philosophy and the Orient.* Oxford University Press, 1971.

———. "Three Presocratic Cosmologies." *Classical Quarterly* 13, no. 2 (1963): 154–76. JSTOR.

Wians, William. "From *Logos* and *Muthos* to . . ." Introduction to *Logoi and Muthoi: Further Essays in Greek Philosophy and Literature*, ed. William Robert Wians. State University of New York Press, 2019. EBSCOhost.

Wiedorn, Michael. *Think Like an Archipelago: Paradox in the Work of Édouard Glissant*. State University of New York Press, 2018. EBSCOhost.
Woolf, Virginia. *To the Lighthouse*. Harcourt, Brace/Random House, 1927.
Zwicky, Jan. "What Is Lyric Philosophy?: An Introduction." *Common Knowledge* 20, no. 1 (2014): 14–27. Project Muse.

Index